LOST AND FOUND WORLDS:

The Memories and Experiences of a
Dutch-Indonesian Immigrant

Amy Van Lawick—Rozenberg

Order this book online at www.trafford.com
or email orders@trafford.com

Most Trafford titles are also available at major online book retailers.

Editor Christine McShane

Printed in the United States of America.

ISBN: 978-1-4669-1016-4 (sc)
ISBN: 978-1-4669-1014-0 (hc)
ISBN: 978-1-4669-1015-7 (e)

Library of Congress Control Number: 2012900612

Trafford rev. 01/19/2012

 www.trafford.com

North America & international
toll-free: 1 888 232 4444 (USA & Canada)
phone: 250 383 6864 ♦ fax: 812 355 4082

DEDICATION

In memory of my son Paul R. Van Lawick

October 1954-November 2003

Whose untimely death occured seven months before this book was
finished, leaving a sixteen-year-old daughter, Nicolette, and all the other
in his family whom love him dearly.

Father: Louis Van Lawick
Mother: Amy (Nemy) Van Lawick
Sister: Linda Van Lawick-Lintz
Sister: Marisa Van Lawick-Saurey
Nephews: Palmer and Parker Lintz
Nieces: Adia and Sofia Saurey
Brothers-in-law James Lintz and Wayne Saurey

I lifted my face and looked up at the evening sky. There were the brightest
moon and most piercing of stars in the heavens. I blinked several times and
realized that I was crying. I thought of my son, my firstborn. No one ever
knows what life holds, I thought, what destiny has in store. A star fell. I reached
for it quickly. Is that you Paul, I asked quietly. Is that you, my son?

Also dedicated to my granddaughter Nicilette Van Lawick. grandson
Palmer Lintz, grandson Parker Lintz, grand daughter Adia Saurey and
grand daughter Sofia Saurey.

PREFACE

I am an immigrant of Dutch-Indonesian descent. I am also a naturalized U.S. citizen and have lived in this wonderful country since July of 1960. To think of it, almost twice as long as I have lived in the Netherlands and Indonesia combined. I'm very proud to be an American. This land has been good to me, but I'm also very proud of my heritage, something I will always cherish and will never belie.

I was born in Surabaja, on the island of Java in Indonesia, formerly known as the Dutch East Indies, and lived in there until the age of fifteen. My parents and I, along with thousands upon thousands of our people, then left our beloved islands around 1950, for both political and safety reasons, to find refuge in The Netherlands.

The Refugee Relief Act of 1953 and its subsequent amendments approved the admission of thousands of refugees to the United States above ordinary quota limitations. Many of us started to enter the United States from that time. My husband and I and our two eldest children left Holland on July 13, 1960, for the United States. We arrived in Hoboken, New Jersey, on the ship, The Grote Bear, and traveled by bus and train to Boston, Massachusetts. It was the beginning of a six-year stay in New England. Our third child was born five years later in Ipswich, Massachusetts.

I have written this book for future generations with Dutch-Indonesian heritage, in the hope that it will give my children, their children, and others a sense of how part of their ancestors had lived in a land so far away. I wanted to tell them about a lifestyle and a culture very different from theirs, which is foreign to all who were born in this country or in Europe, wherever they now may be.

This is a book about a bloodline that is slowly disappearing, through marriages with people of other cultures and bloodlines. It is therefore of great importance to me to preserve, for future generation of this lineage, the knowledge of the ways and lives of their Dutch-Indonesian ancestors. Through this book, I hope to make them to be able to feel and touch the atmosphere of an environment and a culture that no longer exist.

This is my story, but it is Norma van Laren, the book's main character, who leads the reader across those bygone years and into the present. She tells the story of her family and herself with sadness and with great joy. My hope is that it will touch the readers' hearts, move them to tears, but also fill them with laughter.

Amy Rozenberg—Van Lawick
Carmichael, California, 2002

ACKNOWLEDGMENTS

To my favorite doctor, James Bradford Ruben, doctor of ophthalmology and ocular motility at Kaiser Permanente, Sacramento, my enormous gratitude for restoring my vision, enabling me to finish my story and healing my dwindling self-esteem. You always have an extra place in my heart.

My greatest thanks go to my editor, Christine McShane, without whose help and enduring patience this book would not have been possible.

My many Dutch-Indonesian friends were very important to me while I was writing. With tremendous gratitude, I thank Eduard Agerbeek, Francisca Blom, Walter Leydelmeier, Rudi Moll, Louis Pauselius, Wijnand Schardijn, and many others for giving mw information I had forgotten and for giving me access to many books about the old country from which I could acquire precise data about historic events. And for our youth, which we spent there, through happy times and bad times, we are united always. Thank you all so very much!

Amy Rozenberg—Van Lawick

CONTENTS

PROLOGUE

Carmichael, California, 2002

My name is Nora van Laren, and I have lived here in California for 36 years. I was doing my daily laps in the pool and just reached the thirtieth, the last one, with ease. Climbing onto a cement and tile bench, which was built into one side of the pool just a little lower than the water surface, I listened for a while to the relaxing sound of the waterfall. As the water splashed happily over a heap of lava rocks cemented to the side of the pool, I looked at my surroundings with great pleasure.

The backyard was especially pretty at this time of year. It was in the middle of June, and a typical bright and warm day in California. Not yet so blazingly hot as it would be in July and August, but pleasingly warm, with the temperatures in the low eighties and a very low humidity. A perfect day indeed. Large, flowering plants planted in back of the waterfall and also between the rocks gave the whole the deep tropical effect I liked so much and tried to achieve.

All the plants were vividly alive and in the fullest of bloom. My eyes wandered to a clump of bushes in a particular corner of the yard, planted close to the house for protection against the hot sun in the summer and against the cold in the winter. The plants were my prized hibiscus. The flowers, deep crimson and double petaled, were as big as a man's fist. They grew snugly between the dark green leaves, their contrast in color beautifully exposed. Another group of plants, also growing close to the house, were my beautiful gardenias. They too were quite a sight, with their thickly petaled snow-white flowers and thick foliage.

Creeping and draping themselves over the back fence, bursting with clusters of little trumpet-like white flowers, were the star jasmines. For an instant I caught their wonderful fragrance, and suddenly I was hurled back in time. I saw myself as a little girl, some sixty years ago, sitting in another garden, in another place. A tropical land, continents away. The year was 1939, and I was six years old.

Part I

MY DUTCH EAST INDIES

CHAPTER 1

Batavia, 1939

I was six years old and sitting on the front steps of my grandparents' hotel. I was rather small for my age, with big hazel eyes, which sometimes turn greenish. I wore my short dark-brown wavy hair loosely cut. Sometimes a big bow was placed on top of my head, as was fashionable for little girls of my age in those days. If my mother had her way, she'd have me wear one every day.

I was dressed in my school uniform, a white short-sleeved blouse, knee-length dark blue skirt, white socks, and flat black shoes. With my skirt neatly pulled over my knees, I waited for Sudiman, the chauffeur, to bring my grandfather's new black Ford around to take me to the Catholic elementary school at the Groote Post Weg or Big Postal Highway. The school was called Het Kleine Klooster in Dutch, meaning The Little Cloister, of the Ursuline nuns. The school had an excellent reputation. My mother attended the school, as did my aunts, my mother's four sisters.

HOTEL ROZEN

I had just spent a few days with my grandparents, Alfred and Tina Rozen, at their hotel in town. I did this quite often. I loved being with them, and the hotel and its special atmosphere had always charmed me greatly. Also, being an only child could get lonely at times, and somewhat dull, when I was at home with just my parents and the servants. My parents and I lived three houses down the street from the hotel, in a house also owned by my grandparents. At the hotel, there were continuous comings and goings of people, and often there were children I was quick to play with. There were also many interesting things to look at.

Looking over the hotel's vast grounds, I took in the beauty of it all. Right in front of the hotel was a grassy round with, in the very center firmly cemented into the ground, a flagpole with the red, white, and blue flag of the Netherlands fluttering in the soft breeze. It was close to seven in the morning and an absolutely glorious tropical day. It had rained the night before, and droplets on all the leaves of the shrubs and trees glittered like diamonds in the bright sunlight. The sky was a cloudless, brilliant blue.

Suddenly filled with youthful energy, I ran down the steps across the grassy round, all the way to the entrance by the street. I sat down on one of the two low, outward-curving, whitewashed walls that framed the short bridge built over a deep, neatly cemented ditch, used as drainage for the heavy monsoon rains when they arrived.

After a while, I stood up and began to walk slowly back to the hotel's front steps. As I approached the building, I noticed how especially beautiful it looked that morning. It stood gleaming white in the bright sunlight, set against a backdrop of mixed green foliage. It looked so clean and stately, with its two massive white columns on the top of the wide front steps and its orange-red roof tiles.

From the street entrance where I had just been, the graveled driveway separated and wound around the grassy lawn, to meet in front of the hotel's steps. A wide border of bright orange-red zinnias encircled the grassy area, while left and right of it were the lovely flower gardens. I could see the gardeners at work under the all-seeing eyes of Dharmo, the head gardener. A low three-foot-high wall ran along three sides of the huge front yard, coming together at the entrance. The walls were covered here and there with bougainvillea climbers in all sorts of colors. A profusion of flowers in purples, pinks, and reds had been trained over some areas of the low white walls and continued to climb up one corner of the hotel's outer wall.

Here and there, in clumps of three, big hibiscus shrubs were planted, chosen especially for their large, showy flowers and long blooming periods. They washed the garden with flaming color all through the year, a riotous mingling of hues. Blood reds would fade into blush and then into a paler dusty pink, all planted together. There were also the beautiful arbors full of climbing stephanotis, adding their small white flowers and their wonderful fragrance to the perfect arrangement of the whole.

The birds of paradise, orange and yellow bird-like flowers, were everywhere, and royal palm trees, stateliest of all palms, lined the circular driveway. There was a flame tree on the left, which gave wonderful shade to the clusters of impatience, planted underneath as color spots in all kinds of hues.

The grounds blazed with glorious color. I drank in the wonder of it all, on this splendid day. A day I would always remember. An impression I would keep throughout my life.

I came out of my reverie when the car I was waiting for stopped in front of where I sat. The chauffeur got out and held open the door for me to step in.

Seeing that her granddaughter was about to leave, my grandmother—all the grandchildren called her Oma, which means Grammy—hurried from a corner of the vast, open veranda where she and my grandfather were sitting with their manager, Johan Baumer. Johan had worked for the Rozens for many years. The three of them had been in deep conversation about the details of the upcoming day, as their habit had always been at this time of the morning.

My grandmother walked toward me with a smile. She reached down to adjust my clothes, which were in disarray from all that running, and smoothed down my hair. She hugged me and said softly, "Be a good girl, Nora, and pay attention to what the teacher is telling you, would you, sweetheart?" she asked. I nodded and hugged her in return. With her arm around my shoulders, we both went down the steps to where Sudiman and the car were waiting.

"*Slamat pagi Njonja Besar, Slamat pagi Nonnie Ketjil,*" Sudiman greeted us politely in Indonesian, with a big smile on his face. "Good morning, grand lady, good morning, little miss." The greeting was uttered softly with eyes downcast. "*Slamat pagi, Sudiman,*" we answered in unison. We were both very fond of the chauffeur, especially me. He let me help him keep the car spotlessly clean and sometimes even let me help to wash it.

Sudiman was only fourteen years old when he was hired to help Dharmo, the gardener. Later, when he was old enough to drive, after numerous instructions, he became the family's chauffeur. He lived with his young wife, who was a chambermaid in the hotel, in back of the building where the servants' quarters were, and was now a fine-looking young man of about twenty-six. He was dressed in the traditional white cotton long-sleeved jacket and black pants and on his head a black *petji*, the traditional headdress for men of the Muslim faith.

I got into the car and Sudiman closed the door, slid behind the steering wheel, and drove off.

COZY BUT ELEGANT

It was not a very big hotel, with some fifty rooms in all. But it was sought out by guests mostly for its coziness, its quiet elegance, and its excellent care. The layout was typical of that time, with the main building in the middle and the guest rooms, each with a little veranda, on either side of it. The veranda was essential for life in the tropics. It was there, where people could relax in their own privacy in the evening hours, with a tall, cool drink and perhaps a book to read, after a long, hot day at work or wherever it was spent.

The main building was huge and airy, with high ceilings for a good air flow and all the walls painted white. The front steps led up to the big, open veranda with a long, white balustrade on the left and right sides. Eighteen-inch tiles in black and white marble throughout the building kept the floors cool and shiny, with one huge room flowing into another. A set of three tall wooden plantation shuttered doors, painted dark green and neatly spaced apart, led to the enclosed inner sitting room. This room was like the veranda, big and deep, with round tables and cushioned easy chairs placed in groups, and many potted plants here and there, mostly small palms typical of the tropics. The veranda was similarly furnished, except that wicker lounges had been added, and huge conch shells in their usual orange and cream colors were placed on the floor in groups of three in the spaces between the green doors. Here also, in intervals along one wall, elephant ear plants hung in bark and moss containers. Frequently used as wall decorations all through the isles, they brought color to the white spaces of wall between the doors.

The inner sitting room, called in Dutch the *binnen gallery*, was the place where the guests could listen to soft music coming from a radio hidden behind a group of potted ferns. They could read or play a game of chess or checkers.

Opposite the doors, across the room, was another set of doors leading into the open dining room. Here again, one would notice the white-painted balustrades on either side of the big open room. This was the place where the guests would gather three times a day, for breakfast at eight, dinner at two, and supper at eight in the evening. It was a happy place, one of my favorites. On the black and white marble floors, a red runner was laid out.

It ran from across the inner sitting room through the middle of the dining room, all the way to the step-down area that led into the open hallways, which eventually led to the great kitchen storage rooms and bathrooms. The kitchen area was across from the other rooms.

In the middle of the dining room, where the runner was, stood a medium-sized brass gong in a black frame. Amin, the head houseboy, would sound the gong to announce the meals and to summon people to the dining room. The room had a cozy and friendly atmosphere to it, yet there was something imposing about it, too. It had a certain elegance. This was perhaps due in part to the many potted plants scattered all over the room. A couple of good paintings and a silk tapestry hung on one of the soaring walls right above the center doorway, echoing the color of the red runner on the floor. Two shiny brass daggers with handles made of ivory were fastened crosswise in the middle of the silken panel.

It was eight o'clock, and breakfast was being served. Amin had sounded the gong, and people started to fill the dining room. There was a relaxed, almost jovial atmosphere, and everyone appeared to be at ease and pleasantly animated without being loud or boisterous. I was aware of pleasant sounds of chatter and soft laughter, and it filled me with a warmth and peacefulness that I shall always remember.

It was a Sunday morning, and my father and mother and I joined my grandparents for breakfast as we so often did, at the family's special table set up in the corner of the dining room, privately, behind a group of potted palms.

The servants (*djongoses*) went soundlessly to and fro on their bare feet from table to table to serve the guests. Their serving skills and manners were impeccable, always approaching a guest from the left and never reaching across the person they were serving. My grandmother had drilled that into them in her soft-spoken but firm way. They all looked so neat in their spotless white linen long-sleeved jackets, black pants, and black headdresses. With their serviettes neatly draped over one arm they moved quickly, quietly, and efficiently.

The hotel's breakfast menu included several hot cereals: oatmeal, rice porridge, and a delicious tiny green bean porridge cooked and simmered in water, brown sugar, and coconut milk. It tasted delicious and is of great nutritional value. There was also toast and raisin bread, all kinds of cheeses, crepes filled with jellies, and of course there were eggs cooked in different ways—soft boiled, hard-boiled, fried. And there always was a selection of all sorts of tropical fruits, including mangoes, papayas, rambutan—which was coarse and hairy on the outside and glassy white on the inside—mangistan—pretty, purplish, and big as an apple, with milky white flesh inside—and bananas of all types and sizes. The fruits were peeled and cut into pieces, surrounded by ice to keep them cold.

It was always a treat for my cousins and me to gather in the dining room whatever and whenever the occasion. It was fun just to be there and to observe the guests who came from so many different countries. Many were Dutch, like my grandfather, newly arrived from Holland, but there also were English, French, German, and Hungarian people. There were people from Singapore and Australia and of course several Dutch-Indonesians, who came from other nearby islands and other areas of the country, who were being transferred to other regions or work opportunities.

OLD-FASHIONED CONVENIENCES

At the end of the dining room were one or two steps down, which led to a large, tiled area as wide as the dining room but not as deep. Bearing to the left, it eventually went over into an open, long landing with two good-sized storage rooms on the left side called *gudangs*, and next to them two big laundry rooms where the servants did the ironing and folded clothes on long white tables. Lining the walls were deep white shelves for all the linens and towels the hotel provided for the guests to use.

The ironing in those days was done with irons filled with hot coals, which the maids took from the great kitchen. When passing the laundry rooms, one could hear their soft voices singing or speaking to each other. I loved to be there. There always was a lot of laughter among them.

Next to the laundry rooms were nine or ten bathrooms, all of the same size. I have to elaborate on the style and the use of these baths, which were typical of that age and place, for nowhere to my knowledge in the Western world did this type of bathroom exist.

Each bathroom was about eight feet wide and ten feet deep, and the walls and cistern were entirely tiled. Opposite the door was a tank or cistern, built into the wall and also tiled. The cistern looked like a small swimming pool: it was as long as the bathroom was wide (about eight feet), three and a half feet in high, and four feet wide. At one end, like in our contemporary tubs, was a water faucet to keep it filled at all times. A servant kept a close eye on the matter.

Neatly lined up on the ledge of the pool was a row of water pails, which were filled from the pool. A sign on the bathroom wall reminded guests, especially the children, never to enter the pool. The proper procedure was to stand in front of the pool and use the water pails to soak oneself thoroughly by splashing the water over the body, then to use the soap, and then to rinse, washing the waste water down the drain in the floor. There was also a shower against one wall for people who preferred a quick shower to this way of bathing, which for many was unfamiliar. The bathroom floors were cemented and sealed with a highly glossy substance, and the floors sloped slightly to the center of the bathroom, where the drain was.

The toilets were never in the same room as the baths, but were separate in cubicles built in a long row, next to the last of the bathrooms. They were called water closets, after the English word indicating the water tanks high up over the toilets. We called them W.C. for short.

Directly across from all these facilities, again two steps down from the long landing, was the great kitchen, with its flagstone floor flanked at each end with an opening leading to a walled-in water well, a real necessity for this way of life all those years ago. The walls around the two wells were about six and a half feet high, and the immediate area around the wells had a lot of room to work in. It was common to find eight or ten maids in a circle around the well doing their chores.

The kitchen was a mixture of old and modern conveniences. There was nothing brooding about this kitchen, like so many of the big kitchen of those days in the tropics. Most of them were dark, dusty, smoky, cavernous areas. This one was splendidly light, a cheerful place and as spanking clean as a kitchen could be.

On a long whitewashed wall, all manner of pots and pans and ladles sparkled. There were gas stoves on one side of the kitchen and brick stoves built in against another wall. And at one end, near one of the openings that led to a well, were enormous sinks for all the dirty dishes that needed to be washed after each meal during the day and evening.

Behind it all were the servants' quarters, and they used the well closest to these quarters for bathing and their own laundry. The walls surrounding both wells were grown over with the most colorful bougainvilleas, just to make the somber-looking walls more cheerful to the eye.

ISLAND COMFORTS

The two long wings on either side of the main building, separated by graveled walks and plants, were the areas where the guests stayed. Their rooms were large and airy, with ten foot ceilings, and each room was equipped with a ceiling fan, an essential in the tropics.

In the doors and open windows screens were installed to keep out mosquitoes and other unwished-for little creatures, like tiny wall lizards, with their transparent bodies, and geckos, to name just two. People from Western countries were deadly afraid of them, and as a child I hadn't the slightest why that was. At one time I had caught a couple of the little lizards and presented them to one of the guests in a friendly gesture, as a welcoming gift. It was surprising for me to see her almost fall out of her chair in her haste to get away from me and my cute little friends, held protectively in my hands. Seeing an adult behave that way was perplexing. My cousins and I always played with the little lizards carefully; we would feed them steamed rice kernels fastened to a long, thin stick taken from the center of a coconut leaf, called "lidie."

The gecko was a much larger cousin of the little lizards, named *tjitjaks*, after the clicking sound they produce when calling to each other. The gecko was not such a willing playmate. We children would avoid him as much as we could, and he in turn would hide most of the time under the eaves. An interesting legend said that luck and prosperity would befall a person who hears the gecko call seven times in a row. Almost everyone in the Dutch Indies believed it, and everyone would count in silence when at night the gecko called, hoping fervently for the sound of the seventh call. The gecko was named *tokeh*, which is exactly the sound it made when it called.

All the hotel guest rooms were furnished with cream-colored wicker or bamboo furniture. Each room had a dresser, a large wardrobe, a desk and chair, and a big bed. A small wooden commode, painted off white, hid a chamber pot. The latter was of course designed to accommodate the nightly necessities of nature, for the W.C.'s were too far away to reach at night. A small sink was installed in the far corner of each room, hidden behind a narrow screen. It was the duty of the chambermaid to keep the rooms neat and clean and the commodes as spotless and odor free as possible. Each room had its own veranda and a couple of fresh potted plants to make it more pleasing to the eye. A seven-foot wall between the verandas provided privacy.

My grandparents' living quarters were in the front part of the right wing. It was a beautiful open sitting room, full of plants blooming in colorful ceramic pots scattered on the floor and bright panels of batik artfully arranged on the walls. Their private dining room was large enough to accommodate a long, dark teak table with ten chairs and a huge, beautifully carved china cabinet. It was made on the island of Bali, known for its woodcarving throughout the world.

Their bedroom was big and roomy, but almost spartan in its simplicity. The walls were white, as they were throughout the entire hotel, and almost unadorned. In the middle of the ceiling was the obligatory paddle fan. The cool, tile floor was bare except for a rose and wine-colored rug in front of the great bed. Aside from silky wine-colored draperies, applied more as a window dressing than for their usefulness, the only decoration was a handsomely framed portrait of my grandparents hanging above the bed, which was made with their three eldest children when they were still very small.

The room was devoid of other luxuries or trappings of wealth. The few personal items, such as the ivory and silver brushes and hand mirror on the dresser and the writing material on the desk, were laid out with precision and neatness, as if awaiting an inspection. To me, my grandparents' rooms were a tranquil and relaxing place to be. So very reassuring, it was a quiet inner sanctum with an appealing simplicity, a place where one could shed the burdens of the day and lighten one's soul in solitude.

There was in addition a spare bedroom, for whoever of their eight children and their families wanted to stay over. If more than one couple wanted to stay, there were always rooms in the hotel available. As a small child, when I stayed the night, I usually crawled onto the huge bed and curled up between my grandparents. I had the impression that they did not mind this one bit.

TINA AND ALFRED

Tina Rozen, my grandmother, was the only child of a sturdy Dutchman from Friesland, Holland, and a dainty and very pretty Sudanese woman from Lembang in West Java. Small of stature and bone structure, my grandmother had a certain elegance in her bearing that not many of her size can carry off. As a result, many people thought her far taller than she actually was.

Born and raised on the island of Java, on her parents' plantation outside Batavia, she had a keen business acumen inherited from her father, and although it was less obvious than his, hers was nonetheless just as powerful. She was known by many of her business acquaintances to be a tough opponent and negotiator in spite of her gentle approach and soft-spoken manner. My grandmother had no real interest or strong ambition to amass great wealth. Business was a great game of wits to her, the challenge of outsmarting an opponent.

She also had an enormous trust both in herself and in God and always seemed to be relaxed and calm in her business dealings. These characteristics seemed to draw opportunities almost automatically to her doorstep, where she met challenges almost playfully, with a ready smile. Self-assured and devoid of anxiety, she was bound to come out on the winning side of any game—because in her games, there was no greed.

Alfred Rozen, my grandfather, was born and raised in the Dutch East Indies. His parents came from Utrecht, Holland, and had settled in Bandoeng, which is also in West Java. He was quite tall, around six foot one or two, with brown hair and an impressive dark mustache, which he use to pull on when deep in thought.

He came to work for my great-grandfather, Cornelius Rinsinga, on his plantation around the turn of the century. He was twenty-one and had just graduated from the university in Holland, where his parents had sent him to finish his formal education, studying agriculture and business management. He did not like Holland and missed the easygoing way of life of the colonies and the warmhearted manner of the people. He deplored what he viewed as the narrow-mindedness of the Dutch in Holland at that time and intensely disliked the weather, which was often cold and damp. He could not wait to get back to his beloved and sunny islands.

The morning after his arrival back in the colonies, Alfred set off early to meet my great-grandfather, with whom he had been in correspondence for two months, even before his graduation, while he was still in Holland. He had always wanted to work on a plantation and could hardly wait to get started, although in fact he had yet to be hired—nothing had been finalized about his position. In his mind, however, he had studied for years for this moment, and was certain that now his dream was about to materialize. There was no doubt in his mind that he would be hired as the new young assistant on this plantation.

His hired carriage entered the gate. A sign with the name Rinsinga Plantation hung in big graceful letters above it. As he started on the graveled drive, a strong sense of having finally arrived welled within him. The house, seen from afar at the end of the drive, gleamed white in the afternoon sun. It was built on a slight rise and looked more sprawling and imposing than it actually was. Suddenly, he knew with great certainty that it was here where his destiny lay. This feeling became profound when he entered the large veranda. He was met by a servant, who ushered him into a side office inside the inner living room. There he awaited my great-grandfather's return from the fields he was inspecting with one of his overseers.

Now alone, Alfred sat back in his chair and looked about him. From where he sat, he had a clear view of part of the front veranda, and a slight movement caught his eye. In the far corner half obscured by tall potted plants, he noticed a young girl of around sixteen years of age, slouched unladylike in one of the rattan easy chairs scattered across the veranda. Her clothing was uncommon for that era—tan riding breeches, a white fine linen long-sleeved blouse, and brown leather riding boots.

As if she suddenly felt his eyes resting upon her, she lifted her head from the book she was reading and turned her head in his direction. He caught a glimpse of large dark brown eyes under well-defined black brows. Her glossy wavy black hair was cut in a short bob. Her spontaneous smile revealed small, even white teeth in a creamy, tan complexioned, pretty face.

Fortunately for Alfred, my great-grand-father took a liking to him and did hire him as his assistant, because from the very moment he and Tina laid eyes on each other on that day across the vast veranda, they fell in love and knew that they belonged together. They married exactly a year later when my grandmother was seventeen years old, in 1897.

I don't know how often I have heard this wonderful story of how my grandparents met for the very first time, but always brings a warm glow into my heart whenever I think about it. They were so very right together. No one who saw them together would ever deny it.

THE PLANTATION

Alfred Rozen turned out to have the heart and soul of a plantation man. He loved everything about it, from the early morning hours spent inspecting the new yields of the crop brought in the day before from the dried coconuts called *copra*, to the very end product of pure coconut oil, carefully sampled, ready to be placed on the market, to the thorough inspection of the oil presses kept meticulously clean, to the gathering and binding of the leaves in big sheaves used to thatch the roofs of huts in Indonesian villages, called *kampongs*.

The central spine of the coconut leaves was removed and cleaned and made into long brooms and brushes. The fibrous substance that lies between the hard outer shell and the inner hard shell of the coconut was made into scouring pads to clean pots and pans. It also was woven into thick mats to lie in front of almost every front door.

The hard shell of the coconut was used to make women's hair-combs, spoons, and ladles, as well as bowls and cups in numerous different sizes. The functions and products of the coconut tree and its fruit were varied and continuously evolving. Their importance and the dependence of the Indonesian population on these products in their daily lives were clear.

After my great-grandfather passed away in 1907, the entire management of the plantation and its operations came to lie in the very capable hands of the young couple and their overseers. Alfred was then thirty-two years old and Tina was twenty-seven. Their marriage had flourished, and their family had grown to eight children. My father was their firstborn.

Great-grandmother Gesina, still living and in extremely good health, lived on the plantation with Tina and Alfred and their children, whom she adored. She was still recognized by all employees as the *Njonja Besar,* the grand lady of the house, and my grandmother was called *Njonja Besar Moedah,* the young grand lady. My grandfather the *Toewan Besar,* the great master.

In 1910 my grandparents moved from the plantation to their city house in Batavia, and my great-grandmother moved to the city with the family. There were eight children now, and two of them were ready to attend the secondary school. The children had been privately tutored at the plantation beginning at age five.

Here, in the city of Batavia, Tina developed a desire to own and run a hotel and boarding house combined. Alfred, recognizing her sharp intelligence and intuition, gave her free rein and encouraged her one hundred percent in the endeavor. They opened the hotel in the beginning of 1913. Six months later, my grandfather bought an icehouse, which was to me one of many miracles all through my growing years.

Alfred's real ambition was his plantation, however, and he spent at least one week per month, and often times longer, on the land he loved so deeply. He was the one in the family who lived, breathed, ate, and slept the plantation trade, although he would deny it with an engaging laugh when confronted. My grandmother and the children joined him as often as they could, and only the circumstances of schooling and business kept them away for lengths of time. My great-grandmother would stay on for longer periods of time, being utterly at one with the surroundings. Everyone loved the special atmosphere of the plantation.

PLANTATION MEMORIES

One of my earliest childhood memories was of sitting in front of my grandfather on his horse. I recall being kept closely and safely against his chest with his left arm securely encircling me, doing the rounds through the fields of endless rows of neatly planted coconut trees, with one of his overseers closely by his side, pointing out all sorts of things of interest, always pertaining to the crop.

The fieldworkers, men who lived on the plantation grounds with or without their families, would salute or wave to us from a distance. Sometimes we would ride to them, my grandfather saying a few words, jesting with them, which would extract peals of laughter from the group. He took pride in knowing every worker by name, as well as their wives and children. He was known as a kind and just employer.

In my mind's eye I can see the three long tables set out on the front lawn before the big house, when the wages were due to be paid. A line of workers formed, which would split into three when they reached the tables, behind each of which an overseer was seated with a wooden tray before him, filled with little envelopes containing the weekly earnings of each field hand and also of their foremen. My grandfather, standing nearby, always had a friendly word to say to anyone who came to thank him. He would present a cigarette to those who smoked, a wad of tobacco to those who chewed, and candies to take home to the children. These were simple but kind gestures that the workers deeply appreciated.

I also recall seeing my great-grandmother and my grandmother leaving the house in the middle of the night to follow a fieldworker who had come to the house to fetch them. Aroused from a deep sleep, I would peek around my bedroom door and watch the commotion that was going on in those late hours. In times of sickness or when someone's wife was giving birth, the two women would go to the workers' quarters to assist. Sometimes a doctor was summoned to administer medication and special treatment.

My grandparents were deeply involved with their people. A few years later, in the midst of a terrible war, this kindness was returned to our family tenfold.

There were many animals on the plantation, and it was the horses that were my biggest pleasure. When I was four, my grandfather gave me my very own horse. Since he had taken me riding with him since I was a toddler, I was already at ease and quite comfortable on horseback and excitedly accepted the gift. I was a proud little girl! The horse was a beautiful chestnut mare, and she was chosen for me for her gentle disposition. I named her Frieda and loved and cared for her for five years, until the Japanese took her away from me when they occupied the Dutch East Indies.

In my growing years, while visiting the plantation, the monkeys that my grandfather kept were always a source of lots of laughter, yet they played an extremely important role in the operation and management of a coconut plantation. There were twenty-four gray Java monkeys, my grandfather's prized possessions. The females were kept for breeding purposes only. The males were trained to pick fruits, since they were bigger and stronger and their teeth were also much longer and stronger than those of the females.

The special care bestowed on all the monkeys was quite deliberate, as it was with all the animals on the plantation. Looking back, I think those years and those experiences on the plantation instilled in me a great love and respect for everything that lives.

One experience that still makes me smile whenever I think of it was watching the monkeys and their trainers at work. There were six trainers, and each of them was assigned the same two animals. These monkeys were the fastest coconut pickers around. No human could even come close to their agility and swiftness of movement.

A long line was attached to the harness around the monkey's chest. With the two monkeys on his shoulder, the trainer would select a tree with coconuts ripe to be picked. A quick glance up was usually enough to assure the man of his right choice. He stopped at the chosen tree and gave a soft command, "*Najek*," meaning "climb." With lightning speed, both monkeys raced to the top, where the fruits grow in a bunch. They would each grab a coconut and look down at their trainer below. I could see their wise-looking faces and their eyes full of concentration as they awaited their master's command. If the coconut was ripe enough to be picked, they would feel a soft tug on their rope and instantly they would begin to twist the fruit in their little hands. If the stem was a tough one, they would also work it with their teeth, and the coconut would drop in no time at all.

One monkey, a little male, took a special liking to me. He would follow me around like a puppy dog, as soon his cage was opened. He would jump on me to be carried, nuzzling his little face in the crease of my neck with his arms wrapped around me. He was absolutely adorable.

One of my grandparents' special projects was the breeding of pedigree German shepherd dogs. They kept a couple of these dogs themselves. For my sixth birthday, while visiting the plantation on that very special day, I was allowed to choose a puppy. I was elated and chose the darkest of the litter of seven puppies. It was a little male, with the most beautiful markings, which bespoke of his excellent lineage and quality. I called him Prince, and he became my shadow. Three years later, he, too, was confiscated by the Japanese, together with everything the family owned.

Those years spent visiting my grandparents on the plantation on weekends and vacations as well as the frequent stays with them at their hotel in town, had a strong effect on my character. Although the years were short, their effect was potent. For many the memories of childhood are the most vivid, and I have savored my recollections of this happy time—and my formative years—throughout my life.

THE FAMILY

My parents and I lived three houses down the street of on which the hotel sat. Our house was also owned by the Rozen family, together with five other houses located throughout Batavia. It was in an excellent neighborhood on a wide avenue, lined with stately Canary nut and beautiful flame trees, which provided shade, color, and coolness on scorching tropical days.

Entering our front garden, one was greeted with a blaze of color. The flower beds were awash with abundant reds and pinks and whites of impatience encircling the larger and higher shrubs of bird of paradise, hydrangea, and hibiscus. Skirting the gardens were all manner of other shrubs and trees, while graveled paths and an open space of lawn were lined with richly planted borders of zinnias in vivid colors.

The house itself was built in the typical style of the era, with whitewashed stucco, an orange-red tiled roof common to the islands of those bygone days, and steps leading up to a wide and open verandah with cool tiled marble floors. In this house, the tiles were of a marbled dark gray and white and went throughout the entire house, stopping short at the few steps leading down to the kitchen, baths, utility rooms, and other functional areas.

Here again were the big open verandah, the inner sitting room enclosed by plantation shuttered doors, and the open dining room right behind it. All three rooms were of identical proportions, and alongside on the left were the front office or study and the three bedrooms. Each had a connecting door between them, and each had a door to the sitting and dining rooms.

Attached to the house, on the right side, was a small wing that was rented out to a young couple. The young woman, the Dutch/Indonesian daughter of a lifelong friend of the family, was expecting her first child. I could hardly wait for the baby to be born, since Lena, the mother to be, had promised that I could help take care of the baby. This promise came to be prophetic, two years later in 1941, when I was eight, with our beloved islands on the verge of war.

Molly, my mother, was a woman of a wonderful and happy disposition, who laughed a lot and was fun to be with. With a warm and giving nature, she loved my father and me above everything else. She did have a temper, though, and when provoked she could lash out and her tongue could be cutting.

She was very fair-skinned, with very light brown hair and warm brown eyes. All this she inherited from her father, who was a Dutchman born and raised in the Dutch East Indies. His parents came from Zeeland, a province in the southwest of the Netherlands, who settled in the colonies in the mid-1800s, like many before them.

Wilhelm Grotendaal, my maternal grandfather, was a quiet man who wanted to be left alone as much as possible. Therefore, my recollection of him is one of an aloof and cantankerous old man who presented his cheek in a mechanical way to be kissed and who would get back a most mechanical little peck from his grandchildren. I cannot remember him ever hugging me—or any of us, for that matter.

Laura Mellinga Grotendaal, my mother's mother, died young, and my grandfather, who adored her, withdrew into himself and became the man I remember. After her death, he gave one hundred percent of himself to his work and eventually retired as the head of the Department of Topography. He died in the middle of the war when he was eighty-five years old.

Although I did not know her, since she passed away before I was even born, from stories and pictures about her I knew my maternal grandmother as an extremely pretty woman, with wavy deep black hair, olive skin, and the bluest of eyes. She was the offspring of a Dutch father and an Indonesian mother. She bore six children, one son and five daughters.

Molly, my mother was the child in the middle and would laughingly refer to herself as the "Forgotten One." She was far from forgotten, of course, and her cheerful and outgoing disposition was evidence of a very happy childhood, before the death of her mother, when she was seventeen years old.

In contrast to my mother, my father, Albert Rozen was quiet and somewhat cautious by nature. These traits I think were chiefly engendered by shyness, rather than any particular canniness. He was tall, with a regular build and dark complexion. Later in life he became the head of a Department of Financing in Batavia. Although he had an astonishing aptitude for figures and kept the books meticulously, I always had the feeling that it was hardly his vocation. He was apprenticed in accounting when he was eighteen, so after a while it became a way of life for him. I think it never occurred to him to seek a more congenial employer, and since he was not ambitious and lacked the drive his parents had before him, his career remained amidst the accounting books. Because, as the eldest son, he stood to inherit the whole of the plantation someday, my grandparents wanted him to master accounting, since he would be in charge of all the monies involved in all the family holdings. But the war, which was not too far off, changed his life drastically, as it changed the lives of all.

Already in 1939 there were strong rumors of war and unrest in Europe. But who could imagine that it would touch our peaceful colonies? We lived in abundance and comfort and were so far removed that no one was worried, especially not the younger generation. But my grandparents were deeply concerned and aware of the lurking danger.

I often overheard their quiet conversations, when they had gathered their two eldest sons, overseers, and managers for plantation and hotel meetings. My father, with his cautious nature, was also extremely concerned, but he denied all approaching danger with a bravura he did not feel. He probably did this to reassure his parents, who were both in their sixties by 1939, and was trying to spare them the anxieties he felt himself.

We all went on with our daily lives, ignoring the danger signs of an oncoming war, which hung like a dark cloud over our heads, as much as we could. My father continued to organize hunting parties with his friends on weekends, and even took me with him on one or two occasions, presumably to instill in me the art of patiently waiting. I hated those few times I went with him. To me they were occasions of useless killing, and I could never understand how someone could enjoy the destruction of a life. To my father's defense, I have to admit that he never wasted the kills. The wild boars were always brought home to be prepared into meals, as were the geese and many doves. But I never understood the need to hunt if there was such an abundance of meat to buy at the marketplace.

My father often declared that it was a pity that I was born a daughter and not a son. He thought that if I were a boy, I would have enjoyed the fishing and hunting much more. Those declarations, uttered so many years ago by someone I looked up to immensely, are still imprinted on my brain. To this very day, I feel I have to prove myself the equal of men, if not the better of them. It sometimes shows in my aggressive behavior and in discussions I joined as an adult to prove the intelligence of the debaters.

As a twelve-year-old I had to fly kites better, climb a tree faster, and always win in a game of marbles. Right after the war, when I was thirteen, during a time when the military life was still very much a part of our lives, I competed in a shooting match held in celebration of the Queen's birthday (Queen's Day is August 31st, a day to honor Queen Wilhelmina of the Netherlands and all the Dutch colonies). The competition on that day included jeep racing over all kinds of obstacles, field and track events, and the like.

My father, who was still in the military at the time, had seen to it, through many weeks of training, that I could outshoot many a seasoned soldier. He was there to watch the match and gave me the proudest hug when I had beaten my opponent, a young lieutenant. I received a great big medal specially made for the occasion. That day, my father's praise, which I craved, was well worth the anxiety and horror I felt every time I pulled the trigger during those long shooting drills before the festivities.

A PRIVILEGED PERPSPECTIVE

My life is rich with memories of my privileged early life in the islands. But it's not that way for everyone. And my mother once said something to me that stopped me short. She said it years later, when I was a parent with three children of my own and already living in the United States for many years.

We were discussing a vacation plan my husband and I desperately needed. My mother remarked, "Why is it that the modern housewife depends so much on those yearly vacations? I very seldom had one myself." Once I got over my shock, I had to smile about that remark, so completely had she forgotten the luxury in which she was indulged for much of her life. Indeed, with a staff of six servants around her and her small family at all times, a bungalow in the mountains almost twice the size of the house my husband and I live in now, and a place she was always welcome to use at the plantation, the need for a vacation wouldn't be so urgently felt. The fact that I had a full-time job, before coming home to care for my own family of five with no servants to rely on, completely eluded her.

PRECIOUS ASSISTANCE

Our family of three had a houseboy, a cook, a laundry maid, a gardener, his helper, and a *babuh* or nanny. I still remember them all so clearly, but especially Ierah, my nanny. She was Javanese and had lost her husband and only child, a two-year-old son, in the village fire where she and her small family lived. She came to work for our family three years before I was born, as a chambermaid. She was highly recommended by my grandmother, for whom she worked for two years before she came to work for us. My mother was in need of a maid at the time and my grandmother had sent her Ierah.

She became my nanny right after I was born and stayed in that function until long into the war, working for us without any pay.

Ierah was also the one who would feed me deliciously prepared Indonesian dishes and scrumptious little sweet cakes made with coconut milk, in the kitchen, when my mother was not at home. And it was she who dried my tears and tended to my cuts and bruises after an unexpected tumble on the gravelly paths while running or riding my bike. When I was still a toddler, she would carry me on her hip in a sling made of colorful material, called *slendang*. She would carry me for hours while doing her other chores around the house—but only when my mother wasn't home. Mother did not like her to do that too often. She would also sing to me Indonesian songs in her soft but melodious voice. She was always calm and soothing. I will never forget her.

Her great aunt and uncle worked for my grandparents for many years. By the time Ierah became my nanny, they were already retired, since both were in their seventies. My grandparents had kept them on and gave them food and clothing and a roof over their head. They were hard workers in their younger years and loyal to the family. The woman's name I never knew, we all called her Nènèh, meaning grandmother in Indonesian. She used to be nanny to my father and his younger brother when they were little. That was quite a job to do, since both were very spoiled, especially my father, being the eldest son. She spent her days tending the hotel's herbal garden, which grew behind the building, with her husband, whom we all called Kakèh, grandfather. Nènèh's knowledge about the herbal healing powers were extraordinarily perceptive and one hundred percent accurate. In the case of family illnesses, she was summoned when the doctor was not easy to get to.

An incident that occurred when I was seven years old which stands out in my mind. My father was ill and had already been in bed for a couple of days. He ran a high fever and from time to time would roll into a ball and writhe from stabbing pains in his lower back and abdomen.

Our family doctor was on leave and his substitute was nowhere to be found—a not-uncommon occurrence in those times. When the pain became unbearable, my grandmother was asked to come. When she arrived at our house, Nènèh was with her. She carried an old but snow-white pillowcase, most likely a discard from the hotel, on which she had threaded a cord to open and close the bag like a pouch. Inside were several small pouches, each marked with a different sign. The pouches contained the herbs she herself had grown and tended and later had carefully selected and dried. Nènèh could neither read nor write, like many of her generation at that time. Because she was illiterate, this was her way of keeping track of the different herbs to treat different illnesses.

When my father saw her coming into the bedroom he bellowed, "Get that old witch out of here, I don't want anything to do with all her mumbo jumbo." Nènèh ignored him completely and calmly untied her pouch. She then walked to his bed and felt his brow. My father shook off her outstretched hand angrily. She gave him a sharp slap on his wrist and told him to behave and to hold his horses. To her she was still his nanny, and he was still in her charge. My grandmother, standing by, could hardly suppress her laughter. Her adult son was still a small boy under Nènèh's hands.

Nènèh asked many questions, which my father grudgingly answered. After a while she precisely laid out all the tiny bags next to each other on a small table that stood in the far corner of the room. As far as I could see from where I stood, which was near the door, there were more than twenty pouches. Nènèh seriously and painstakingly studied the little bags for a long time. She then picked one up and held it to her heart. Her lips were moving as in silent prayer. Then she nodded and smiled to herself, suggesting to me that, yes, the one she had picked was the right one. She could feel it in her bones. She then left the room and went to the kitchen. When she returned, she carried a white big mug filled with a steaming tea. My father roared when he saw the tea. No, he was not even going to touch it, let alone drink it. Nènèh came quickly to the bed and spoke sharply in Indonesian, "You either drink this every day for a week or you will die, it's your choice." And with that, she turned and walked quietly away. To my mother, who had followed her out of the room, she gave instructions to watch for pulverized residue in his urine, which my father would pass in a few days. Two weeks later, my father was as good as new, and when the doctor finally examined him, he was pronounced totally healed and the kidney stone gone. The herb that Nènèh had given him to drink as a tea is called *kumis kutjing* (whiskers of a cat), since the flower of the herb resembles a cat most precisely and even imitates the little mouth.

At another time, Nènèh healed my grandfather of a threatening eye disease. It was a case of advanced cataract, nowadays easily cured but in those times it meant certain blindness. Like my father, my grandfather did not believe in Nènèh's herbal knowledge. He called it "a lot of hocus pocus."

Nènèh, however, saw the seriousness of the slowly progressing disease as she observed how uncertain my grandfather had become in the way he walked. And when she saw his inaccuracy in judgment of distances, she ground fine an herb, also used as a decorative plant, with thick and furry pink and purplish leaves, and diluted the slimy and pulpy mass with tap water and poured it through a strainer. She then instructed my grandmother to put some in an eyeglass, and my grandfather was to bathe his eye twice a day with this solution for as long as a month religiously—perhaps somewhat longer if necessary. My grandfather, with no other means left to solve his problem, relented and did what Nènèh had told him to do.

To this day I still see him bent over the sink in his bedroom, bathing his eyes precisely as Nènèh had ordered. The film that had formed over his eyes became gradually thinner and slowly disappeared.

These two incidents astonish me when I think of them. What a just and accurate diagnosis in both cases—and many more—made by an illiterate woman of nearly eighty years of age with no education. Nènèh helped and healed many of us in the family for many years, until she passed away in 1944, near the end of the war.

SPIRITS AND SUPERSTITIONS

In Indonesia, as in many tropical regions, superstition persists in many forms and actually is a way of life for many in the population. I heard several stories as a child, and when I was a teenager, I even went with my friends to investigate, to see if the stories were true, as people claimed them to be.

To this day, I have to admit, reluctantly, that I really do not know. I have witnessed some weird incidents that made me believe that the unexplainable does exist, although some of them I would discard with a shrug of the shoulders as, in my grandfather's words, "a whole bunch of mumbo jumbo."

When I was a child, my nanny Ierah told me that everything and everybody has a spirit or guide, and to this day I strongly believe this to be true. She talked about the wells that were on all our properties, for example. "Do not ever go even *near* a well," she would warn me. The wells have water-spirits living in them, and therefore the wells are their domain." "Always have the utmost respect for these wells, and never throw things into them that do not belong in the water, and especially never look down into the well. The spirits will pull you down, and you will never see your parents ever again." The effect of these stories did work very well for a while. But after a time, the gravity of what I had heard wore off, and I thought it strange, that the story seemed to pertain only to children. The servants themselves did not hesitate to look into the well when drawing up water to do the dishes, washing the laundry, and to bathe themselves, and they never got hurt. I got the strong feeling that Ierah wanted only to protect me from the danger of falling into the deep well, and this was the best way she knew how to, by instilling in me intense fear of the wells.

The Indonesian people do believe in the water-spirits—in all sorts of spirits, for that matter. They believe strongly in the fact of their presence near these deep and dark water-holes to keep the wells clean and pure for the people to use, and sometimes one could find small offerings of flowers and food within the walls surrounding these wells, to appease these *penunguhs* or spirit-guards.

They also believe in appeasing the spirits when building a house or opening a business. The custom calls for offerings of delicacies, fruits, and flowers put in small ceramic bowls and placed in the four corners of the building. A *dukun* or shaman would walk around and through the building with a bowl of holy water in his hand, softly murmuring prayers, asking for protection for the owners against misfortunes and negative influences from the outside world, sprinkling holy water here and there as he went along. His helper walked right next to him, praying with him while carrying the incense, and also begging the spirits for health and prosperity to come to the owners who had hired them to perform the ceremony.

When I was a teenager, after the war was finally over, I would roam through just such ceremonies with a group of my friends. We would go wherever we could find one and would gorge ourselves on all the delicious foods left in the corners after the people had gone. Otherwise it would be left for the neighborhood dogs and cats to eat.

Another event that was always an attraction for us children was the *Kudah Kepang*, a street show given by a group of people who would tour the cities and towns to earn their living. The show existed of a few men sitting astride fake horses, representing the horse itself. The audience stood in a wide circle, watching with great expectation. The men were quickly brought into a heavy trance and began to gallop wildly within the circle. The horses were made of tightly braided coconut leaves or fine strips of bamboo, thickly interwoven, completely with ears and tails. They were neatly painted in all sorts of colors, with eyes, mouth, and other characteristics of a horse.

To demonstrate of how deeply the men were hypnotized, grass and chaff sifted from the rice paddy were fed to them as one would to a horse, which they hungrily devoured. Water in dirty pails was now brought into the circle and placed before them. The men drank from the pail with great thirst.

The highlight of the show, the moment everybody was waiting for, was next. While whipped into a frenzy, the men who had taken on the entire personality of a horse neighed, kicked, reared, and bucked. Coarsely stamped glass was now brought into the circle. Some of the glass was being fed to the men, who seemed to eat it with great relish. The audience was totally captivated. Excited "ooohs and aaahs" could be heard throughout the throng of people who had gathered to watch. The rest of the stamped glass was now thrown on the ground in the center of the circle. The men were perspiring profusely in the hot tropical afternoon and drank water frequently. Then, on a sharp command from the hypnotizer, they rolled and writhed on the heap of glass. The audience gasped and stood petrified.

Another event of mass hypnosis—which is what it probably is—occurred when I was eight years old, just before the war began. My grandmother often would have a servant fetch to the hotel one of the many street vendors who daily traveled the city streets to sell their wares in handcars they would push, or in big baskets hanging from a yoke they carried on their shoulders, perfectly balanced.

It was a mango vendor and his son whom the servant brought in from the street. The son, a sturdy young man of around twenty, did most of the carrying, and the father, middle-aged, would call out what they had to sell and would relieve his son of his burden from time to time. The servants led them straight to the front steps of my grandparents' apartment at the hotel.

Good deals were usually made this way, if the merchandise was considered to be of good quality. The entire contents of both baskets were then bought for a more than reasonable price, since the happy vendors could now go home without their heavy loads on their shoulders.

I still remember the scene clearly, both the father and son emptying their baskets carefully, while the servants carried the fruits away to the storage rooms to be used the next day for the guests. Suddenly, the father asked if he could peel and slice up one mango for us to try. We found it odd, since he had done this before he'd made the sale. There was quite an audience on my grandmother's veranda: my mother and I, both my aunts and their children, my grandmother, and the few personal servants who worked for my grandparents. Each of us was given a small slice of the mango, until only the stone was left in the vendor's palm. He then asked if he could plant the seed in the very corner of a flower bed nearby. My grandmother nodded her agreement. The man dug a small hole carefully in the very corner of the flower bed as not to disturb the plants, placed the seed in the hole, and covered it with dirt. Now both men invited all of us to come down the steps to watch carefully and attentively. Both men became very still in their utmost concentration, and, to our astonishment, a tiny green point became visible through the black soil after a moment, then a sprout emerged. A tiny plant started to form, and, miraculously, the plant began to grow right before our eyes. It reached a height of three to four feet and a fruit started to form on a small branch

The mango grew to full proportion and ripened on the spot while still on the tree. The older man picked the fruit. A drop of white fresh sap appeared at the tip of where the fruit had been attached. He then peeled the fruit with a clean knife and again gave each of us a small piece to taste. "This one will be twice as sweet than the one before," he said with a smile. We all tasted the fruit and all agreed that it was indeed sweet. We all then applauded, the two men graciously bowed, and they left waving to us happily. They'd had a good day and, with time to spare, decided to give us a show, as a small bonus, I suppose. We children were very impressed.

THE FAMILY BOUTIQUE

My grandparents also owned a clothing store, which was at first a boutique that they owned together with their youngest daughter, Gilly. It started out as a fun investment. Gilly had a superb sense of style and her color combinations were extraordinary, even if a little daring for the time. She also had a real knack for design. My grandmother had given her full rein in managing the boutique and in designing her own fashion line. Aunt Gilly had another boutique in Singapore, which she mutually owned and managed with her Hungarian husband, before their divorce in 1938. She therefore had plenty of experience in the fashion business.

Following the divorce, her ex-husband returned to Europe, and they parted as very good friends. He gave Aunt Gilly the store to keep, recognizing her great talent as a designer. No one knew where her artistic gifts sprang from, but her taste was matchless and her flair unrivaled. Aunt Gilly possessed incredible talent and, coupled with her inborn energy, it made her a woman to reckon with in the Southeast Asia of that time.

Apart from her great talent, she had a finely tuned understanding of the public's desires. She also possessed an uncanny knack of "knowing" ahead of time what people wanted and liked and—more importantly—what they would buy. Together with my grandmother as a major shareholder and partner, whose grasp for financial matters was equally astute, the two women were unsurpassed in their combined business strength. My father, who was their accountant at the time, found that all their complex monetary schemes stood up to his scrutiny and won his constant though astonished approval.

Aunt Gilly was just like her mother. She was twenty-seven years old when Maison Gilly came into existence. After living in Singapore for six years after she was married, she decided to move back to Batavia, to take up designing and the management of the store. My grandmother was elated, for she knew Maison Gilly was in extremely capable hands.

In 1940 Aunt Gilly's designs for this particular year's collections were even more striking then the years before. The lines were elegant, understated, and superbly balanced by fine detailing. She had also cleverly combined colors for entirely different effects. Only Aunt Gilly could have put together such unusual mixtures of colors. Navy blue for instance, highlighted with apple green, vivid cyclamen with lilac, blues combined with violet, and greens sparked with a deep rose.

They all worked very well together and her designs, because of their clean lines and simplicity, created an elegance women loved and craved—something my grandmother's excellent eye for business was quick to recognize. Instantly she hired ten more *djajits*, seamstress and tailors, in addition to the five she already had employed a few years back. She also had the store enlarged. And so, in the fashion-starved elite society of the Dutch colonial cities of that time, Maison Gilly became a phenomenal success.

I remember the *djajits*, each sitting on his own *tikar* or woven mat, in their traditional cross-legged way, tailor style. They were all male. Each had a sewing machine in front of him, and each was equipped with a pair of sharp scissors, a big pincushion full of pins, and a measuring tape around his neck. They sat in rows, neatly arranged on the floor. I also remember the two long tables at the very end of the large open room. One was used to measure the cloth and precisely lay it out on the paper patterns Aunt Gilly had made. The other table was used to cut the fabric in accordance with the pattern.

Later, a men's boutique was added to the steadily growing store, and even more tailors and seamstresses were hired. Two more salesmen in the men's department now completed the expanding staff.

THE ICE FACTORY

Another aspect of the family enterprise was the ice factory, which provided the hotel with huge ice blocks and stocked three big refrigerators and freezers. In those days, freezers and refrigerators were a luxury usually found only in restaurants, food stores, hotels, and the homes of the well-to-do. There was a constant need for ice in the hot climates of the tropics, so financially the icehouse, as we called it, did extremely well.

It was a matter of intense interest to me, especially when the crew released the big guardrail latch way up high to let the ice blocks slide down the chutes, sending them with incredible speed down into an enormous heap of sawdust at the opposite end of the huge space below. When I visited the icehouse with my father, he always made sure that his hand was firmly wrapped around my small wrist. We always stood at a safe distance in case one of the huge blocks came loose.

On the walls of the icehouse were all matter of hand tools, including many different ice picks. There were straight ones, used to separate huge blocks into smaller pieces, also curved ones and ice saws. Against another wall heaps of burlap bags were stored lined up racks. The ice blocks were wrapped in burlap and made ready for transportation and delivery to whoever had ordered them. The trucks that transported them were heavily insulated as well—quite unusual for that period. Sawdust was added for even better insulation to battle the melting process in the hot and humid tropical weather. Upon delivery, people would store the ice in long wooden boxes lined with thin sheets of metal, very much in the same way the trucks were insulated. All in the service of preserving the ice just a little longer.

Sadly enough for me, the icehouse was sold to another investor in 1939, when I was six years old. I had always liked the icehouse and Mr. Anton, who had been its supervisor for many years. He sported a large handlebar mustache just like my grandfather's. I also missed the long visits to the icehouse that my father and I used to share for as long I could remember.

MOUNTAIN RETREAT

The family's bungalow, way up high in the mountains, just outside a small town by the name of Tjitjuruk, was another highlight for an active and curious youngster as I was at the time. We would retreat to the bungalow when the city temperatures reached oppressive highs. Sometimes the group was just my parents and I and the chauffeur and the houseboy, leaving the other servants to care for our house in the city for a few days. And sometimes we would share the house with other family members, which was even more fun.

The bungalow had four big bedrooms, a large inner sitting room, and a deep wraparound veranda, which there in the mountains was glass enclosed. The temperatures here were much cooler, especially at night. The bungalow had no electricity, and the entire house was equipped with the kerosene lamps, which made a soft hissing sound. In the evening, their bright lights were reflected in the glass panels that surrounded the veranda, creating a festive air. The crickets and frogs in the ponds and thick foliage around the house gave a natural concert that added to this lively yet peaceful atmosphere.

The bungalow was built high on a rise, to avoid the chance of flooding, surrounded as it was by creeks. Sitting on the back part of the veranda in the still of the morning, enjoying a cup of freshly brewed coffee, one could follow the rice field terraces, extending for miles in magnificent shades of green—an immense pleasure to behold.

Long, thin lines could be seen coming out from the tiny huts, built way up high on stilts on the very edges of the *sawahs*, or rice fields. The lines were connected to scarecrows and rattling tin cans, which were kept in continuous motion by someone in the huts, to keep away the swarms of birds that flew over the *sawahs*. From our bungalow vantage point, this way of life seemed wonderfully laid back and serene, and the panoramic view was magnificent indeed.

Also from this side, one could see a narrow, winding path that snaked its way down until it disappeared under the thick foliage of bamboo and other shrubs and trees. If you listened carefully, a soft murmur could be heard from the tumbling and dappled creeks that ran across the property near where the bungalow stood. The path led to a small natural basin and a little water-fall splashed down between huge ferns and bamboo. It poured into the basin, which was formed by boulders, before it continued its course into one of the creeks.

This spot was my idea of a little piece of heaven on earth, and I raced to it, as soon as the car pulled up in front of the bungalow. My father followed, running happily as a child after me. We both were panting and perspiring when we reached the waterfall. I kicked off my shoes, took off my dress, and splashed into the water. My father also took off his shoes and shirt and went in with his walking shorts still on. We immediately headed for the *pantjoran*, constructed years ago out of a big piece of hollow bamboo as an extension to guide the water away from the slippery wall, more toward the center of the pool. Father and I both stood under the water, enjoying every deliciously cool and refreshing moment.

After a while, Mother came down the path to join us. Asim, our houseboy, directly in front of her, swinging a house broom from left to right against the undergrowth on both sides of the path. He had the biggest grin on his face while doing this, because he knew my mother's fear of snakes and anything that crawls extremely well, since he was called to her assistance on numerous occasions to remove things that even slightly resembled a crawling creature.

Mom brought towels for us when we came out of the water. For a while we all sat on the mossy rocks, taking in the beauty and tranquility of the place. Asim sat a little apart from where my parents and I sat, as was the custom. He pointed out all sorts of interesting things to me. He detected a wild *djambu bol* tree, better known as wax guava or mountain apple tree in the Hawaiian Islands. The fruit resembles an apple, but its texture is finer and softer than the flesh of an apple, with a more intense flavor known only in tropical fruits.

Asim also pointed out bushes laden with wild berries. The berries look somewhat like raspberries, but the color was bright orange-red and they felt velvety to the touch. Asim picked handfuls for me, which I shared with my parents. The berries were deliciously plump and juicy and very sweet. Suddenly he looked intently to the ground right in front of him. He called me over and pointed to a couple of tiny wells in the loose sand. With a twig he carefully poked in the wells and out came two little creatures. Ever so carefully he picked them up and put them in the palm of my hand. They were the *undur undur*, which means "walking backwards," after the peculiar way they travel, appearing to move backward, or so it seems to the human eye. At Asim's request, I put them back where he had found them. Soon we were ready to go up to the bungalow, which my father and I hadn't yet entered since we had arrived.

It was lovely and cool inside. All the windows had been opened and the house aired out by Kuss, our chauffeur. There was a cool mountain breeze blowing through the house, and the enormous *djati*, or teak trees, surrounding the bungalow also helped to keep it cool.

The two servants retreated to the kitchen after a while to prepare the evening meal for all of us. Asim had bought necessities for our supper and lots of fruits for after the meals. The two servants were pretty good cooks as long as the meals were kept simple. We shared everything we ate with them, which they took back into the kitchen after we were finished, with the exception of pork. Asim and Kuss were both Muslims and, as adherents of the Islam faith, could not consume or touch pork. It was a very important issue, especially when hiring a cook, to know if they were willing to handle pork.

The three days in the mountains went by much too soon and before we knew it we were heading back to the city and its responsibilities.

AN UNFORGETTABLE BIRTHDAY

It was 1941, and almost at the end of January. My grandmother had extended many invitations to family and friends for my upcoming eighth birthday in the middle of February. This birthday stands out in vivid detail for me, because it was the end of an era. It was one of our last happy and glorious days together. It was the end of what it had always seemed to me a trustworthy and balanced life, cradled in the security of my family's strong embrace.

As in all the previous years, my birthday celebrations were always held on the plantation. The house was large and sprawling, and it had more than enough room to accommodate a large crowd of people. Many celebrations were given here just for that reason, and because of its lovely surroundings and inviting, wide lawns where children could play and tumble. Also, the plantation, with its wonderful old house, was not too unreasonably far from the city. Situated as it was, just off the old Antjol road toward downtown Priok, a forty minute drive by car would bring us right to its steps from where we lived in the city.

Children's parties were as important and meticulously organized as were the parties given for the adults. The front veranda underwent a transformation. Festively adorned with garlands, bows, streamers, and an abundance of flowers, it became a lovely and festive place to be.

A magician and a movie kept the children interested and entertained. Delicious aromas came floating through the air from the kitchens. Everyone helped to get the feast ready for the following day, and even the servants were giggling while walking to and fro with flowers in vases and garlands over their arms. Cakes and small jelly-filled tarts baked in the ovens, and their aroma filled the air.

On the day of my birthday, I woke early. Unable to hold still any longer, I slipped out of bed. But before I could do anything else, the door to my room opened and Ierah came in, apparently to check if I was already awake. I started to chatter excitingly. She warned me softly to be very quiet and not to wake the others. My parents and Ierah and I had arrived the evening before, as had a couple of aunts and uncles and their children as well.

Ierah handed me my slippers, a fresh towel, and my bathrobe, and she herself carried a tumbler with my toothbrush and toothpaste in it. The two of us marched toward the bathrooms for my morning bath. As she had since I was seven, Ierah waited patiently outside the door. She usually had a difficult time getting me out of the bathroom, but not today. I was far too excited to spend much time bathing and came out of the bathroom way too soon for Ierah's taste. She eyed me suspiciously. "Let me see your teeth, did you brush them long enough?" she demanded. "And your hair, it is still dripping wet, you haven't even dried it." She toweled my hair until it was dried to her satisfaction.

Back in my bedroom I dressed quickly in the clothes Ierah had laid out for me the night before. I put on my open-sandaled shoes and combed my hair. Ierah put a ribbon in it, although it rarely lasted for long. After a while it was mostly found on the lawn, in a tree, or stuffed into one of my pockets and occasionally it just disappeared.

Almost immediately after Ierah turned her back on me to prepare my breakfast, I ran to the monkey cage outside. The monkeys ran toward me inside their cage, especially Coco, the little male who always clung to me, pressing his face against the coarse chicken wire and sticking out his little arm to be petted. I dashed into the main kitchen, returning with handfuls of tiny bananas, kept mainly as a treat for the monkeys. Chattering excitedly when they saw their favorite food, they rushed toward me, clinging to the side of the cage. I distributed the bananas as fairly as I could, painstakingly seeing to it that every one of them got a share, reprimanding the ones who were too aggressive.

Now Ierah came to fetch me, urging me softly to go back inside the house to eat my breakfast before it got cold. It consisted of a generous mug of piping hot Ovelmaltine, a chocolate drink, very much like the Ovaltine that we know, a soft-boiled egg fresh from the plantation's own chickens, a bowl of hot cereal, called Havermout, which is rolled oats, and a small bowl of fresh fruits, neatly cut up.

In my excitement on this special day, I could hardly eat at all. I took a couple of spoonfuls of my porridge, I ate the egg and drank half of the chocolate milk, but ate all of the fruit, running off as quickly as Ierah had seen to it that I wiped my mouth.

My cousin Eric, who had arrived with his parents the night before, had also awakened by now. He was a year older than I, the oldest son of my father's younger brother Ed. He and I were the closest in age of all the other cousins and when together, we were inseparable. Our adventures often made the servants groan and our parents moan and roll their eyes.

While waiting for Eric to have his morning bath, get dressed, and eat his breakfast, I went outside. Filled with excited energy, I was contemplating doing cartwheels on the lawn when I remembered that it would be wet with dew. Instead I walked around to the side of the building and gazed across the back terrace, past the monkey cage obscured by oleander bushes, past the chicken coops where the big white ducks were kept, all the way to the three acres of fruit trees, planted a few years before I was born.

There were mango trees in a long row, of all different kinds, as well as banana trees in a small grove by themselves. The bananas came in all different sizes and flavors, from the ones the humans preferred to the monkey treats. There were also the fruits that were used only for cooking and some that had seeds the size of tiny pebbles, used mainly for fruit salad.

There were many rows of *nangka* or jackfruit trees with their enormous fruits, which can easily weigh twenty-five pounds or more. These fruits grow closely to the tree trunk, hanging from a short but sturdy stem. They are mossy green in color and their shell is tough and thick, covered with a short, soft stubble. The fruit can be found all over Southeast Asia and has also been transplanted to the Hawaiian Islands.

Jackfruit has a strong, sweet aroma when fully ripe, and the flesh is thick, deep yellow, and chewy. When it is still very young, it makes a wonderful thick vegetable soup. Adding coconut milk and hard-boiled eggs and serving it over white steamed rice and fried pork rind is one of my favorite dishes.

Then there were the durian trees, growing in a designated area. Their fruits resemble the jackfruit in color, but they are rounder in form and smaller in size, weighing from five to twelve pounds. These fruits have a much harder outer shell and are covered with firm, short, but extremely sharp spikes. The durian area was off limits to children.

Papaya trees were also grown on the plantation. The fruits are huge, like watermelons, but more slender and yellowish. Again, they come in different varieties: there were the ones only the birds ate, small and pale yellow inside. The ones people consumed were much larger, almost orange in color, and extremely sweet. Papayas are delicious served icy cold with a slice of lemon on the side. That was a treat after the siesta period—a rest period so needed in the tropics between the hot hours of two and four in the afternoon, when the temperatures are too hot to do anything else. Even so, sometimes children climbed out of their bedroom windows, escaping their parents and their nannies, to roam around unattended.

Papaya leaves made into a bitter tea served as a blood cleanser, and the stems, when freshly picked, produced a milky white sap that was used to assist in the extraction of thorns and splinters. The sap, when placed on the tiny puncture wound for a little while, would push out the thorn or sliver that was lodged in the flesh. We children were treated with this sap almost constantly by our nannies, since our shoes left our feet almost as soon as they were put on.

All over the world, papaya is used in meat tenderizers. It also makes an excellent household remedy in case of bee stings. Made into a paste and applied to the area the bee has stung, it extracts the poison and the stinger as well.

The plantation's fruit and vegetable harvests were distributed throughout the entire plantation population, ending up in the field hands' kitchens as well as in our own. We all benefited from the profuse yield, and nothing was wasted.

Eric, finally dressed and fed, came running out of the house. By this time, the adults were emerging from their various bedrooms. It was time for Eric and me to disappear before we were detained by our parents. We had made plans the night before to go horseback riding all over the grounds toward the river. We had a lot of exploring to do before the party started at five o'clock. It was now seven thirty in the morning, four and a half hours to the midday meal, which was being served earlier than usual today in connection with the party.

Eric and I ran to the stalls in great haste, avoiding the chance to be called back by our nannies. Panting heavily, we arrived at the stalls, which were located near the fruit orchards. Salim, the stable boy, greeted us with a big grin on his face. "*Tabeh Nonnie, tabeh Sinjo,*" greetings little Miss, and little Sir, he said. We loved being with Salim and helped him with whatever he allowed us to do.

My horse Frieda neighed softly when she saw me and shook her head and mane. She also saw the carrots we picked up at the entrance, which were kept there to give to the horses as little snacks through the day or well earned after a workout. The horses were already brushed, fed, and watered when Eric and I arrived at the stalls. We led them outside by their reins, threw ourselves on their backs, and broke into an instant gallop, which made the chickens scatter, their peaceful morning disrupted. The two German Shepherd Dogs my grandparents kept raced out of the house to follow us, no doubt knocking down a couple of servants in their excited pursuit. When passing the house, we deliberately turned our heads away, applying the "What you don't see, doesn't hurt" philosophy, and galloped away. We turned right at the end of the lawn to where the coconut groves were planted in endless rows as far as the eye could follow. The paths, wide enough for our ponies to gallop side by side, were meticulously groomed.

Everywhere we looked we saw field hands doing their chores—removing weeds, checking the crops, climbing up and down the trees. There were the monkeys with their trainers in areas where the coconuts needed to be picked. We slowed our horses down a bit, and the two dogs, calmed down now after their workout, sniffed out the area.

The workers greeted us as we passed them with their hands together touching their forehead, as was the custom. Kamir, one of the oldest foremen, beckoned us to stop. When we saw what he held in his hands, we immediately slid down off our horses and squatted down beside him. A green and not fully ripe coconut had fallen down during the night, perhaps knocked down by a fruit bat or something. Kamir hacked off the top of the young coconut easily with his sharp cleaver, punctured a hole in the soft area that he knew precisely how to locate, and gave it to us to enjoy. We drank deeply from the coconut milk, which was deliciously sweet but not overly so, carefully taking turns. After we had finished drinking, I gave Kamir back the coconut, knowing that the best was yet to come.

Kamir hacked the fruit in two. The young coconut meat was still glassy white and not yet firm. Kamir gave us each a piece of hard coconut shell, which he had carefully cleaned, to scrape out the meat. It was deliciously sweet, velvety soft, and creamy. We devoured the unexpected treat and thanked Kamir for his kindness. He wished me a happy birthday and announced that both his granddaughters would be at the *rumah besar*, as the plantation house was called, at five o'clock. They were to sing to me with a group of other children of plantation employees, in honor of the celebration. This was a tradition held for all the Rozen grandchildren who chose to celebrate their birthdays on the plantation.

After the singing, the group of young singers would be given small bags filled with candies, several tiny jelly-filled tarts, and as much lemonade as they wanted. These children may have enjoyed the event even more than the birthday child, since being the focus of all this attention was quite embarrassing. The birthday child was seated at the top of the steps leading to the front veranda in a decorated chair, listening for half an hour or more to the songs, while forty or more pairs of eyes stared up in a group from the front lawn. Still, we understood that this was a tradition and recognized the importance of it all. It was a gift from them to us, which we needed to accept graciously, and it also a treat for the young singers as well.

Eric and I waved to Kamir and the others and directed our horses at a trot to the river, which also was the plantation's boundary. When we arrived, we saw several young boys in the shallow water, bathing and scrubbing their water buffalos. We knew the boys by name; they came from the neighboring villages, and we often saw them doing their chores. They always were quite shy at first and kept their eyes downcast, until we spoke to them in a friendly manner.

Today, of all days, I decided to give them a helping hand with the bathing of their animals and waded with both dogs into the knee-deep water. Eric followed suit. Peals of laughter rang out when they saw us wading toward them. They offered us the coconut fiber to scrub their animals with.

The sun was now high in the sky, and it was getting hotter by the minute. The water looked enormously inviting. One of the boys, each of whom was not older than ten, climbed onto the back of his buffalo, and I decided to do the same on another buffalo. I had never climbed one before: the buffalos were slick and their backs are much broader than that of a horse. I slithered down and fell into the water with all my clothes on, to the enormous amusement of the boys and Eric as well.

Not to be deterred, I noticed how another boy got on his charge. He grabbed it by a horn and flung himself on its back. I did the same and succeeded. Eric found another buffalo to scrub.

The hours flew by and we were enjoying ourselves until I started to feel tiny stings, sporadic at first, that grew into an agonizing itch all over my body and on my head. Eric was experiencing the same discomfort. When we asked the boys what this could be, they explained that the buffalos were covered with lice, which they were trying to get rid of. They were not harmed in any way by the lice and so did not think we would be bothered by them. The itch by now was so bad that we could not sit still. We slid down from the buffalos and lay in the cool water, which helped to alleviate the itch a little. We felt bites on our heads and all over our bodies. Eventually we dashed out of the water, ran to our horses, called the dogs, and galloped home, all the time scratching and slapping our bodies.

We rode straight to the stables and left the care of our horses in the capable hands of the stable boys. We always rode the horses bareback, so there was no saddle to be removed, and the horses needed only to be rubbed down, watered, and fed. It was a task that we otherwise enjoyed doing ourselves.

It was eleven o'clock when we entered the house. We must have been a terrible sight, with our wet hair standing out every which way and our soaked clothes covered with mud. Even the dogs had to be hosed down, since they too were covered with mud.

The household was in an uproar. Our nannies shrieked and ran toward us. My mother flew out of her chair when she saw us, and Eric's mother joined her in consternation. Our fathers stood in the background staring at us, and I detected a glimpse of a smile on my grandfather's face when I glanced at him quickly.

Oma, always in control, knelt down and asked us questions. As soon as she saw us scratching uncontrollably and heard our story, she ordered petroleum to be brought in. Our nannies then ripped off our clothes as we walked and hustled us unceremoniously into separate bathrooms. Twittering all the time like a pair of overexcited birds, they applied the petroleum all over our bodies and rubbed some in our hair as well. Ierah left it to work for a few minutes and then rinsed me off. After the rinsing followed the soap lathering and scrubbing, many times over. Ierah was not about to take a chance of leaving behind any lice or ticks on my skin or hair. My skin felt raw and tingling all over. Finally the torment ended, and she rinsed me off one last time, scolding me and twittering in my ear all through the ordeal. She ordered me to wait quietly for a moment while she got my clean clothes and slippers, coming back in record time, not trusting me for one second by myself. For the second time that day, Eric and I were dressed and combed.

It was noon when the two of us hesitantly entered the dining room. The adults were already seated, and six pair of eyes looked us over. My mother motioned for me to sit between her and my father, and Eric's parents did the same with him. My grandparents, as always, sat at either end of the long dining table. Nothing more was mentioned about our adventure. Later we learned that my grandparents had requested that the lecture be postponed until the next day. They did not want the birthday celebration to be spoiled for me and the others.

Eric and I ate in utter silence, while the adults exchanged pleasantries all through the meal. We were relieved beyond all expectations and thought perhaps, if we kept very still, our mischievousness would be forgotten altogether.

It was a little past one o'clock when we left the dining room. The men went to sit on the front veranda to smoke, and the women followed a little later. Iced coffee and tea were served, and the children were sent to our rooms for an afternoon nap, after we finished eating our fruits.

Ierah already had a game set up when I entered the bedroom, as she always did before my nap. It was either a game of checkers, which she played poorly, or so she claimed. But I had the strong suspicion that she wanted the game to end as soon as possible. Sometime it was a game of cards or jacks or the like.

One game I was particularly fond of—the *tjangklok* game. It is played by two people. It involves a piece of wood of approximately two feet in length, ovally shaped, about two and a half inches thick, in which fourteen holes are carved. There are six holes on one side and another six across from them, with one bigger hole at each end of the board. The game is played by filling the holes with colorful tiny pebbles or seed pods, dropping them one by one into the holes until nothing is left in the hand. The idea is to get as many as possible into one of the big holes at the ends. *Tjangklok* takes forever to finish, which may be why I liked it so much. It could keep me out of bed for the entire siesta period. I didn't think I would be able to sleep, but my mother told me that I fell asleep almost instantly after I climbed into bed, exhausted from the day's adventure.

Ierah woke me an hour later, and my mother came to my room to instruct her as to how I should be dressed for the party. She then turned and gave me a loving hug. I eyed her suspiciously. No reprimands just yet, I thought. However, she did remind me softly to at least stay neat and clean for the remainder of the afternoon.

It was now nearing four o'clock, and the guest were to arrive soon. The first to arrive were four of my best friends from school, accompanied by one of their chauffeurs and nannies. Some of my aunts and uncles and their children then arrived, and then my great-grandmother, together with my father's youngest brother and his wife. Now in her eighties, Gesina, my great-grandmother, preferred her apartment in the hotel to living at the plantation. She was cared for by two of her favorite long-time servants, who returned with her to the city. They all had presents with them, which were placed on a long, decorated table.

Now the mortifying moment had arrived. The decorated chair was positioned atop the stone front steps. The children of the plantation employees began to arrive from their quarters about a mile from the big house. More and more gathered on the front lawn, accompanied by a few of their parents. Some were so little, they came carried in a sling on their mother's hip. One of the parents was the organizer and choirmaster.

I sat in the chair, prompted by my grandmother. Next to me on a low table were trays of jellied tarts and the rows of little bags filled with candies I was to hand out after the singing. The children clapped their hands when I sat down and wished me happy birthday in unison: "*Selamat ulang tahun*," "Happy birthday, little Miss!" And then they began to sing. After the singing, they approached the steps shyly, first the tiny ones carried by their mothers, and then the young singers, who received the candy, tarts, and lemonade in paper cups. They accepted the treats, laughing and joking with each other. Eric and I had played with some of them often when we were on our secret excursions away from the big house and our families. It was always great fun to be with them since they knew secret places, and their mothers made delicious little bites that we never got to see on our table at the big house. Eric and I use to steal food out of our kitchens and bring it to them as a gift in return.

It was now past six and total darkness had arrived. The young singers started to take their leave, waving and thanking us for the treats. Even the little ones waved their chubby little hands and smiled, so cute all dressed in their best. My grandmother saw to it that the children stayed in good health, and Eric and I often brought them fruits and milk and such. Those who lived on the plantation grounds had their own vegetable gardens, and they had their own chickens and ducks behind their compound.

The magician was now ready to perform his tricks. Always a favorite in our circle of children, he never ceased to amaze us, holding our attention for an hour or more. When he was finished, we clapped our hands and stomped our feet and used the noisemakers we were given. After more refreshments, we were ready for the movie. The screen was already put up and a technician started the first reel. It was a Laurel and Hardy movie, a hilarious performance that made us squeal with laughter. Even the adults thought it was funny, and the ones who thought it most hilarious were the servants, who were standing in the background. They tried to maintain some decorum since they were in the presence of their employers, but with little success. Weak with laughter, they fell against each other in the darkness.

After the movie, we sat down at long, prettily decorated tables, set up to accommodate the many guests. When asked what I would like to eat for my birthday, I had requested saffron rice. The yellow rice was served with numerous side dishes of chicken, beef, fish, and eggs, simmered in all kinds of sauces. The yellow rice was also a symbol of good luck for the celebrated. It was brought to the table in a huge cone, decorated with ornately carved slices of cucumber, tomatoes, and eggs, surrounded by all sorts of finely shredded pan-browned coconut mixed with peanuts and finely ground dried shrimp. It was delicious. Each table had a cone of saffron rice in the middle and a dozen or more side dishes. Each cone was decorated with a wreath of the beautiful *kembang sepatu*, the hibiscus, the region's precious flower.

The opening of all the presents followed the feast. From my parents I received a ping-pong table, completely with net and paddles and ping-pong balls. My grandparents gave me an adult bike—I was the proudest ever. The seat had to be adjusted to the lowest setting, but that did not matter one bit to me. The guest began to take their leave around ten o'clock, since it was a children's party.

In all the years since that time, the details of that happy day have stayed with me. The celebration of my eighth birthday party at the plantation was indeed like a closing of an era, never to be recaptured, for our family and for all of the people of colonial Dutch East Indies.

FAMILY TRAGEDY

By 1941 the rumors of war coming to our part of the world could not be ignored any longer. Europe was now completely under German domination, except for Italy, which they quickly made their ally. In the Dutch East Indies, men were called for military duty, and women were being trained as military truck drivers at the General Motor plant in Tandjung Priok, an important harbor about an hour's drive from the city of Batavia. Australian troops were being sent to Singapore to reinforce the British troops already stationed there. Citizens were asked to gather everything aluminum to help the airplane industry. One could feel it in the air, the enormous tension of getting ready to do war. Japanese families left the colonies, the men to return, not even a year later, as military officers of the Japanese army.

In September 1941, personal tragedy came to the Rozen family. My grandfather contracted pneumonia and had to be hospitalized. He contracted the disease while checking on his crops out in the huge barns during a tropical storm. A planter in heart and soul, his first concern was his crops. The barns sometimes could not withstand a storm of great volume and would leak, which would moisten the dried copra, causing it to mold. He and his overseers went out in the stormy night to make sure that this would not happen by covering the dry copra with enormous sheets of oiled canvas to protect it from the water.

My grandfather sent his overseers home but himself stayed out too long in his soaking wet clothes, working with two young Indonesian men whom he had asked to stay on to help him finish the job. By the time they were done, many hours had passed, and my grandfather was chilled to the bone. His body temperature dropped rapidly. The following night found him in bed with a raging fever and a dry, hacking cough.

My parents and I were back home in the city and my grandmother had gone back to the hotel. My grandfather, who had stayed on alone at the plantation as he often did, was taken to the Saint Carolus Hospital in Batavia by his loyal chauffeur with great speed. Siti, the plantation's housekeeper, had in the meantime telephoned my grandmother to inform her of her husband's condition. Soon she got a second call, this time from their doctor and personal friend, urging her to come to the hospital at once.

The next morning at five thirty, even before my father had left for work or I for school, my grandmother stopped by to pick us up on her way to the hospital. Others of the family were informed and summoned also. We were to gather in the hospital waiting room. My grandmother, my parents, and I were the first ones to arrive. "Ah, there you are, Mrs. Rozen," Dr. van Leeuwen said when he saw my grandmother. He hurried through the great swinging doors of the waiting room. "Your husband had been asking for all of you, but I can permit only two at a time to go into his room." She stared at him. "Your husband is very weak," the doctor continued quietly, avoiding her eyes. Her stare became more penetrating. "My husband isn't in real danger, is he?" The doctor responded, "He is very tired from all that coughing and the high fever. Please, come, he's waiting to see you."

My grandmother took me by the hand and said to my parents, "We'll go first. Why don't you two follow fifteen minutes later?" Grandmother and I followed the doctor down the corridor, trying to assess the gravity of the situation. How fast everything went. It was incomprehensible. Instinct told my grandmother that the doctor was hedging, and this frightened her. Somehow I knew that Opa was going to die that night.

When we reached the door of my grandfather's room, the doctor turned to us, his face unreadable as he said, "We have sent for a priest." My grandfather was Catholic, while Grandmother was Protestant. "A priest—but why, doctor?" Oma asked with rising alarm. "Your husband asked for him. He is very weak, worn out. Please don't excite him." The doctor opened the door for us. "Mrs. Rozen, let's not waste time." He ushered us in and closed the door softly behind us.

We hurried to the bed, our eyes sweeping over Opa, who lay propped up against pillows. We could see his exhaustion. His face, still handsome, was wan in the cold light, etched with lines of fatigue and dark smudges under his eyes, which brightened at the sight of us. Grandmother's smile did not falter for an instant. She bent over her husband, whom she had left at the plantation just four days ago in excellent health, and kissed his cheek carefully so as not to disturb the oxygen mask.

I sat down on a chair next to the bed, swallowing very hard. My grandfather lifted his hand weakly and beckoned me to come closer. He touched my face and smiled at me. "I love you very much, honey," he said weakly. I could no longer suppress my tears and they spilled down my cheeks and splashed onto Opa's hand. "Don't cry, sweetheart. There's nothing to cry about." "Oh Opa—Opa—" My grandmother, tears streaming from her eyes, took a deep breath and tried to pull herself together. Softly she untangled my fingers from grandfather's hand, kissed me on my head, and asked me to be strong, wiping away my tears. I stepped away from the bed and let her have a moment with her husband.

"Alfred," she said. "Alfred, listen to me now. You must fight. Try harder dear. Please fight to live," she implored. She gathered my grandfather's body into her strong arms and cradled him close, pressing him harder against herself, as if trying to infuse her dying husband with her own enormous strength and her own stubborn will. She then laid him back on the pillows, her lips shaking, her face white and strained.

There was a rustling sound as the priest came in, carrying a black bag. My grandmother and I moved away, tears streaming, hearts surely breaking. We watched the priest bending over grandfather, seeming like a harbinger of death. I wanted him to leave. The room was very quiet; the only sounds were the faint swishing of the priest's cassock and his low voice as he absolved Opa of his sins. Sins, what kind of sins, I thought bitterly. Opa never did anything to hurt anybody. He had only given love to everyone he knows. The priest now anointed Opa. I turned away and looked out the window. It all seemed so wasteful to me.

The door opened, and my parents came in. I threw my arms around them and they both embraced me lovingly and asked me softly to go with grandmother so they had some time to be with Opa. I turned around one more time to look back at my grandfather. He smiled and winked at me as he always did. That was the last time I saw my grandfather alive. He died at three o'clock the next morning. Cause of death, double pneumonia. He was in his late sixties.

CHAPTER 2

WORLD WAR II

Two weeks after my grandfather passed away in September 1941, my father was called for military duty. In the meantime, whole armies had been formed. My father was one of the last to be drafted. He and his age group, which was over age forty, became Landstormers and *Stadwacht* soldiers of the K.N.I.L. (*Koninklijk-Nederlands-Indies-Leger*), which translates into English as Royal Netherlands Indies Army.

In early December, following the attack on Pearl Harbor by the Japanese, my father came home for the last time on a one-night leave to say goodbye to his family. He announced optimistically to my mother and me that he would be back in no time. "We'll have them whipped before you even have time to miss me," he said cheerfully.

I knew that my father was play-acting so as not to burden us with fear. I had seen and heard enough, when he and his brothers and the managers of the plantation and the hotel and the other family holdings were together, how serious the discussions were and how tense and concerned everyone looked. With my grandmother presiding at one end of the long dining table and my father at the other, where my grandfather used to sit, I sensed the undercurrent of concern. Sitting in the next room, surrounded by my coloring books, I felt the seriousness of it all. The word *war* was frequently mentioned.

The next day, my mother and I accompanied my father, one of his brothers, and a friend to the railway station. It was a silent ride through the rain to the station. My mother and I were staggered when we arrived: crowds of troops, many from other regiments besides the Landstormers, were filing through the gates, and the gloomy, dirty platforms were jammed with hundreds more. Women and girls of all ages and classes, wives and mothers and sweethearts, were saying farewell to their men. My father, my mother, and I clung to each other, while my uncle brought the military bags on board.

"You'll be fine, both of you," my father said, tightening his grip on both of our hands. "And don't worry about me. Just take care of yourselves." We were now biting our lips, striving for composure. "It is you who must take care, dear," my mother said softly. Finally, my father had to break away from my mother and me as we clung fiercely to his arm, trying without success to hold back the tears. But my mother's white face was filled with immense courage as he took his leave of her.

THE WAR AT HOME

Months before, citizens were instructed by the government to built bomb shelters against expected attacks from the air. Most were just big holes, six to seven feet deep with about a ten foot circumference, with wooden steps leading to the floor. Some shelters were built into the buildings themselves and completely reinforced; this provided protection in case of the building's collapse, although, in case of a direct hit, it was useless.

The hotel was required to have a shelter, and so a hole was made in the garden, as big as an oval swimming pool, to accommodate so many people. It was heartbreaking to see the beautiful garden ripped apart. My grandmother, always the strong one in the family, explained to me the importance of having the shelter nearby. But I could see the pain in her face when her beloved garden was destroyed. The same thing had to be done at our house, too. One side of the beautiful garden had to be entirely uprooted to make way for a big, gaping hole.

The air attacks commenced soon thereafter. Everyone had a helmet, a flashlights, and a piece of rubber to bite during the air raids, which occurred mostly at night. Needless to say, it was from then on that our beautiful, tropical, peaceful nights became nights of endless fear and horror, with people even afraid to go to sleep. On several nights we had to literally dive into those awful bomb shelters, with seconds to spare for the little protection they gave us. The servants pressed against us for protection, shaken and afraid. On mornings after such close calls, we were grateful to still be alive.

I remember that my mother and I got an invitation from an old family friend to stay with her and her family for a while, in the beautiful mountain town of Sukabumi, where she and her children lived. Her husband had also gone to war. It was just a few hours away from Batavia. "You will be safer here than in the capital city," she said. "Stay at least until the air raids subside." My mother and I went, strongly against my grandmother's wishes, who thought it wiser for the family to stay together as much as possible in these dangerous and trying times. My mother had taken me out of school, as many mothers had done, not wanting their children to be away from them. Anyway, the schools were not fully operating at this point.

We were in Sukabumi for about a week when, in a sporadic air raid, a nearby elementary school was bombed. Perhaps it was accidental; who is to say in wartime? The school was situated just three blocks away from where we were staying. The next morning we walked to the site to see the damage. The destruction was devastating and complete. The entire school building was completely demolished, and, before my mother could turn me away, I saw bits and pieces of human remains scattered all over what once had been a school and a schoolyard. Over 200 children had been killed, and with them many teachers and the principal of the school, since the attack took place in the middle of the day. A military crew worked quietly through the rubble, looking for survivors, of which there were none. The smell of decay already filled the air. We walked away, utterly devastated.

The next day we returned to Batavia, my mother now realizing that in time of war one cannot be sure where the safest place might be.

In March of 1942, the Japanese took control of the capital of Batavia, and life changed forever for the European population. Their hated flags, white with the red ball in the center, fluttered wherever one looked. The fear of bombardments was now replaced with the fear of rampaging Japanese soldiers. People kept quiet behind the closed doors and windows of their homes. Even the dogs were kept inside. At night oil lamps were burning low. No one dared to use bright lights for fear of inviting unwelcome guests. We lived in a hushed world filled with anxiety and terror.

Asim, our houseboy, and Ierah, my nanny, were the only servants we were able to keep in our employment, and they turned out to be loyal to our family beyond imagining. We had to let go the chauffeur, the gardener, the cook, and even the laundry maid. Money was very tight, and we had to be very careful with the little we managed to keep hidden in the house in different places.

One morning in mid-April, Asim came with the news that military prisoners of war were going to be transported through the city in long lines, either walking or in military trucks, before being taken overseas. He had heard this over the grapevine, but he could not say to where exactly. "*Tuan*, the master, could be among the ones in the transports." We had not heard from my father for four months and had no idea where he was or what had happened to him. My mother asked Asim if he knew when this was going to happen and where. "Tomorrow," he said. "They will be on

Gunung Sari, the street right behind us, during the late morning hours." I did not say anything but vowed to be there to see my father. At least there was a chance of seeing him before they shipped him off.

The next morning I woke up with butterflies in my stomach. I could hardly eat the breakfast Ierah cooked. Asim, very attuned to my moods, looked at me askance. "Why are you so nervous?" he asked me suspiciously. And then suddenly he said, "Don't you dare go out into the street to see if your father is in the transport. That's what you are planning to do, aren't you?" he asked nervously. "People get shot for doing just that. They bring them to the *Kempe Tai*, the Japanese military intelligence bureau, and they get tortured. Do you know that?" Asim was shaking me now, besides himself with worry.

Before he could do anything else, I jerked myself loose from his grip and ran out of the house, across the yard, and into the street. Asim was right at my heels, in the meantime, screaming for my mother, "*Njonja*, mistress, *Nonnie*, little Miss, wants to see if her father is with the prisoners of war. I'm following her." I did not stop running until I reached the street through which the captive soldiers would pass. I stood pressed against a big old tree on the side of the road, Asim right at my side. We both were gasping for breath after the long run.

The march was already going on. There were long lines of weary-looking men, marching in rows of four. Japanese soldiers guarded them on either side, holding rifles and bayonets in their hands. They looked ridiculous, the rifles almost too big for them to handle, but they were extremely dangerous in their euphoria of being the victorious conquerors—trigger-happy and showing off their power over their prisoners. Tears streamed down my cheeks as I scanned the endless lines of marching men.

It was difficult to recognize anyone, and the captives were marching across the street from where Asim and I stood. Suddenly I saw him. I saw my father. He looked down while he was walking, with his head bowed, in utter defeat. I saw him for just a moment. I forgot to be careful and screamed on top of my lungs *Pappie!* meaning Daddy. He winked at me and stuck up his thumb, and then he was gone. When I turned around, there were two Japanese soldiers on either side of us. We were lucky, because one of them spoke fluent Indonesian. He probably lived in the colonies all his life until Japan called him back to fight us.

Asim explained calmly that I had wanted to see my father one more time, and that when I saw him I forgot to be quiet. "She is just a child," he said. One soldier frisked Asim and me while the other one kept his rifle aimed on us. The soldier who spoke to us in Indonesian warned me never to do this again. We might not be so lucky. In response I spat on his boot and stared at him defiantly. He looked deeply into my eyes and said to Asim, "This little one really hates us." Asim replied, "You took her father away. She loves him very much and you have destroyed her world." The soldier turned away, but not before I saw the sadness in his eyes. It was like a silent apology.

Asim and I walked home unharmed, where we found my mother in tears, beside herself from worry about our safety. She hugged us both for a long time, sobbing, until the tension left her. She thanked Asim for being with me, and I promised her never to do such a thing ever again. She was happy to hear that we'd seen *Pappie* and that he looked relatively all right. It was another year before we heard from him again.

OPA HAN

After my grandfather's death, my grandmother leaned more and more on her managers, at both the plantation and the hotel. Johan Baumer, the hotel manager, was grandmother's confidant for many years and a wonderful friend of the family, in addition to being an excellent employee. Johan was born and raised in the colonies but was of German descent.

His wife had long since left him and had taken their three girls with her back to Germany, never to return to the Dutch East Indies. Johan was not about to follow her. It was a mistake, he once admitted a long time ago, to marry someone who did not "belong" in the colonies. She never took to the tropics that Johan loved so much and had made life miserable for both of them and their three children. He missed his daughters very much at first, but as often happens, the family ties weakened with time and eventually unknotted altogether.

The hotel became his home and the Rozens his family and his entire life. He was devoted to us all, and the Rozen grandchildren called him Opa Han. He spoke fluent English, having lived in Singapore in his younger years. With impeccably correct German, Dutch, and Indonesian as well, he was a real asset to the hotel trade.

Already a true friend of the Rozens, he gave my grandmother the advice and support she needed now that her husband was gone and her sons made prisoners of war. They became inseparable over the years, although they never could marry, since Johan's wife would not give him a divorce. He and my grandmother stayed together until his death in 1949, at age 75.

LOSS OF THE PLANTATION

In December of 1942, our beloved plantation, great house, and acres of land were confiscated by the Japanese. The terrible and unavoidable had come to pass. A safe and peaceful haven was jerked out of the hands of the family who had cared for and made it all happen for two generations. The great house became a sort of mess hall for Japanese officers, and acres upon acres of plantation were destroyed and the coconut trees uprooted to become a huge junkyard for their discarded tanks and all kinds of ugly military vehicles.

Although we had expected this to happen for years, when it finally did the family was in shock. We sobbed for days after the terrible news—except for my grandmother and great-grandmother. They stood there, embracing each other, in terrible silence. Grandmother's mouth was grimly set and her eyes glittered with hatred. She did not speak for a long time, and when she finally did, her first thoughts were for her dead husband. She said, "Thank the Lord, Alfred has been spared this enormous and terrible loss. He would not have been able to bear it. The plantation was always his whole life." Although I did not say anything, I thought, "No Oma, this is where you are wrong. You always were his whole life."

FROM LUXURY TO SURVIVAL

The hotel became now a pension, meaning a boardinghouse. There were no travelers any more, only people who wanted to stay a long while, to be with other people, perhaps for reasons of safety. Furthermore, it operated as before, but of course on a much more frugal level. The lavish meals that once were served were now quite simple. Still, there was plenty of nutritious food to be presented to the boarding guests, though not so elegantly now. We still owned plenty of chickens, and they gave plenty of eggs. We also could buy fish from the street vendors and at the market, although the prices were extremely high. We had no milk, but for the babies and for us there was a wonderful substitute, soybean milk. It proved to be healthier, and the babies grew fat and firm.

There was no beef and no pork, since all the meat resources supplied the Japanese armies. We could occasionally get hold of cow's liver and heart and could collect the blood if the servants were early enough at the slaughterhouse. The hotel or rather pension cooks were extremely resourceful in working all of this into dishes that were delicious as well as nutritious. All the rooms at the pension were full, but now people rented on a monthly basis. And of course my grandmother had to lower the prices considerably, since no one had a steady income and everyone was living on their savings very carefully, not knowing how long the war was going to last.

My grandmother still had an income from the boutique store, which now produced uniforms to supply the Japanese armies. This income, although minute given all the work involved, was under much scrutiny by the Japanese, but it was steady as long as it lasted and considering the capricious nature of the enemy. Also, Opa Han had an income as an interpreter at the Japanese Intelligence Bureau, the *Kempe Tai*, where he was employed because of his German heritage. These two financial sources were to support the entire Rozen family for some time.

Opa Han was also the real reason my mother and I were able to avoid the concentration camps for as long as we did. If not for him, my mother, being so fair-skinned and blond, had no way of denying her direct lineage with the Dutch, who were hated by the Japanese. Their slogans screamed from the city's billboards "Asia For Asians Only," and these exclamations dripped poison into the minds of many Indonesians, mostly the young who were unhappy with the Dutch regime. One of them was a young engineer named Sukarno, who had studied abroad and whom the Dutch government had exiled to a remote island because of his rebellious and mutinous behavior against the Dutch government.

Mother and I still lived in our house with our two servants, Asim and Ierah. Lena, our Dutch-Indonesian tenant, and her infant son needed to find a source of support, since her husband, like all able-bodied men, had been put into one of the many concentration camps spread all over the Dutch East Indies islands.

Out of pure necessity, she took a job in a restaurant and bar frequented by many high-ranking German officers—a situation of which she was not aware at first. She left her son with us when she had to be at work. She became involved in a relationship with one of the officers who regularly visited the restaurant and bar. He became very fond of her and provided for all of her needs. They eventually fell in love with each other and moved out of our house, after my mother asked her to do so, not wanting to have anything to do with the enemy. After a while, we learned of her pregnancy and, again a while longer, of the birth of a baby girl. The German officer, Lena, and the two children settled into a happy family life of their own, not too far from where we lived, until the war ended and her husband returned.

TJIDENG CAMP

One morning around 4 o'clock, a loud banging on the shuttered doors aroused us from sleep. Peeking through the shutters, we saw one of the dreaded Japanese trucks in front of our house. The truck was enclosed, and immediately we knew what this meant. The Japanese had set up camps all over the Dutch East Indies to intern European civilians, mainly Dutch, on order of their Emperor during the period 1942 to 1945.

Opa Han had warned us months ahead of time that this moment might come. At the *Kempe Tai*, his boss had left the department and another officer had taken his place, a younger man who worked precisely by instructions. He refused to sign a consent to keep my mother and me out of the camps any longer. My aunt, my father's sister, was also fair with blond hair, a throwback that is often noticeable in Dutch Indies families. She married a full-blooded Dutchman and had a blond, blue-eyed daughter who was then eighteen years old. They too had stayed out of the concentration camps, living with my grandmother in the pension, because of Opa Han's connections, which were now abruptly severed.

It was December of 1943 when we were taken from our beds and our homes. They stopped first at the hotel to pick up my Aunt Rita and her daughter Sara. My grandmother and Opa Han arrived at our house shortly thereafter, breathing hard and quite alarmed. My grandmother so overpowered by her fears for our safety that for once she was totally speechless, stood as if turned to stone. She had just time to embrace us and to whisper in our ears to be strong and that she would be in touch with us constantly.

Asim and Ierah clung to us, tears streaming down their cheeks, promising to take care of the house and Prince, my beautiful German Shepherd Dog. The Japanese soldiers had to separate them forcibly from us, and my grandmother had tried to calm them. Later I found out that Prince was taken from the house the next day. I had noticed how one of the officers looked appraisingly at him when he escorted us to the waiting truck. Asim and Ierah were helpless to prevent it.

After a few more stops to pick up more prisoners, we recognized the route the truck was taking with sinking hearts. We were headed for the most feared camp in Batavia. Tjideng Camp was notorious for its crazed and cruel Japanese camp commander, Lt. Kenichi Sonei (later Captain). The man was weird with a form of dementia that came out strongly when the moon was full. When this happened, he would dream up with the most horrific punishments.

We remained in Tjideng Camp for a year and a half, until the Japanese capitulation in 1945. I remember an episode that happened shortly after we arrived at the camp. It was 1:30 in the morning and everyone was asleep, when loud yelling awakened us. Heavy with sleep, we were led out to an ancient mango tree, which had two almost horizontal, low-growing branches, perhaps 24 inches in diameter. On one of them, grotesque in the eerie moonlight, was Sonei, dressed in only a loincloth, doing what to Western eyes would have seemed to be a wild and strange barbaric ritual dance. We were grouped around him and made to watch. After he had danced himself into a frenzy, he ordered his soldiers to give us each a shovel to dig our own graves.

My mother and I and all the other newcomers were panicked and started to cry in fear. We could not understand why the others who had been in this camp so much longer acted like nothing was happening. Later we discovered that this strange behavior had happened many times before. After the appalling dance, Sonei would sink to the ground and was led away by his officers. Everyone was allowed to return to their beds.

The food served to the prisoners in the camp was Japanese. Everyone was allowed a daily bowl of rice firmly pressed into the bowl, lots of Japanese tea, one big piece of salted and fried fish on top of the rice, and a cup of watery vegetable soup. Sometimes, perhaps for variation of this meager diet, a thick piece of pickled Japanese horseradish was slapped onto the rice, replacing the horrible soup. And once in a great while, there were fruits.

Asim and Ierah, who risked the danger of being shot to death if discovered, brought us precious eggs and milk. They came carefully, surreptitiously, and at long intervals so as not to arouse suspicion. They met us at a spot along the fencing that was somewhat remote, near the cassava patches. The children were responsible for tending the vegetable gardens. We watered them and weeded the entire area diligently, knowing that there would be even less to eat if we didn't.

Boys stayed with their mothers until they reached the age of twelve. After that, they were separated, which always provoked tearful goodbyes and tremendous emotional upheavals, since no one could predict when they would see each other again. Heartbreaking scenes accompanied these separations.

Some of the women prisoners were appointed camp leaders, and one functioned as the head camp leader. This woman was in daily contact with the capricious and erratic Japanese leaders.

Late one night, another transport of women and children from another camp was brought in to Tjideng. The women and children were bewildered and tired and, like us, undernourished. They were supposed to bow deeply before the guards at the entrance of the camp, where they had been dropped in the middle of the night. But in their condition and in the dark, they just could not function as the Japanese wanted them to. Sonei, the demented camp commander, noticed the sloppy way in which the bone-tired women and children greeted his soldiers. He had worked himself into a frenzy again, frothing with manic anger. Suddenly he roared with rage and ordered his soldiers to strike the prisoners. In no time at all, screaming women and children were trying to parry blows from the soldiers. The children, whose blows were many but lighter than the savage beating of the women, screamed from exhaustion and fear and from seeing their mothers so brutally treated. When we saw them the next day, the women were badly bruised, some could hardly walk, and some could not move at all.

About six months later, Sonei was replaced as camp commander by a much milder mannered man. But it was just months before the Japanese capitulated, and a few months before we were all on the road to freedom, or so we thought. My mother and I had entered the concentration camp much later into the war than most women and children. We were the lucky ones, considering. Most people had to endure Sonei and his cruelty for much longer, and many of them did not live to see him removed. The Japanese were clever enough to have Sonei removed before the war was over. Otherwise the women would certainly have shredded him to pieces by hand.

After the Japanese capitulation in August 1945, Sonei was captured in Batavia by our British allies and was court martialed. Throughout the trial, that most cruel and brutal of all the prison camp commanders sat meekly, with downcast eyes. He even apologized for all the horrors and intense pain, both physical and emotional, that he had inflicted on his prisoners. However, this play-acting was not successful. In September 1946, after being imprisoned for a year, the brutal monster Sonei, captain in the once-powerful Japanese army, was given a death sentence. On December 7, 1946, on the fifth anniversary of the bombing of Pearl Harbor by the Japanese, Sonei stood before a firing squad and was executed. For those who experienced his cruelty, he did not deserve less.

FREEDOM SLOW IN COMING

Our freedom came slowly and not at all as we had envisioned so many times, while lying on our hard, thin mattresses late at night, too weary to fall asleep. In my mind's eye I saw endless lines of marching troops, triumphantly waving colorful little flags with English, American, and Australian colors on it. Nothing like that turned out to be true.

For us in the camps, freedom came in soft whispers at first, from our faithful servants who suddenly were allowed to enter the gate, one by one, to bring us extra food and clothing. We hugged them and cried and hugged some more and heard the whispered the news of having seen Japanese troops driving away in countless trucks at night. The soldiers all had white bands around their arms, they said, the sign of having laid down their weapons.

Then, one morning, the unbelievable happened. The camp commander asked us to gather at the field where every morning we had our roll-call or "appeal," rain or shine. Without preamble he blurted out two words in the Indonesian language, *"Perang abis,"* the war is over. And as if to convince himself of the fact, he added, *"betul betul,"* it is really true. He then instructed us that everything would go on as usual until further notice. Except that there would be no more roll-calls in the morning hours, and fruit and bread was added to our diets. After those announcements, he marched away with the bowed head of a defeated man.

We returned to our home in Batavia, but it was to be a very brief homecoming.

PRISONERS OF WAR

Only twice in our camp time, did we hear from my father, who had been transported to Japan with thousands of other prisoners of war. While in the Japanese prison camps, they were made to work in the cold, damp coal mines. They were allowed to send a few lines to their families at home, just to let them know that they were still alive. We too were allowed to write to them a few sentences, which were heavily censored. The writing was to be done in the Indonesian language and was tightly restricted.

Sometimes the letters were months old, but still we longed for them, since they were the only contact we had with our loved ones. The Red Cross, the organizer of this correspondence, was swamped with thousands of letters like ours as well as notifications of people who had perished and people who had been transported to other regions. In this whirlpool of confusion, many letters became lost or wrongly delivered, as one might expect. My mother was a victim of such a horrible mistake. Twice she received notification of my father's death, and twice she refused to believe it was true. Both times, after a moment of intense silence, she declared with unwavering certainty that if this were true she would undoubtedly have felt it. Her strong belief brought my father back to us, about half a year later.

A NEW ENEMY

By August 1945 the entire Dutch East Indies was freed from the Japanese occupation and domination, under the command and leadership of Lord Louis Mountbatten, the brother-in-law of the Queen of England and the commander-in-chief of the Allied Forces. All of Southeast Asia was now under the command of the Allied Forces.

Now something strange and ironic was about to happen. The Japanese, who were for three years our jailers and prison guards, were now ordered by the British to protect citizens of Dutch extraction against the more and more aggressive and rebellious Indonesians, who now made hostile threats to anybody who was Dutch or partly Dutch. Camps were again put together in great haste, this time not to imprison but to protect us against a new enemy.

These were mostly the new generation of Indonesians, the students or *permudah*. These students who were stirred up by the Japanese against the Dutch and also against the Dutch-Indonesians. The Japanese, in the throes of their defeat, did their utmost to instigate hostility and whispered their poison into more than willing ears.

Slogans on walls and huge banners started to appear—"Asia for Asians only" and the word *Merdeka*, meaning freedom, was seen everywhere. The slogan "*Merdeka, Tetap Merdeka*," which means "Indonesia is free and will stay free," fluttered from high buildings and tall poles in the wind. The newly designed Indonesian flag, the Red and White, was everywhere. The Indonesian people were split in half. The older ones were tired of war and destruction and wanted to go back to the more peaceful and tranquil atmosphere of colonial times. It was a familiar world that they had accepted. Although oppressed in many ways by the Dutch and taught to be submissive and humble, they also recognized its great order and meticulously organized government, which they respected and trusted.

But the young upstarts were restless and filled with hatred against the Dutch, who had occupied their country for over 350 years. The Japanese gave them the opportunity to break free from the yoke they had shouldered for so long. However, in their haste, hatred, and hot-headedness they did not see that, to hold their country's leadership in their own hands, would require years of intense education. They needed to acquire knowledge of a solid and well-organized government and, even then, many mistakes would be made every day, as in any other country in the world. They did not realize the enormity of the task of leading their country correctly and safely. Spurred on by a young, irresponsible leader and diligent Japanese collaborator, Sukarno, they created chaotic situations, the impact of which is still felt now, some sixty years later.

The Indonesia of today never regained the prosperity it had once known, when it was under Dutch administration and rule. True, much of its riches had disappeared into the Dutch treasury, and the wealth of the Netherlands had indeed been built from the richness of its colonies, especially from the treasures that came readily out of Indonesian soil. Oil, tin, and copper, to name just a few resources, brought millions of guilders in profit to the Dutch. And it was the spices of the colonies—the desire for which sent Christopher Columbus to the New World—that made the small and rather insignificant country of the Netherlands one of the richest countries in the world.

In the meantime, murder and destruction rampaged through the streets of Batavia, and all other major cities in the islands. Young extremists were leaving death and ruin in their wake while in a half-crazed state of mind. Mostly armed with only sharply pointed bamboo spears, they nevertheless were deadly and very dangerous.

Our own men had still not returned home. Many were sent to Manila, in the Philippines, to recuperate from their three-year ordeal as prisoners of war. Americans and their Red Cross were responsible for nursing them back to health. My father was among these men.

Here at home, the Japanese were little by little being shipped back to Japan. The handful of British, British Indian, and Australian soldiers still in the islands were not a large enough force to keep the Indonesian rebels under control. We were waiting every day for more troops to protect us. It was in these stressful times that we were released from the concentration camps and allowed to return to our homes.

In Batavia, our house was still intact. Some pieces of furniture were missing, perhaps sold by the servants for provisions. It did not matter much. We were back in our own house, alive and well, and under the circumstances that was what was important.

Lena, the young Dutch/Indonesian woman who had lived with her baby in the wing of our house, came back to live there again, now with her two children. She had stayed on there after we were incarcerated, and her presence, with that of her German lover, had certainly saved our house and household effects. The German officer left as soon as he heard of our release, knowing that he was not welcome in our home. However, he stayed in close contact with Lena and the children, of which one was his.

The pair really seemed to love each other. He felt responsible for all three of them and provided for them in a most caring way. And when the time came for him to return to Germany, they both appeared to be heartbroken. He knew that he would never see his adorable little daughter again, or her mother.

Lena's husband was due back from the war soon, and we all knew of his hot-tempered nature, fearing for mother and child. When he did return, Lena, out of fear and despair for her baby daughter's well-being, gave her away to a friend with whom she had worked in the restaurant-bar, where she had met the baby's father. This kind of story, so heartbreaking and sad, is a typical occurrence in any war, anywhere. Two people, who were supposed to be enemies, fall in love. It is one of the many tragedies of war.

UNCLE PETER

My mother and I had been living in our house for about a month, when late at night a loud banging on the front door awakened us. It was a recurring nightmare, in an instant a replay of what had happened a year and a half earlier. This time it was Indonesian soldiers who demanded for us to come with them, although they were not unkind and quite polite.

Later we learned that they were the sons of old servants of my grandparents, who had worked for our family for many years. These young men had volunteered to get us, since they feared we would be treated unkindly if strangers were to get to us first.

My mother and I were needed to identify the body of a man who had been shot to death earlier in the evening, not too far from where we lived. The soldiers recognized him as my mother's brother, but they were not sure. We knew about Peter's deep and diligent involvement with the underground guerilla fighters. We suspected him as the leader, and our hearts were heavy as we came along.

Arriving on the dreadful spot, we saw a shape on the side of the road, covered with the Dutch Red, White, and Blue. Above the body the Indonesian flag was raised on a makeshift pole. The message was loud and clear: the Indonesians had conquered the Dutch. And it was indeed Uncle Peter's body—my mother's one and only brother whom she had always adored.

Ashen faced, she turned and walked away, almost regally, after she'd acknowledged and identified the body as that of her brother. I walked right beside her. After posing several questions we could not answer, the soldiers escorted us back to our house. They apologized and expressed their condolences. My mother looked at them coldly and did not say a word. They left swiftly and quietly, and we entered the house.

Once inside the house, my mother broke down, bursting into tears. She sat on a chair in her bedroom and the tears ran down her cheeks. I sat close to her on the floor with my head on her lap. She stroked my hair. She then wiped her eyes dry with her handkerchief and stared at the opposite wall, her eyes dull, her mouth trembling. We were both stunned and disbelieving of what we just had witnessed.

After what had seemed an eternity, my mother got up, forcing her shaking legs to move forward, holding on to me as she never had before.

"Get your pajamas and sleep here with me," she said to me softly. I was bone-tired and quickly did as she said. When I came back into my mother's bedroom, I found her lying motionless, staring at the ceiling, her eyes dark pools of sorrow. When I came to her to kiss her goodnight, she started to weep again, her tears streaming down her face unchecked. I quickly climbed in bed and lay down beside her. There was a soft knock on the bedroom door, and Ierah came into the room. She knelt down on the floor next to where my mother was on the bed and began to stroke my mother's arm.

Slowly, almost hesitantly, my mother began to speak in a whisper, hardly audible at times. "Poor Peter, he was too young to die," "His wife and children have to be warned," and "Where is his body now?" She wanted Uncle Peter's body, and as irrational as the idea was under the present circumstances, she wanted to give him a proper burial. The thought of her brother's body lying neglected somewhere haunted her.

My mother lay in her bedroom, unaware of the hour, watching the night descend. I had fallen asleep as soon as my head had hit the pillow, exhausted from all the happenings earlier in the evening, and with the flexibility of my youth, I was able to sleep a heavy sleep, dreamless and healing.

The next morning we returned to the same spot where my uncle's body had lain. His body had been removed and, to this day, what had happened to him has never been discovered by any of his loved ones.

Shortly after my uncle's murder, his wife, my Aunt Irma, passed away. She had lived surprisingly long, considering that she was a seriously ill diabetic who for the entire duration of the war had no medication. She was kept alive with all kinds of herbal remedies and a constant and strict diet of no sugar and no salt—deprivations that are easier to live by in a war, with fewer temptations to fight.

PROTECTION CAMPS

I have now arrived at the moment in my story when we had to leave our home for a second time. The newspapers, now functioning again, were filled with stories about "protection camps," where all the Dutch and Dutch-Indonesian citizens were to await the arrival of reinforcing troops, which were on the way. We also awaited the return of our own men, who continued to recuperate from the horrors of prison camps and forced labor, at least physically. As to their mental rehabilitation, there was no assistance. They were on their own to straighten themselves out, just as their women and children had to do.

The family gathered at my grandmother's hotel, taking only the most urgent necessities. We imagined that it would be for only a couple of weeks, no longer, until troop reinforcements would make us safe again in our homes. The troops had begun to trickle in, and we had hopes of a speedy return to our own homes.

In the meantime, however, Gesina, my great-grandmother, who was now in her late eighties, refused to go. She said that, since she was old and purely Indonesian, she had nothing to fear. Siti, my grandmother's trusted housekeeper, who always had taken care of the plantation house in my grandmother's absence, volunteered to stay to take care of great-grandmother during our absence. It would be quite eerie to be alone in the big hotel. But my great-grandmother's wishes were firmly set in her mind, and it was only for a week or two anyway, or so we thought.

Our stay in the protected camps lengthened to a month and, while we were there, my great-grandmother fell ill. She was brought to the hospital by my grandmother, who was permitted to leave the camp daily to check on her mother and Siti. Great-grandmother died that month at the age of 88.

Now the hotel and our house down the street were completely empty. When we returned to them once again, these properties were only a shadow of what they had once been. The young rebels had ransacked the buildings thoroughly. Furniture had been removed, and what had not been taken had been destroyed. The beautiful gardens, or what was left of them after the digging for the bomb shelters, were in shambles. My grandmother stood there with Opa Han, dry-eyed and stiff, as if hewn of stone. She said with a deep sigh, "We don't seem to be the only ones," looking at her neighbor's house, where a high-ranking Dutch official had lived with his family for years. Their house was in an even worse state than the hotel and ours. Even the walls surrounding their property were broken in many places.

The lovely street where the hotel and our house stood had been a beautiful neighborhood. It was one of the older ones, but always wonderfully kept up. The old homes on that street were full of distinction and grace, and the people who lived there were mainly people with high positions in government or very rich business people and families with old money.

The beautiful tile roof of our hotel was broken here and there, as if someone had been shooting from inside the building through the ceilings and through the roof. The walls were sieved with bullet holes. The connection of the family with my Uncle Peter, the Dutch guerilla leader, had unleashed the rebels' anger and hatred, and in their fury they just wanted to kill and destroy.

Ever practical, my grandmother quickly turned to her old Chinese business acquaintances for assistance. She found other accommodations for the family in houses owned by these rich Chinese merchants, in the dignified and genteel neighborhood of Oranje Boulevard, a street lined with gorgeous flame trees on either side. The homes were all stately, with long driveways and huge sprawling lawns. Neglected but still impressive in their layout, they appeared relatively sound under the circumstances. After the Dutch, who had rented these homes, were imprisoned during the war, the Chinese owners themselves came to live in them to protect their property against rampaging soldiers, Japanese and Indonesian alike.

In these homes we lived comfortably for many months, awaiting the return of our husbands, fathers, sons, and brothers—the ones who were lucky enough to return.

Although in terms of possessions, we had lost everything valuable and dear to us, the family was largely intact. Everyone was still alive except for my grandfather and great-grandmother on my father's side. And on my mother's side my grandfather and of course my uncle were no more.

ONE LAST LOOK

One day, my grandmother decided to go to the plantation to observe and estimate the damage it had suffered. Although she was warned several times about the enormous destruction she would encounter, she was determined to go. She was accompanied on this sorrowful journey by my mother and me, and her second son, Ed, who had already returned from the war, and his family. My cousin Eric, his son, was also there, as was Opa Han.

Despite the warnings, the shock was devastating for everyone, but most of all for my grandmother. This indomitable woman, who was in complete control under the most trying circumstances, started to tremble, clasping her hands together to stop them from shaking. Her body stiffened as she observed the devastation done to her beautiful plantation. "Oh my God!" she cried, slumping back against her son, who put his arm around her shoulders.

We all stood there, where once had been a beautiful lawn surrounded with beautiful plants and flowers. It was now full of old and rusty Japanese military vehicles. The house, the beautiful and comfortable home that we all considered our haven, stood crumbling in front of us. Windows and doors were broken, many were taken from their hinges, some dangling crookedly in the window frames. The walls were even more sieved with bullet holes than at the hotel and our house in the city. The beautiful tile roof was completely destroyed, and there was no roof at all in many places.

I ran to the monkey cage. The door stood open, the cage empty, with grass growing through the cracks in the cement floor. I went to the stables, where there was more destruction. The fruit trees still stood, but the weeds were knee deep, with a forlorn fruit here and there between the leaves and branches. Without realizing I was crying until I felt warm tears on my arm, I sobbed for the beauty and the comfort that was gone.

In my mind's eye, I saw my grandfather in happier days, riding his horse, Johan, his manager and best friend next to him, and his overseers. I could almost hear him whistle as he often did when riding through the orchards. His orchards, acres and acres of them.

I looked toward the plantation grounds and sucked in my breath sharply. For miles, I could see uprooted trees, lying on the soil. I could now see the cottages clearly where the workers used to live, now abandoned and desolate. As desolate as I felt in my heart. I felt a soft tap on my shoulder and turning I found my cousin Eric behind me. His face was wet and his eyes were red and swollen. "Oma wants to leave," he said softly with a shaky voice. "Come on Nora, let's go," he said with a sob in his throat.

My grandmother saw us coming, and she knew all too well our great love for the plantation. She embraced us both and pressed us against her heart, and said, "You know, it's going to be just fine. We still have each other." She then released us, and I saw her straighten her back and raise her head. It took all of her self-control to speak normally, for she was still shaking. Of us all, her anger, hurt, and total disgust was greatest for those who had done this to her family's cherished home.

This was the home in which she was born and raised. It also was the home in which she had lived with her beloved husband and had borne and raised eight children. It was the place to which her husband had given all his energy for most of his life, turning it into a smoothly organized, profitable, and productive plantation. It was his pride and joy, and to all the family it was a welcoming haven of comfort and serenity.

Oma walked away slowly but with great dignity. Opa Han walked beside her. His concern for her was clear to see to all of us. The silence in the horribly neglected garden was tangible. Everything looked so unreal. I saw grandmother's eyes misted over, when she turned around for the last time, to look again at the devastation. Then she walked away, placing one foot before the other, moving automatically. We all returned to the two waiting taxies.

RETURN TO NORMALCY

Slowly, safety in the streets returned with the coming of the troop reinforcements, English, Irish, Scottish, British Indian, and Australian alike. And many of our own men were also returning. The rebels were now kept under strict control, and curfews were being discontinued.

My father was sent to Manila, in the Philippines, to recover his health and strength. We heard from him regularly, and he continued to improve. His weight was 80 pounds when he was released from the Japanese prison camp and was now 145 pounds. Although still on the lean side, since his height was 5'10", he was much healthier, so that he was almost ready to be released from the hospital. Along with many of his compatriots, he was now ready to return to active duty, and our family reunion would take place soon, he wrote. We would be notified by the authorities when this would happen.

Ierah was now the only one of our servants who was still with us. Asim had left, for we did not have the money to pay him. He had stayed together with Ierah all through the war and even a few months after it was over, working just for the little we could share with them, a roof over their head, and food.

During the year and a half that we were in the concentration camp, Ierah and Asim were totally on their own and watched our house for us. When she could, my grandmother gave them money, but it was difficult to come by. They also put their lives at stake for us, smuggling food amid tight Japanese security through the fencing around the camp. Not many would have wanted to risk their safety and lives for their employers. They did this several times, throughout those awful long months.

When Asim finally had to leave us, he begged our forgiveness for doing so and asked for our understanding, with tears streaming down his cheeks. He clung to me and I to him. He promised to come and see us as often as he could, which he did, until we had to leave for the Netherlands. But that was years later.

After Asim left, I saw him in my mind's eye, sitting, as he so often did, on the floor, right behind my chair at the dining table, swatting at mosquitoes, if he saw them, with his serviette. When my mother asked him why he was doing this, his answer was as always, *"Nonni di gigit njamuk, kasian"* The mosquitoes are biting the little miss, I feel sorry for her.

I also remember him riding his bike, right next to mine, not wanting me to go alone too far. It had always irritated me beyond reason. At eight, I thought myself grown-up enough to go anywhere I pleased, and sometimes I was incredibly rude and unpleasant to him for not allowing me to prove that. He was the one who overindulged me with homemade Indonesian cookies and puddings, which he had made himself in his free time. They were wonderfully delicious, made with lots of coconut milk and brown sugar, made tasty and fragrant with *pandanus* leaves, which are used often in Indonesian desserts. When asked why he did all this, he always answered softly with a shy smile, "I was in the next room, cleaning, when the little miss was born, and I heard her first cry. I was the first one of all the other servants to carry her, remember?"

I used to play school with Asim, and I taught him to write and read and how to do easy arithmetic. I was amazed at his quick understanding of the numbers and how swiftly he adapted to writing and reading. I told my mother about him and when she saw that I was right, she decided to tutor him even further. Asim won her respect on several occasions for his quick wit in grasping complex mathematical matters with ease. And he was overwhelmed with gratitude for my mother's efforts to educate him a little.

We were not surprised when Asim informed us about his plan to open a small business in a huge marketplace. He planned to open a stand at the end of the war, selling odds and ends. He would do very well on his own, we knew. He was very capable—and besides, we could not pay him wages just yet, which were long overdue.

From a staff of six servants, we now had only Ierah. She assured us that she wanted to stay with us as long we needed her. After that she would return to her *dessah* (little village) and take care of her aging mother, working during the day picking tea leaves on a nearby tea plantation for her own support. I did not want to think when that would be. I did not want to lose her too, so soon after Asim had left. I still missed him very much.

FAMILY REUNIFICATION

In April 1946, we received word from the military authorities that we were to reunite with my father at the end of June. At that time we heard the news, he was still in Manila. We were to be assigned to a ship to go to Balikpapan in Borneo, together with many other women and children. It was exciting news.

I may have been more excited at the prospect of being on a big ship, cruising the Indian Ocean, to an island I never had been to before, than at the prospect of reuniting with my father. I hadn't seen him for four years. What would he be like? And what about me? My feelings were confusing. I was now thirteen years old. I had changed in many ways. One grows up very fast during a war. I wasn't the little girl who looked up to him with adoration. My mother conversed with me as she did with her adult friends. We had gone through terrible times together, shared decisions, with our lives at stake, with enduring consequences.

My father had been through terrible times as well, which nearly cost him his life. At one point, in Japan, while he was working outdoors, there was a surprise air raid. Shrapnel from a bomb grazed his back. He had just time to throw himself flat on the ground when another bomb exploded.

He was ill with dysentery, as many were in the camps, and he was hit in the face several times by his Japanese tormenters for working and moving too slow. He never spoke of these horrors. A friend of his told us, who had been with him in the same prison camp. We learned from my father's brother, who had the good fortune to work in the camp's soup kitchen, how he secretly brought my father soup, every day, when he lay in the prison camp's infirmary, deadly ill with pneumonia. "It was a miracle he lived through all the bodily misery," my uncle said, somber with the memories of that miserable time.

We left Batavia at dawn on a Thursday morning in June. My grandmother and Opa Han brought us to the harbor of Tandjung Priok. We had to pass the short road that eventually led to the plantation. Anxiously, I took a sidelong glance at my grandmother, while Sudiman drove quickly by the iron gate. I sensed the sudden change in my grandmother immediately— her body rigid, eyes dull, face a stone mask. When she turned to me and squeezed my hand, hers was icy cold.

At the Batavia city limits, a drizzling rain started, but when the car roared up the Antjol highway, we began to hit brighter weather. The rain stopped and although the sky was dull and overcast, the sun was beginning to filter through the gray clouds. Sudiman, chauffeur to my grandparents for over ten years, knew the road well, anticipating the twist and turns and many bumps, slowing down when necessary, and picking up speed when there was a smooth stretch of road.

Sitting quietly in my corner of the car, I formed a picture of the plantation house in my mind's eye, and saw that lovely old house as it used to be, so full of beauty and warmth and which I loved as much as my grandparents did. I imagined myself riding my horse over the land, racing my cousin Eric, riding bareback as fast as the wind, with my hair flying in all directions. We never used the saddles my grandfather had bought for us, always using the same excuse, that we didn't want to overburden the horses.

I closed my eyes and there was a throbbing in my head. I dared not think about what once had been. I was as determined not to think about all we had lost as I was to close my mind to all the misery we had been through. Oma looked at her watch and said, "We are almost there, Nora. I will miss you very much while you are away. Write to me often, will you, dear?" she asked tremulously. My mother, who sat on the other side of grandmother, gave her a big hug and said softly, "You know we will always be in touch with you, Mother." "Yes, that I know, honey," my grandmother answered.

I looked at my grandmother with tears in my eyes, and for the first time I noticed how frail she had become and how vulnerable she looked at that moment. But I also knew her enormous strength in times of despair and confusion. She was a true matriarch in every sense, the strength and backbone of the entire family, and if she was demanding and sometimes even imperious, she was also understanding of heart and extremely loving to all her children and grandchildren. Years ago, even her opponents acknowledged she was an extraordinary woman of her time.

VOYAGE TO BORNEO

We had made excellent time and were among the first to arrive in the military hall where we were to gather. After that, Opa Han and my grandmother walked with us onto the ship to choose an area to put away our baggage. The lower decks were full of thin mattresses laid down neatly next to each other, with about twelve feet of space in between. It was plain that this was no pleasure cruise ship, but a transport ship in its most basic form. Opa Han and grandmother left immediately after the signal for departure was given. It was a tearful farewell, but knowing we were to see each other again soon made the parting somewhat easier.

Mother and I made lifelong friends on that voyage, and with some I am still in contact with here in the United States. We sailed for five days and reached Borneo on the day scheduled. The island appeared huge and forbidding from a distance. Our ship had to drop anchor out in the water, and military boats carried us to shore, which I thought very interesting and exciting. I especially liked the part where the soldiers had to carry each of us to the shore, after the boats had landed, to avoid getting us and our baggage wet. I was reluctant to let go of the soldier's neck on arrival. He was a cute one, with sparkling blue eyes. At the age of thirteen my interest in the opposite sex was indeed starting to unfold, much to my mother's discomfort.

After all the unloading was done and our belongings were gathered, we again marched into another building, full of military personnel. Suddenly I saw my mother in the arms of a slender looking man with glasses on. I looked again and recognized my father. How he had changed! He looked so much older than in my memory, and different because of the weight loss and the eyeglasses. I flew to him, while he was still looking around for the little girl he had left behind four years ago. We hugged each other and than hugged some more. His eyes filled with tears and he said with wonder in his voice, "Good heavens, I have left a little girl and I have found back a young lady."

When the first excitement of seeing each other back had subsided, I wandered off by myself, giving my parents the opportunity to reunite. Carla, one of the new friends I had made on board the ship, saw me and came over. The first thing she said was exactly what I had experienced when I saw my father. "My Dad looks so different from how I had remembered him," she blurted out, a puzzled look on her face.

We both felt a little lost. After having had our mother's undivided attention to ourselves for so long, it was suddenly hard to share them with someone else. We had become somewhat isolated from our fathers, after all these years of their absence. Guiltily, I recognized a pang of jealousy, when I saw my mother so totally involved with someone other than myself. "Well, fine," I thought sulkily, "I can find my own way around," and walked away.

When all families had been reunited, we were again loaded up onto military trucks, this time driven by our own military men, and escorted to the barracks, which would be our home for a full week. The men once again separated from their families for just a little longer. After that our destination would be announced by the military leaders. I was pleased to notice that Carla and her parents were in our group and would be most likely be housed in the same area with us, since her father and mine shared the same battalion and company.

The week in Balikpapan was not a family vacation. The water had a horrible taste, even after it was boiled. The tea and even the coffee tasted like petroleum. In fact, there was petroleum in the ground and in the water, and it seemed to be everywhere. After bathing, a film could be detected on one's skin and in one's hair.

Balikpapan was where the B.P.M., or Bataafse Petroleum Maatschappy—better known much later as Shell Oil—had a cluster of oil refineries. Saturated with oil, the area was a steady source of income for the Dutch and had been for years, filling the already overflowing coffers of the Netherlands treasury. Our military was needed to protect these riches, and they were also needed to protect the companies, their employees, and their families.

HORROR IN SANGA SANGA

We were finally settled in a small town called Sanga Sanga, located alongside the Mahakam River and somewhat deeper into the interior of Borneo. The boat ride on the Mahakam was quite interesting to say the least, and although a far cry from being comfortable, I did not think there was a dull moment throughout the entire trip. Alongside the shoreline, we detected several tree trunks, or so we thought, partly in and partly out of the water, until one of the soldiers told us to watch carefully as he aimed his rifle just a little away from the target. The rifle went off with a reverberating noise, and the bullet splashed in the water next to one of the "tree trunks." There was a wild commotion, and the shoreline was suddenly cleared of what had looked like driftwood. The crocodiles, which of course they were, suddenly disappeared and were nowhere to be seen. I looked at my mother and saw her shudder, and the other women shuddered with her. Nowadays, most of these beasts end up on the shelves of expensive stores, in the form of handbags, leather belts, and fashionable shoes all around the world. Only very recently has the Indonesian government, with American advice and financial help, taken steps to preserve and protect its wildlife.

Arriving in Sanga Sanga, we were given shelter and accommodations in a sprawling wooden building, formerly used by the *Kempeh Tai*, which was well known for its extremely cruel methods of extracting the truth from its captives. The large rooms were divided into smaller rooms, with wooden partitions to accommodate a family. Our little family of three was given three small rooms, two makeshift bedrooms and a living area with big windows. The main kitchen was located in the back of the building, on the opposite side from where the bathrooms were situated.

I was elated to learn that Carla and her family were given accommodations in the same building, on the opposite side. We were inseparable from then on, roaming the fields outside the premises and the neglected grounds surrounding the building. The building was built on stilts to let air circulate, with a crawl space about three feet high beneath it.

One day Carla and I decided to investigate what was underneath the building. It was cool and dry when we crawled in, but dark. We were about to leave since the entire space seemed to be empty, when Carla stumbled over what seemed to be a ball in the dimness. It was not much smaller then a regular ball children play with. Suddenly she picked it up and threw it away from her with such a force, giving a ear-piercing scream. I recognized it for what it actually was as soon as Carla did, and screamed with her in unison. We bolted out of the crawl space as fast as we could. People came running out of their new-found quarters to see what all the commotion was about. Soldiers came running with them. We pointed, mute and shaking, at the crawl space. A soldier went in on hands and knees and came out with the object of our horror in his hands. It was a human skull, with the hair in some places still attached to it.

More soldiers now went inside the crawl space and by the end of the day six more skulls and skeletons were dug up. They appeared to be all male, this diagnosed by the military coroner, who had been immediately summoned after the gruesome find. The victims had been tortured to death by the Japanese, no doubt in order to extract information from them. A thorough investigation was now undertaken, and more atrocities revealed. A tiny closet wedged between the bathrooms, which was thought to be a broom closet at first, was revealed to be a water-dripping torture chamber, a type of torture the Japanese preferred even over the pulling out of fingernails one by one. The little bench on which victims sat was still in place. A metal band was still attached to the wall to keep the victim's head in place, while steadily the drops of water would drip on his head for hours and sometimes for days on end, until it would drive the victim mad. After a treatment like this, victims would confess to almost anything, whether guilty or not, just to make the awful dripping on their heads stop.

CHAPTER 3

POSTWAR INDONESIA

We stayed in Sanga Sanga for four months, and Carla and I thoroughly investigated the entire surrounding area of the compound. We stumbled on a dry oil well not too far from our military base, which the natives had declared haunted, since two workers had fallen into a deep pit nearby the site and were accidentally crushed to death by machinery. We spread the word about the story, and before long a midnight trip to the "haunted" site was organized by our camp commander, a Captain van Brink. We had very little entertainment in those four months in Sanga Sanga, and we jumped at the idea. In fact, we would have jumped at anything that would break the monotony of daily life while awaiting military orders sending the battalion to protect another region.

The trip was planned for a moonless Thursday night, the night Indonesians believe to be spirit-night. Only one flashlight was permitted, carried by a young lieutenant. The group of participants grew to about 30 and included parents and their teenage children. We traveled in six jeeps. Eerie silhouettes of the oil drills were dimly visible all around us and continued for miles further. The smell of raw oil was everywhere.

The oil drills, poised at precarious angles, or so it seemed in the darkness, did their strange nodding game. Everything seemed to be in motion around us. Some were soundlessly moving, and others made eerie creaking noises. Carla and I clung to each other, giggling nervously in anticipation. Some of us sank ankle deep into the muddy mixture of oozing oil. Those to whom this happened gasped and exchanged alarmed glances. Suddenly a white, ghostly figure appeared from behind some old field equipment. a flashlight held under a kerchief obscuring his face and distorting it grotesquely. The group screamed and flew in every direction, stumbling and running into each other. The men, our brave soldiers, regained their composure almost immediately after the scary moment, but we had the satisfaction of seeing them flinch after all.

The young lieutenant, who was indeed the ghost, roared with laughter, accompanied by Captain van Brink. The two men slapped their thighs and tears ran down their cheeks. The group milled about, punching and slapping them in good fun. Suddenly, a strong, permeating fragrance of a Plumeria or frangipani type of flower, called *kembang kembodja*, filled the air. These particular flowering trees are found only in cemeteries throughout all of Indonesia. The analytical and critical part of my mind rebelled, even at that young age—there must be an explanation, I told myself, all the while running as fast as I could, together with the others, to our waiting jeeps. Well, there was no explanation. Even the captain and his young lieutenant were quiet as we returned to the safety of our compound and our houses.

Certain things in the tropics are better left alone. But some day, as with anything else, we may solve the mystery of such phenomena as we experienced that night. In part it is the mass consciousness of a nation, of people who believe in the same happenings, that fuels the vibration and energies surrounding us. The vibrating energies, the sound and light that create and encircle us, bouncing from human to human and anything that lives, connect us this way with one another, without any separation. An old Buddhist monk I came in contact with shared this wisdom with me a long time ago, and I have never forgotten it.

MOVE TO MENADO

In October of 1946, our military family, which was the 62nd company of the KNIL, left Sanga Sanga, Borneo, to be stationed indefinitely until further orders in Menado, the capital of the Minahasah, in the north of the island of Celebes. We again embarked a ship, which would take us across the waters from island to island. We felt like a huge family. The war was over, and still we were picking up the many pieces. But it was comforting that we all did this together.

I missed my grandmother enormously. I wept in my bed at night, thinking about her, but I also remembered her indomitable manner and, sitting up, straightened my shoulders and raised up my head. I drew strength from the thought of her, which was her legacy to me.

On the second day of the voyage, in the quietness of evening and surrounded by a calm ocean, a deep and warm voice rang out, singing the American favorite "Home on the Range," accompanied by two guitars and a harmonica. It came from the quarters where all the single military men stayed. Someone unfamiliar with the colonies might say, "Now why an American song, in the middle of the Indian Ocean?" Most of the songs we listened to and sang were American, and so were all the movies in the theatres. We were constantly exposed to many aspects of American culture. Now the sound of a clarinet joined with the sounds of the other musical instruments, and someone else beat an empty metal drum from somewhere on the ship. The music sounded wonderful that night.

The very next evening, the wife of one of the sergeant-majors played a boogie-woogie on a piano, which stood in the corner of a large open space. She played well, and soon the sounds of the immensely popular songs "In the Mood" and the Andrews sisters "Drinking Rum and Coca-Cola" came bouncing off the keyboard. Everybody sang, and this little impromptu band kept us entertained for the remainder of the voyage. No one complained. It was so nice to be able to laugh again.

A fifteen-year-old girl named Elly also joined the music group. She had a warm, alluring voice, surprising in someone so young. Years later, she and I sang together in the same band for a short while, when we were back again in Batavia, in the well-known swim and dance clubs of Mangarai and Tjikini.

When we reached Menado Harbor, it was around six o'clock in the morning. The rattling noise with the lowering of the anchor awakened everyone on the ship. People left their cabins in a hurry to see what was happening. As I came on deck, I was stopped by a scene of perfect wonder. The rising sun summoned the flowery scent of the island, and the light breeze carried it toward us on the ship. The beaches surrounding the island seemed almost white in the bright morning sunlight, and glittering. The many shrubs and trees in every hue of green served as a gorgeous backdrop, here and there interrupted by bright red and yellow spots. It was a magnificent sight in the early morning hours: glittering white beaches against a backdrop of green foliage lush with dew. The sunlight striking from a certain angle had turned this lovely panorama into a fairy land. Behind all this beauty, the majestic blue-green mountains seemed to embrace and cradle the scene, like protective guardians.

A few hours later found us already settled in our new quarters. Large and comfortable homes, which had been abandoned during the war, were cleaned and made ready for our use. The homes had large rooms and verandahs, which were partitioned to create more living space and privacy, for three small families or couples were assigned to each house. With memories of living in overcrowded and horrific concentration camp conditions, our new home was like a little paradise.

My parents and I and two other couples occupied the same house. It had three bathrooms and three WCs and a large kitchen to share. The neighborhood, before the war, had been a lovely one, built on a bluff overlooking the ocean, with a path leading down to the beach below.

GROWING UP IN MENADO

We ended up spending three years in Menado, until I was almost fifteen. It was wonderful to grow up near this lovely beach while in my teenage years, and if teenage problems burdened my heart and thoughts, I would sit quietly on the beach and contemplate. It always helped to clear the cobwebs from my mind.

We could see the shimmering water in the distance, and on quiet nights we could hear the surf down below. Fishing boats moved about in the distance, with their kerosene lamps reflected on the dark waters. We could hear the fishermen chanting while throwing out their huge nets. "*Hallé hallowang,*" they would chant in unison, "*Hallé kamudi,*" or so it sounded to me, listening to them from afar. I never knew what the chant meant, or even if I heard the words correctly. Coming from another island, I was not quite able to understand their dialect. The chant sounded mysterious and alluring in the still of the night, and some voices were deep and extremely clear when the wind and water carried them toward the shore.

While sitting on the front verandah with my parents and the other couples and with the fragrance of the evening primrose heavy in the air, it was hard to believe that a monstrous war had just ended, and the islands were licking their wounds in the aftermath. Peaceful as it was there, I had a premonition that bad times were not over yet and the worst might be still to come.

Still, life went on at a regular pace. Right behind us lived a colonel with his wife and two teenage children, a girl my age and a boy a year younger. They were a Dutch family but born and raised in the colonies. The girl's name was Frieda, and we quickly became great friends. Together with Carla, who lived one street over from us, we formed an inseparable trio, and the practical jokes and teenage pranks we thought up were plentiful and notorious.

One dark cloud on our horizon was school. The war meant three and a half years of no school discipline or drill. Although wise beyond our years in some ways, we were far behind in education and discipline. In Menado I began to attend a school run by Catholic nuns.

In one respect, I was luckier than most my age. During the occupation, when all Dutch teaching was prohibited and only Japanese teachings were allowed, I had the opportunity to progress in my education after all. A friend of my mother, a teacher, tutored me at home until we entered the concentration camp. In this she took great risks of punishment and torture if caught. As a result, I was only a little over a year behind for my age group in my education.

My friends, Carla and Frieda, were not that fortunate and were placed two grades lower than I. To our chagrin, the three of us were put in different classrooms, although we were always together during recesses and lunch breaks. We hated the regular school drill and discipline, which was hard for us to submit to after being free of it for so long. The nuns were tested beyond their endurance in trying to educate us and bring us to order. And so, to no one's surprise, one day the three of us were home at a time when we were supposed to be in our classrooms, because we were suspended.

It was because on this day we decided never to go to Confession again. Weekly Confession was a requirement in a Catholic school, but for us, who had received no religious training in this matter, it was meaningless. Friday afternoon was the appointed hour for all of us to stand in long files and walk to the church, which was located right next to the school, for Confession. My friends and I resented this drill and on this day refused to go. When asked the reason for our refusal, I answered that we found it unnecessary to go to Confession if we had not sinned. Of course we were sent to the office of the Mother Superior. She and another nun talked to us for almost an hour, as we sat, stiff and morose, glaring out the window, refusal written clearly on our faces and in our body language.

What were these two women speaking of, I thought? Their vocabulary was filled with strange words—forgiveness, understanding, sin, compassion— that we did not understand. What had they been doing for the past three and a half years, while we lived through the war? Living protected in their snug and safely walled-in convent, perhaps? In the arrogance of youth, we felt pity, disdain, and disbelief. One after another, we stood up and walked out of that dark and oppressive office, away from these two women who were saying one thing after another that sounded absurd to us.

Elated by our sudden freedom, we ran across the schoolyard and all the way home. We found a way to sneak in undetected and changed into bathing suits. I looked for the long stick I always took with me on my trips to the beach and found it near my bed. We planned to wait for each other at the edge of the bluff, where we usually met. The path to the edge was a narrow one, flanked left and right by low grass and bushes. There were lizards, *binjawaks*, living in the underbrush. Not half as big as the komodos, smaller and much more slender, they are nevertheless quite a sight. They are harmless creatures, feeding mostly on the vegetation surrounding them, with us humans scaring them constantly away from their cool resting places underneath the low shrubs. They had the habit of scooting out of their hiding places in great haste and crossing the narrow path right in front of you. I was never very fond of these encounters, which scared me every time they happened. So I carried my stick to beat against the low bushes while walking down the path.

Looking over my shoulder constantly, afraid that someone could see me from the house, I quickly climbed down the steep wooden steps that had been built a long time ago. I lived closest to the bluff and arrived just before Frieda and Carla did. It was a hot and humid day at the end of November, and perspiration trickled down our faces and bodies. The sand was burning hot underneath our feet, and with relief we reached the cooling waters and dove into the gentle surf. We swam for awhile and treaded water, keeping an eye out for jellyfish. One could feel their stings right away when they were near.

As we frolicked in the water, something clung to my finger. It was a tiny seahorse, and Carla had one too in her hand. They were amazingly delicate, these little creatures of the sea, and extremely graceful. Its little tail was wrapped around my finger, and it seemed perfectly at ease while it looked at me from round eyes. I kept it wet and cool by dipping it in the water several times, expected it to swim away every time I did so. However, it stayed snugly wrapped around my finger for the longest time, until I had to undo its tiny tail from my finger and let it go.

We swam back to the beach and sat down with our feet in the water, talking and joking with each other. Frieda noticed a starfish close to where we sat, thrown by the surf onto the beach. Its bright yellow color was still fresh when we turned it over, the mouth in the middle of its body still quivering and contracting. It was very much alive and quite a large one, the size of a small platter. We picked it up carefully and returned it to the water, where it swam straight to the bottom and settled itself peacefully.

Our beach—it was ours the moment we saw it—was laid out prettily in a bay, encircled by groves of coconut trees. Some grew on the bluff and some on the steep slopes down to the bottom, edging the beach. Coconut trees like the ocean air and do very well near it. My grandparents' plantation, which we still spoke of as "our plantation," was also near the sea.

A strong wave of nostalgic thoughts and emotions assaulted me, seeing these graceful trees so nearby. I saw again the plantation grounds and my grandfather riding his horse through them. I saw the lovely setting of the gardens and the sprawling house, where so many happy events had taken place. I saw my grandmother sitting on the front verandah, leisurely reading, in the quiet of the afternoon, while everyone else was taking a nap. She sometimes would go into the small office, off the side of the verandah, to look over her books. Waking up from my nap sooner than others, I would crawl onto her lap and snuggle against her body, still somewhat groggy. She never showed irritation at being interrupted in whatever she was doing. Instead, as always, she put everything aside, giving me her undivided attention.

From afar I heard Frieda asking, "Shouldn't we go home now, Nora?" This brought me back to the present with a thump. I nodded a reluctant yes, and with heavy hearts we picked up our towels and started the climb back up the bluff.

Entering the front yard, I saw my mother sitting on the front verandah. Uh-oh, this does not look very good, I thought. She did not smile, as she usually did when she saw me. "You have been swimming at a time when you should have been in school," she said flatly. She also held a piece of paper in her hand, which she waved angrily. My mother was a sweet and loving person, but she also was known for a fiery temper when provoked. Her face was flushed, and that was not a very good sign, either. It meant that she was working up a storm inside. She'll let me have it in a minute, I thought, and I was right.

The note in her hand came from the Mother Superior, brought to my mother by one of the school office workers while Carla, Frieda, and I were down on the beach and in the water. My two friends probably are going through the same ordeal, I thought, which helped me a little to face the situation I was in.

My mother told me that I was suspended from school and that she now had to do her utmost for me to be reaccepted. I looked down at my feet and begged her not to make me return to that school. I asked if I could go to another school. I told her my reason was that I refused to do what I did not believe in. She listened quietly, after her first anger had subsided. I could see the struggle in her face, trying to understand. She herself was a devout Catholic, and she had seen to my Catholic upbringing, including receiving first communion, when the war came. She was quiet for a long time, and then finally spoke. She said she needed some time to think this through and then, of course, she had to discuss the situation with my father. In the meantime, I was grounded for a certain length of time.

Nervously I awaited my father's return from work at the end of the afternoon. My parents talked for a long time. I avoided being near them as much as possible. At supper time, my father kissed me as usual and gave me a hug. Briefly he touched on the subject, to let me know that he was aware of what I had done and agreed with the punishment my mother had announced. We ate supper in silence, which made me very uneasy.

The next morning I was asked to get dressed neatly and quickly. In a rented *sadoh*, a horse and buggy, my mother and I went to register me at another private Christian school. My friends Carla and Frieda returned to the Catholic school. I was elated and promised to bring home good grades—a promise I always kept. It was a good school, boys and girls mixed together. And I attended it for two more years, until my father was demobilized from the military in late 1948, and we moved back to Batavia, where he resumed his civilian career in the financial department he had always worked for.

VISIT FROM AUNT GILLY

In January, my Aunt Gilly came to visit us in Menado. She now worked at the Australian Embassy in Batavia as an interpreter. She spoke beautiful English, which she perfected during the years she lived in Singapore. Aunt Gilly and my grandmother had sold the clothes boutique they owned together and had made excellent profits—one of the few good things that had developed for the family during and after the war.

Aunt Gilly had never been in Celebes, and my father had arranged to take her, as well as my mother and me, on an island tour, including the well-known mineral baths in the mountains. While they were engaged in conversation, I sat back, regarding my aunt. The sun pouring through the open windows bathed her in its bright light. She really had that special kind of beauty that looks best in the daytime, I thought. And she is so full of energy. Of all my grandparents' children, she is the one who resembles my grandmother the most. My grandmother must have looked like her when she was Aunt Gilly's age—the same thick, dark, short-cropped hair, the same wide-spaced deep brown eyes, with an impish expression. And Aunt Gilly seemed almost unaware that she was such a beauty. Certainly she was devoid of personal vanity, and that was the greatest of her charms. She was filled with a radiance and a vitality that was almost sensual in nature. Men always swarmed about her.

She had told us that she was engaged to be married to an Australian gentleman she had met at the Embassy. We were extremely happy for her, especially my father, who was very fond of his youngest sister and always seemed to worry about her just a little.

The next morning, bright and early, we all piled up into the jeep that was assigned to my father for his personal use and that of his family. A huge basket with all kinds of goodies had been packed full by our new servant, Maria. The Menadonese are mostly Christians and therefore have Christian names. But I have never seen so much of the black magic rituals than when we were in Menado and throughout the entire island.

The ride to the mineral baths was a wonder. Wild ginger graced the mountain slopes in red, pink, and white. Everywhere were ferns of all sizes and palm trees of all different sorts, some heavily laden with clusters of red and yellow berries the size of marbles and oblong in form. The fruit inside the colorful skin is glassy, white, and tasted a little like a young coconut—delicious when mixed into a tropical drink made of a little bit of rose syrup, water, and crushed ice. The name of this fruit is *kolang kaling*, when found in a jar on store shelves.

After an hour and a half, over a bumpy road, we arrived at the baths, noticeable from afar by the rising steam among the heavy foliage. The place was in a natural state, with no guide rails or wooden pathways, no signs, no rules or regulations. One was just left to one's own intelligence and judgment. It was very peaceful. The birds in the trees sang a happy song, and the mountain air was crisp and clear. Maria had included a huge thermos filled with hot coffee and warm *Serabih* cakes in the picnic basket. The cakes are light and airy and resemble American pancakes. After a leisurely breakfast, consumed in these wonderful surroundings, we chatted for a while longer, enjoying the atmosphere.

The water in the basin at our side looked mysterious, with steam swirling around and above it. After a while we all decided to enjoy its beneficial and therapeutic powers. The temperature just right, delicious to the skin in the chilly mountain air. My mother, who could not swim, clung to a piece of rope that was tied to the trunk of a big tree nearby. The pool was not deep, the water barely reaching my chin. But according to my mother, even ankle-deep water was deep enough to drown in.

We stayed in the water for quite some time. Although it had a bit of a sulfur odor to it, it was not too unpleasant. After we felt thoroughly waterlogged, we clambered out of the basin and bundled ourselves into large, fluffy towels.

By one o'clock in the afternoon we were hungry enough to eat practically anything in sight. There was cold fried chicken and *empal*, fried thin slices of marinated beef. There also was a cool pickled dish of cucumber and thinly sliced carrots, sweet and sour in taste. There also was hot chili sauce, called *sambal*, fried shrimp chips, and steamed white rice. And for dessert, Maria had included fried bananas. All of this was neatly packed in food containers, called *Rantang*, stacked on top of each other and fitting into a frame with a handle to carry it all. Everything tasted delicious and we applauded Maria in silence, taking note to thank her for the wonderful picnic.

Thinking of Maria brought back other memories of another time in my life and of my sweet and dear Ierah. Although hired not in that capacity, she could cook wonderfully, and she often did when the cook was not able to come in. I missed Ierah very much and longed for her gentle care. I also missed Asim. Theirs were the faces of my formative years, part of my world. I saw them only one more time, shortly before I left my beautiful islands for good.

We had planned to show Aunt Gilly the famous sea gardens the next morning. She was as excited as a little child with the prospect of this event, She looked so young and full of life in her expectations of the next day. A sea garden is a particular spot in the tropical ocean or bay where gathered together the most colorful of fish and other sea creatures, such as sea anemones and starfish. The sea gardens were well known for their colors, beauty, and variety. They were one of the things that had not suffered from the war's destruction.

When we arrived at the beach, my father rented one of the winged boats, which lay neatly side by side, waiting for customers. He chose a sturdy looking one big enough to accommodate four people plus two boatmen. The boat was amazingly stable in the water, and roomy enough for all of us to sit comfortably. This was before glass-bottomed boats had been invented, so we all just hung over the sides, looking down into the clear water.

In the stillness of this January morning, the beauty of the sea gardens caused Aunt Gilly to catch her breath in admiration. The sun was high in a cloudless blue sky, the water sparkled, the air was limpid, and the soft breeze kept us cool and refreshed. The only sound we heard was the rippling water against the boat. Even the boatmen were quiet, captivated by such beauty.

This is perfection, I thought. This is God in all his glory. And no church with its dogmas and man-made rituals, rules, and regulations could have extracted from me a deeper and closer feeling of oneness with my creator than these precious moments in nature, recognizing and absorbing its perfected glory. In such moments I completely connect and submit my entire being to the creator of the whole.

Aunt Gilly, sharing a similar powerful emotion, reached for my hand and squeezed it knowingly. Curiously enough, it was the same gesture my grandmother used to make, when we shared an experience. My parents, equally captivated by the splendor of the sea, held hands while they admired the wonders. We all sighed, marveling at the beauty of it all. We saw sea anemones in clusters all over the sea bottom, clinging to rocks, in a huge mingling of incandescent hues. Some were blood red, some a deep coral that edged into blush, with white, yellows, and blues adding their delicately fresh tints to the lavish setting of different sea creatures that rambled about. It was a gorgeous sight to behold and to remember.

On the way home, we stopped at a wayside stand and bought a variety of fresh fruits. We also drank the juice of fresh young coconuts opened for us by the vendor. After we drank the juice, he hacked the fruits in two so we could eat the soft pudding-like flesh, just as we had done as children. Deliciously sweet.

Aunt Gilly went back to Batavia the next day. She married her Australian gentleman and left for Australia that very same year. My parents and I did not attend her wedding, which was small but very elegantly done, according to my grandmother, who wrote us a long letter about it. It was the last time we ever saw Aunt Gilly, and I always remember the wonderful days she spent with us in Menado. We corresponded with each other frequently, but we never met ever again.

GROWN-UP CELEBRATIONS

It was then February and my fourteenth birthday was about to arrive. My mother had arranged a celebration in the officers club downtown. Carla and Frieda and their parents were among the invited, and the band that had been put together on the ship, and which had developed in to a full-fledged orchestra, had been engaged as the evening's entertainment. The pianist, who lived in the same house as us, had taken care of the arrangements.

I remember many times when the band came to together to practice in our house, since a baby grand piano stood in our living room. Those were happy times, filled with lots of music. And that's when I started to sing for the band for fun and picked up certain techniques just by listening to the radio. Still, I hated to make public appearances and used to bribe the older singer with everything I had to sing for me instead.

But this time it was my party and I looked forward to it with great excitement. I loved to dance and had many "teachers" since I was twelve years old, because of the shortage of single female partners in the adult age group in our military circles. At first unwilling, I was many times literally dragged onto the dance floor, but I then started to acquire a taste for dancing. I especially liked the jitterbug and jive, dances that were immensely popular at that time. Of course my parents were always near keeping an eye on me.

The birthday was great fun, and I never lacked for a dancing partner all evening. At midnight we all went home tired but happy. It had been a wonderful party, long talked about afterward.

Another occasion for celebration was Queen's Day, August 31st, a big holiday in the Netherlands and the Dutch colonies. For this big day of fun and games, events were planned weeks ahead of time.

Target shooting matches were organized for military and civilians alike. Jeep racing and ability driving contests were put together. The driver of each jeep would choose a mate, who sat next to him and together they were supposed to conquer all kinds of obstacles, like driving over a wide seesaw while the mate holds a full glass of water, and trying to pluck a ring from a horizontal hanging bar. There were track and field events, basketball games, and soccer.

A young officer chose me for his jeep mate. I knew him well. He was a frequent visitor in my mother's Eatery, which she had opened on our rear verandah. It was an opportunity for single military men, for a small price, to occasionally avoid the horrible fare from the military kitchens. The Eatery became so popular that we had to hire two more kitchen maids to help Maria to keep up with the great demand.

My father, without my knowledge, had also entered and registered me in a shooting match, against a young lieutenant as my opponent. In Sanga Sanga, I was taught to shoot, which I had accepted as a challenge at first. However, after a while, through regular practice and repetition and my father's constant prodding, I began to excel, especially in handling the machine guns called Owen and Stan-gun. I knew all their shortcomings intimately. Both had a tendency to pull to the left, when the metal became hot from so much firing, and I knew how to compensate for this aberration. Actually, I hated these drills, but every day, for the next two weeks, my father and I went target practicing, right after he came home from work. As always, I still wanted to impress him and so I went along against my wishes.

Finally the day of the games arrived. A band played the Dutch anthem and everyone stood at attention. Then a colonel gave the sign for the games to begin. The shooting match was first, which I liked. I was nervous but controlled. When my opponent, the lieutenant, walked by to take his place next to me, he reached over and ruffled my hair in a patronizing gesture. This gesture made me furious, and I vowed to beat him on the range.

In short, I won the 100-meter shooting match, both with the Stan-gun and the Owen, and the public burst out in loud laughter when I reached up and ruffled my opponent's hair in turn. However, he was a good sport after all, laughing whole-heartedly with the audience and giving me a big hug. The prize was a lady's watch, but the look in my father's eyes was the grand prize I was craving. His eyes shone with pride and he boasted to whoever was near about how his young daughter had beaten a seasoned military man in a shooting match.

I was only too glad that this part of the day was over. Now I could enjoy the further events of the day. My jeep partner and I also won a prize, a second prize this time. It was the biggest cake I had seen in a long time.

MY FATHER'S SILENT HISTORY

Just about the time of the Queen's Day celebrations, I became aware of an unsettling feeling about my father. All was not quite right with him, I felt. Already quiet, gentle, and somewhat timid by nature, he became even more withdrawn. He had never spoken about his camp years in Japan. And when his military buddies exchanged camp stories while visiting, my father was always quick to change the subject.

I only could imagine what those years would have done to someone of my father's disposition. Surely severely wounded emotionally, not to mention physically, during those terrible war years, he must had received many blows to his self-esteem as well, working in the coal mines deep in the bowels of Japan. Not dressed or shod adequately to tackle the cold winters in those damp and cold mines, he contracted pneumonia so severe that he was given up for dead. That was when my mother received the first notice via the Red Cross of his apparent death. The second time she received such a message was due to a mistake in the spelling of his name.

My father also contracted dysentery and almost died from the disease. His body already weakened from his illnesses, he could not perform his work as fast as the Japanese demanded, and he was frequently beaten because of it.

All these stories we learned from his friends, men who were with him during those camp years. There were also 500 American soldiers in the camp with my father, and only 27 survived. My father never spoke a word about all this, but he had been seeking consolation in the bottle instead. He had been drinking for the past two years, ever since he was discharged from the American Red Cross in Manila.

My father was very discreet and careful, knowing that my mother would strongly disapprove of his behavior. My mother, who had never drank a sip of alcohol in her entire life, had no understanding of his problem and blamed it entirely on his strong preference for the spirits, and not on what the liquor was doing for him.

My father began to hide the bottles of whiskey in all different places. And more than once, I saw him reaching deeply into the drawer of an old commode and taking out a bottle. Once I saw him starting to pour himself a drink and then hesitated, grimacing, perhaps at the thought of my mother's disapproval. He played this little game until his death in July 1980, when he was eighty years old.

RETURN TO BATAVIA

In November of 1948 we learned that our KNIL battalion in Menado would soon be demobilized, and a regiment of soldiers of the Koninklijk Leger or Royal Army was already on its way from the Netherlands to finally release the KNIL men from their military duties, so they could resume their civilian lives with their families, where they had left off when the war started.

Letters had been exchanged between my father and the Department of Finances in Batavia, his former employer in government, and his return to this office was already expected and assured.

Carla's father and his family was to return to Surabaja, the second largest city in the colonies, to resume his civilian life there. But Frieda's father was a high-ranking army officer by profession, and so she and her family would stay behind.

Feelings of mixed emotions emerged. Adults and children alike were saddened by the forthcoming separation, for a tightly woven band of friendship had been formed during these military years, a spontaneous love and camaraderie among families that had been through so much together. Still, the prospect of resuming our civilian lives, so cruelly disrupted by the war, and returning to familiar surroundings also brought happiness and joy. The reunion to come with my grandmother and the rest of the family played an important role in our minds and hearts.

In January of 1949, after many tearful farewells from all our friends in the military, especially for me from Carla and Frieda, my parents and I returned to Batavia, where my father was reestablished in his civilian position as head of the Department of Finances, exactly a week after our return.

I entered the H.B.S., which means Hoger Burgelijke School in Dutch and is equivalent to a university preparatory school in the United States. It was located not too far from where my Uncle Jack had found us a house, which we shared with another married couple.

My grandmother, now seventy years of age and still blessed with good health and a sense of humor in spite of all she had lost, was now living with Aunt Helen, my father's younger sister, and Uncle Jack, occupying a separate wing of the main house. Still very much in control, calm and self-assured as always, she lived on her own attended by two of her old servants, following the death of Opa Han almost two years earlier. She had lost a little weight and had become quite hard of hearing over the years, but her mild manner, which belied a stringent wit, was still very much intact. I did note the webs of tiny wrinkles around her eyes and mouth. But I also saw that her cheeks were still firm and her eyes, which could turn flinty in anger, were not at all the watery wavering eyes of an old woman. They were still very alert and knowing.

Uncle Jack was of Dutch-Jewish descent. He was a jovial and happy-go-lucky man by nature. I will always remember his loud, booming voice and his jokes and roaring laughter. Although far from being "stinking rich," as he always clowned and bragged of becoming, he was quite well off. He dressed elegantly and expensively, after my Aunt Helen tactfully persuaded him to curb his affection for flashy ties and gaudy jewelry. Most of his rough edges had been smoothed away, and he was now even sophisticated to a certain degree. He walked with a confidant swagger, always with a smile on his face. Aunt Helen had a refining and gentle influence on him, without destroying his natural outgoing and happy nature.

Uncle Jack loved play-acting and belonged to a nonprofessional actors' club before the war. He owned a construction business, which reached soaring heights for a while, immediately after the war. During that glorious time in his business, his singing and whistling became even louder then usual, and everyone could hear his two most favorite songs for days on end: "My Bonnie Lies Over the Ocean" and "You Belong to My Heart." They brought smiles to people's faces. He had a warm and deep baritone, and his exuberance was contagious. He hated both his first and middle names, "Isaac Levi" and changed them, to Jack, but he was enormously proud of his last name, which was Spielberg, and of his entire ancestral heritage.

At school, I was elated to be reunited with Elly, the little songbird from the Menado years, with the deep, alluring voice. She was seventeen, two years older than I and one grade ahead of me in school. We came together often after school, and from her I learned of the well-known band in Batavia called Reggie Haas, which was looking for two female backup singers, who later were to be promoted to solo singers. Giggling from excitement, we decided to give it a try, but first we had some serious practicing to do. We chose "Sentimental Journey" and "Harbor Lights" as the songs we would sing at the audition. To our wild surprise, the two of us got the job. We walked home, stumbling with delight at our good fortune. Our parents gave us their permission to sing with the band, provided that our grades in school were maintained. A drop in this category of performance would mean an immediate stop to our singing careers; also the hours had to be kept within reason.

Because of our ages, we were scheduled to perform only on weekends, in the afternoons, and Saturday evenings from eight to eleven, with one of our parents always near to keep an eye on us. However, our careers in the music business lasted only six months. They ended abruptly when our grades in school started to downslide. Tearfully, we said our goodbyes to the band members and turned our attention to school and homework, diligently studying for hours on end, to make up for what had slipped during our singing careers.

The government had given the school board instructions to give to students the opportunity to complete a grade, which normally would take a year, in six months' time. This was in order to make up for the war years, when going to school was prevented by the Japanese. Because of this accelerated schedule, our homework load was tremendous. I really don't know what we were thinking when we assured our parents that we could handle both the singing and the hectic school schedule easily. I am now sure that it was done with the misguided confidence and ignorance of youth.

COUSINS AND FRIENDS

My cousin Eric, now sixteen years old, attended the same school as I and was one grade ahead of me. He had grown much taller and had began to fill out and was much broader in the shoulders. He wasn't my little playmate anymore, the one I used to boss around when we were small. He was now a handsome young man, his hazel eyes so very much like my own, reflecting his delight at seeing me again. When we met, he smiled widely, embraced me, and said with a laugh "You have shrunk, little cousin . . . What's the matter with you?" I told him not to get too confident, that I could still beat him in many things, with a big grin.

In a sudden flash I remembered an episode that happened when we were five and six years old. Our mothers had gone out to play bridge one afternoon in one of the clubs they frequented. Eric was deposited in my nanny's care to spend the day with me, until our mothers returned. He brought his dog Fifi, a miniature poodle, to play with my dog at the time, a miniature pinscher.

When Ierah had gone to the kitchen to help the cook with the meals, she instructed us to play quietly together until she summoned us to the table. We promised exactly that, already giggling with mischief. I suggested playing barber, and Eric readily agreed. He would be the client and I the barber. I ran to the laundry room, took a white sheet from the shelf, and draped it neatly around Eric, who sat patiently in front of my mother's dressing table. He had one of my father's newspapers in his hands, just as he had seen the men do, sitting in the barber's chair. I then took out a pair of scissors from the drawer in the dressing table and began to cut big chunks of Eric's dark-brown wavy hair. After a while, while watching me intently in the mirror, he said uneasily, "I don't think my mother will like this haircut you are giving me, Nora." I assured him that it would look much better in a moment. After all, I had just begun. I cut and cut, and huge patches began to appear on Eric's head. I then decided to cover his entire head with my mother's Pond's cream, just as I had seen the barbers do with the men, except that they used Brilliantine. Pond's cream will do just as well, I thought, and applied it plentifully to Eric's head. As a finishing touch, I reached for my mother's talcum powder, distributing it generously all over Eric's head and face. The result was terrifying yet hilarious. Eric looked in the mirror and burst out in laughter. We both screamed with glee.

Fifi then joined us in my parents' bedroom, where all the racket was taking place, to see what was up. The moment we saw her, we decided to give the dog the same treatment. Eagerly we took turns cutting huge chunks of fur off the dogs body, taking the utmost care not to harm or hurt her. Then we took turns with the Pond's jar, which was empty by the time we were through, and then again the talcum powder. Since Fifi was a black poodle, the effect was a hilarious transformation.

Eric and I were just finished with our masterpiece, giggling all the way through, when we heard Ierah coming into the dining room softly humming and carrying a large tray filled with steaming dishes. I can still hear her blood-curdling shriek when she caught sight of Eric, and another one shortly thereafter when she spotted the dog. The dishes rattled dangerously on the tray when she set it down on the table. A stream of words poured from her mouth in Indonesian, her voice reaching heights I never knew she could produce. Then she pressed her hands together and seemed to pray to Allah. Servants came running from all different directions, making lots of noise when they saw Eric and his dog. We thought them all extremely silly. It was not all that bad, nothing that a little water and soap would not fix.

Asim, who was in the storage room, polishing the silver, took charge immediately. He dragged Eric and the dog into the nearest bathroom, past the kitchen and the storage room.

Ierah, still speaking rapidly in a shrill voice while she cleaned the mess in my parents' bedroom, shook her finger close to my face and told me emphatically that this was going to cost her job, that it would be mainly my fault, and that she hoped that my next nanny would be old and ugly and someone I did not like at all. This would serve me just right, she went on and on, running out of breath and becoming flushed with agitation.

For my part, I lost interest in Ierah's tirade as I had become very hungry. I gravitated toward the dining room, where the food was set out for me and Eric. With Ierah still working in the bedroom, I served myself a generous portion *semur ajam*, one of my favorites, an Indonesian chicken dish prepared with lots of onions and simmered in soy sauce. I skipped the steamed white rice and veggies entirely. After I had loaded my plate, I helped myself to lemon iced tea from a pitcher on the sideboard, carefully not spilling a drop. As I finished my food, Asim, Eric, and Fifi came into the dining room. Eric and the dog were both clean but looked terribly mutilated. For the first time, I worried about what our mothers would say when they came home. I swiftly drank my tea and avoided Asim's accusing eyes, for he knew that I was the instigator of the hair-cutting plan. I slipped out of my chair, sauntered out of the dining room, and disappeared into my own bedroom, where I took out my coloring books.

As much as a five-year-old can, I thought about what I had done for a while, and what would happen when the mothers came home. I prayed to the Lord that Ierah would stay on, to take care of me. I just could not imagine a life without her. On impulse I ran out of my bedroom to find Ierah, who was now busy cleaning off the dining table. I pressed my face against her body and wrapped my arms around her waist. Without a word, she knelt down and held me close for the longest time, brushing my hair out of my face with her hand, and I knew that everything would be all right.

This childhood reverie was interrupted by Eric, who looked at me strangely. "Hey Nora, you were miles and miles away," he said with a half grin on his face. "Could you cut me in on it?" he asked. I told him what I had been remembering, and he burst out laughing with his own recollection of that day.

TEENAGERS TOGETHER

Eric had a friend, Eddy Barens, a seventeen-year-old boy who was amiable and polite and very popular. He was the best soccer player at our school. Many times other soccer clubs had tried to get him away from us, but Eddy was extremely loyal to our school and would never leave us for another club.

Eric dated a girl named Ingrid Meyers at the time, and the four of us and a couple more friends were inseparable during those years. We frequented the movie theaters on Saturday nights and the ice cream stands and parlors in Pasar Baru, meaning the New Marketplace in Indonesian, the most popular shopping area at the time in Batavia. The ice cream parlor, Toko Oen, a Chinese-operated store, was most popular, but so were smaller ones, where one could get the most wonderful snow cones and other delicious icy drinks made with young coconut, drenched in a rose syrup in a tall glass and packed full with finely shaved ice. There was also a green gelatin, made from leaves that grow on thick vines, that was considered healthy and cooling to the stomach, called *Tjen-tjaw*. There are poor imitations of *Tjen-tjaw* in cans on the shelves of the Asian stores now, but they taste nothing like the fresh product we used to have in our drinks then. The gelatin, cut in small cubes and mixed with pieces of exotic fruits, was put again in a glass with syrup, water, and tiny ice cubes to make a wonderful cooling drink. Such treats were savored by many in the warm and humid climate of the Dutch East Indies.

On Sundays we would venture further and away from the city. One of our favorite places to visit was the botanical gardens in Bogor, which was called Buitenzorg in Dutch. Buitenzorg or Bogor was a small town in the foothills, an hour away from Batavia. The botanical garden and the university of agriculture were the highlights of the otherwise sleepy little town. The botanical gardens were magnificently put together, reflecting decades of planting and landscaping. The Dutch governor general of the time lived on its grounds, surrounded by the exquisite gardens, laid out and flanked by pathways and avenued by rows of royal palms and tall teakwood trees, all offering shade on a scorching day. Stylized flower beds were awash with color. Variegated greens, lushly inviting, sloped away into the distance, highlighted with patches of pink and white bougainvillea, The cheerful little white trumpets of the jasmine vines, entwined in and hanging over arbors, filled the heavy air. Skirting the gardens were all manner of shrubs and trees, for Buitenzorg botanical gardens contained more specimens than any other park in the Dutch East Indies. Towering majestically above the shrubs were the flame trees, festooned with orange-red blossoms. Rocky paths and wide open spaces of lawn, as smooth as deep green satin, were enclosed by additional shrubs and trees and richly planted colorful borders.

Along these pathways moved the public and we mingled with them. The scene was idyllic on this splendid day. The peaceful surroundings made one forget the still unsettled situation in the government, and the grim realities of war three years ago were pushed back into the far corners of one's mind. We were lulled into a sense of false security. The years ahead were full of promise, and change was ripe in the air. I suddenly felt a strong foreboding that this was the last time I ever would see this park. A cold steel band enclosed my heart as I looked around me, blinking several times to make the pictures in my mind vanish. I saw myself with thousands of my people on big ocean steamers pulling away from the colonies. It was just for a short moment, but the images were clearly and sharply etched. I shook my head and looked around me, seeing only happy faces wherever I looked.

It was the postwar era and this year especially seemed to be the year when society danced and partied and flirted and sailed and hunted and laughed away the days of fear and pain that lay behind them. It filled everyone with a false sense of security. Things could only get better from now on, people thought—but wrongly.

There was a bandstand in the park, and benches had been built around it. The bandstand, a pagoda-like structure, added to the exotic and oriental ambience of the tropical setting. We settled ourselves on the benches as the band finished warming up and commenced their program with the Dutch national anthem. We listened to the music for a while, and then Eric suggested going for a long walk beneath the trees. But the feeling of doom, which had come over me earlier, stayed with me all through the day, stripping it of its joy.

Eric, who knew me well, glanced at me a couple of times with genuine concern. He took me aside and asked what on earth was the matter with me. I told him about my foreboding. He did not laugh or tried to appease me. He simply looked at the ground for awhile and when he lifted his head, his eyes were serious. He threw an arm around my shoulders and together we walked for awhile in complete silence and away from the others.

The days went by as usual for me and my friends, and I had somewhat forgotten about the strange experience I had in the botanical gardens. Actually, I did not forget but pushed it back to the far recesses of my mind and succeeded in enjoying life the way a normal teenager of those times would, always looking to the weekends and to the fun they would afford. One Saturday, in the late afternoon, riding around on our bikes, eight of us rode past a Islamic mosque, which was packed with people of the Muslim faith. The faithful were kneeling inside, packed as tightly as herrings in a tin. Their footwear lined the wide steps of the mosque, in long, neatly arranged rows. There were hundreds of pairs, sandals and shoes of all kinds of designs and sizes, waiting patiently for the owners to claim them when they came out after their prayers.

We looked at each other and began to laugh softly, recognizing the opportunity of a practical joke. Swiftly we climbed from our bikes and ran up the steps, grabbed as many shoes we could carry and threw them in a heap on the sidewalk, scrambling them thoroughly. Then we left quickly and hid behind thick bushes with our bikes, which surrounded the mosque's premises. Not long after, the first of the faithful came out. They had a surprised look on their faces and then started to cackle like a bunch of overly excited chickens. More and more people came out and discovered their footwear missing, then rediscovered it in the huge heap down below on the sidewalk. We fell against each other from laughter. The Muslims were now themselves in a heap, trying to get to their footwear and to make a pair that was theirs. Stealthily we came out of our hiding places, jumped on our bikes and laughing and hooting we rode away, looking over our shoulders as we went.

I mentioned earlier in the book the traditional offerings to appease the gods that people arranged in brand-new buildings, both professional offices and family homes. The tradition was also followed to bring to the dwellers excellent health, prosperity, love, and harmony during the time of their occupation. A *dukun*, or shaman, would be called in to perform the ceremony, which would consist of holy and magical words and the sprinkling in the four corners of the building of water he had blessed and prayed over prior to the ceremony. The most delicate dishes, flower pieces, and fruits were then laid down in the four corners of the building, and incense was burned right next to food and flower arrangements. At that point the ceremony was completed and the people would leave.

Our group would enter the empty buildings and feast on all sorts of the most delicate foods and fruits. It was a total sin, so we reasoned, to let these wonderful foods go to waste or be devoured by rodents. So why not have a feast amongst the eight of us. And so we always did. We developed a "nose," detecting such ceremonies all over the town, and were always trying to encircle the buildings from afar to lay claim as soon as the people left. There were other groups up to this kind of mischief, so we had to watch out for and beat them to the bounty.

SEMARANG AND SERENITY

In April of 1949, my father was asked to take a position in Semarang to replace a colleague for at least two years. Semarang is a port city in northern Java. I was heartbroken to leave my friends and especially Eric. They all promised to visit me on the Big Vacation, which in America is called summer vacation. With a heavy heart, I followed my parents. Also, I was getting into the last six months of my studies and hated the idea of going to another school. My grandmother and Aunt Helen and Uncle Jack offered for me to stay with them until I finished school. But my parents were afraid that something might happen in these uncertain times and wanted me near. My father already had reasons to believe that something was afoot.

The house in Semarang that was assigned to us was quite comfortable and had a lovely inner court. It was fully furnished and two servants were already there to take care of us. Not too far from where we lived, we found two families whom we knew during our Menado years. One man was a captain, now happily remarried, and a good friend of my father. He was now the head of the police department in Semarang. Another man was Richard Beems, who had settled with his wife and two daughters very close to where we had our house.

Next to us, in a magnificently kept house and grounds, lived a extremely rich Chinese businessman and his wife and only daughter, who was my age and attended the same school I did. Her name was Lucy, and she was so much fun to be with. The family was Catholic, but Lucy's grandparents were very much still Buddhist. They all lived in the same beautiful house, as Asians always take care of their parents in their senior years.

Like my grandmother in Batavia, Lucy's grandparents occupied a huge wing of the main house. They spoke halting Indonesian but were still fluent in Chinese. They were friendly, serene old people and were very soft-spoken. I loved to be with them. In a way, they reminded me of my grandparents. One of the rooms in the wing they occupied was arranged and made into a small Buddhist temple with a beautiful altar. The colors were typically Chinese, with lots of gold and orange-red and black. The odor of incense was always present, and the fragrance of freshly picked flowers always filled the air. I had reached an age in which curiosity was a fact of my life. Eager to learn and full of questions about all matters, I was strangely drawn to the philosophy of Buddhism, which Lucy's grandparents practiced. Slowly, by observation at first, and later by asking endless questions, I began to comprehend more and more about this wonderful philosophy, or way of life, so much older than Christianity. My questions were always answered in a calm and serene manner, and Lucy's grandparents instructed me with incredible gentleness, love, and soft-spoken patience.

This was no fire and brimstone way of teaching, I thought to myself, with some fanatic minister or evangelist or priest preaching with thundering voice from the pulpit to an awestruck audience, banging the pulpit with his fist to get his message across. Lucy's grandfather taught me not ever to look for refuge to any one besides myself. He spoke and taught me to follow a balanced, moderate path that is honest, straightforward, and impeccable. He also taught me how to live without excessive confusion, which creates anger and fear. Live without clinging, vacillation, or greed, he said. Basic sanity means being in tune with things as they are. "Make your first priority your spiritual life and develop a warm, kind, and loving heart, along with a sense of empathy and friendliness." But he also said that this included developing integrity and character, not just seeking short-lived "high" or mystical experiences. In other words, truth is about getting free, not getting high on whatever it may be.

Lucy's grandfather—his name I have never known, I always called him Grandfather—also taught me something about money. In the Western world, there is a saying that everyone knows, "Money is the root of all evil." Buddhists would totally disagree. They say, "Ignorance is the underlying problem. How we relate to money can promote either good or evil. It is helpful or harmful, depending on whether we use it or abuse it, and whether we posses it or it possesses us." It is something I have never forgotten. But then again, my own grandmother could have told me that, years ago in her own form of wisdom.

My Chinese teacher also talked about the idea that everything is connected with light and sound and cause and effect. "It's all surface," he said, mere temporary appearances. All things, by definition, are impermanent, like dreams, or echoes, or mirages. They, and everything else, are empty and relative, arising because of cause and effect, or interdependent origination. They are merely an expression of various conditions temporarily coming together, like the sound of a drum, for instance. There is nothing concrete or absolute.

Much later in life, very slowly, all these teachings became much clearer to me, than when I was sixteen years old. I did not become entirely Buddhist—no, not really so. Lucy's grandfather had opened my mind beyond Christianity. I understood that there is so much more than meets the eye, and so much more than just the teachings of the Christian Church, in a way that few people comprehend. Much, much later in life, I had a deep and thorough discussion with an elderly Catholic priest, a family friend of a good friend of mine. This wise and intelligent gentleman told me that if he and all the clergy would discuss what they really know with the public, the entire congregation would run out the church door, as fast as they could, never to return, since no one other than just a very few would understand the immensity and complexity of the teachings. And guided by ignorance, which creates fear and misunderstanding, most are not ready for the deeper aspects of the existence of the "whole," which takes years of theological study even to comprehend just a little. The priest concluded, why confuse the people, if they are satisfied with a few Hail Marys, going to church once a week on Sundays, and making donation, he said with a wry smile. But his eyes shone with great love and understanding.

Buddhism also taught me that the main cause for life's difficulties and suffering is desire or craving. Because all of us consistently desire various experiences and things, we continue to suffer. The object is not the problem. It is our attachment with what we desire or crave that causes the suffering. It is the inner clinging, in not giving up when something is denied to us, that entangles us in the endless net of suffering.

COUSIN ERNA

At about the same time, during my Buddhist phase, the disturbing news about one of my female cousins reached us in Semarang. My cousin Erna was seven years older than I, which made her twenty-three at the time. She was an extraordinary beauty. The only child of a younger sister of my father and her Dutch husband, Erna was breathtakingly lovely. Her skin, a translucent olive, was flawless. Her eyes, a smoky green, made the initial impact and were startling to find in a person of her coloring. Deeply socketed yet large and set wide apart, fringed with silky black lashes, they appeared to give her face a certain radiance. Her features were perfectly balanced, her brow smooth, a small upturned nose, high cheekbones, and a rounded chin. Her eyebrows matched her rich dark brown hair, which was parted in the center and fell in glossy waves to her shoulders. Her mouth was full-lipped and turned up at the corners when she smiled, which gave her a look of innocence and a suggestion of vulnerability. Aware though she was of her own beauty and the impact it made on other people, she had no vanity. In some ways she was even self-effacing at times, striving to find something special in others, which was her greatest charm.

Erna had the misfortune to fall in love with a full-blooded Indonesian young man whom she met through her work as an assistant manager in one of Batavia's largest, most sophisticated hotels. Hotel des Indies would now be considered a five-star hotel and was certainly a fine and elegant one in those times. The Indonesian young man, Kusnadi, was a counter clerk there, with impeccable manners, and the guests frequently asked to be helped by him. Tall for an Indonesian, with a well-proportioned frame, he walked with an innate grace and elegant manner, yet was entirely manly. His features, finely chiseled in a tannish face, were pleasant and always wreathed in smiles. It was easy to see why my cousin had fallen for him.

Their courtship would have lasted undetected for a long time had not Erna become pregnant with Kusnadi's child. Not knowing what else to do, she confided in her mother, who took matters into her own hands immediately, by sending her daughter out of town into the capable hands of a doctor who was an intimate friend of the family. Kusnadi was sent packing with a considerable amount of money in his wallet and told never to set a foot in Batavia again. He was never seen or heard from again.

After the abortion, Erna stayed with the doctor and his family for a couple of weeks and was then sent to live with us for a while to regain her strength, physically and emotionally. Erna was devastated by the experience. She had not only lost her lover, whom she loved with all her heart, but also her unborn child. I remember her sitting for hours in her bedroom, staring with blind eyes through the window. She looked so vulnerable and forlorn, it broke my heart. How immensely cruel society was. Such a relationship with a pure Indonesian was unheard of in our circles. How insane, I thought to myself. What about our own sweet and lovely and gracious great-grandmother, whom everybody doted on in our family and from whom we all originated. She was purely Sundanese, from the same background as Kusnadi. My great-grandfather adored the ground she walked on, and so did all her family. Who are we to interfere in Erna's life? I did not understand and was confused about it for a very long time.

FLIRTATION

Around that same time, I accidentally came into contact with a young police officer named John Huizinga, a Dutch-Indonesian young man about 24 years old. He was in the motorbike brigade and rode proudly on his beat, which was in front of the school I attended, although graduation was just a few months away. He made it a point to sit on his motorbike underneath a huge old tree near the school grounds, watching the traffic, especially when school was dismissed in the early afternoon.

One afternoon, I was among the milling teenagers cavorting exiting through the school doors, jumping on bikes and motorbikes. In my haste, I accidentally fell against John and his bike, making a huge gash on the gas tank of his motorbike with the handlebar of my bike. The impact of my fall almost toppled him from his seat and also knocked his cap askew. I looked at him horror-stricken at first, then burst out in a nervous giggle when I saw his cap positioned in such a silly angle on his head.

He looked at me with great disdain, and I'm sure he thought me one of those silly teenage girls who giggle all the time. He straighten his cap determinedly while I stuttered and mumbled my apologies, feeling like a bumbling idiot. He surveyed the gash in the tank with irritation, then, without a word, started his bike and rode off. I inhaled deeply with relief, jumped on my bike, and rode homeward at great speed, thinking what an conceited and pompous man he was. After all, it was purely an accident. I did not do it purposely, I reasoned, and with that I decided not to waste another thought on the man.

However, a few days later I found myself sharing his company at a dinner party at the house of Mr. van Daalen, a business associate of my father, to which my parents and I were invited. John was Mrs. van Daalen's nephew, and apparently they were enormously fond of each other. I could not believe my eyes and fervently hoped that the ground would split so I could disappear in it unobserved. When John and I were introduced, he looked at me with an amused smile on his face and explained that we had already met earlier in the week, in a most peculiar way. However, he did not elaborate as to the "how" of it. He winked at me and the gesture made me furious. He treated me like a child, and I felt patronized and annoyed with him.

I offered my hand, looked him straight in the eyes, and gave him a faint smile that was coolly indifferent. Feeling a certain degree of defiance, I turned around and walked away. But later, after we all sat down at the dinner table, John took over. Without really seeming to do so, he dominated the conversation, discussing everything from the theater to colonial and world politics, as well as sports of all kinds. He did so with a charm and élan and intelligence. He also managed to successfully bridge the brief but acute sense of awkwardness that had prevailed at the onset of the meal. I found myself being drawn into the conversation quite naturally. Much later again, over coffee and dessert, as well as brandy for the men, John kept us all entertained with hilarious anecdotes, displaying a marvelous sense of humor. My reservations about him started to crumble.

Late in the afternoon as we thanked our hosts for a lovely dinner and a wonderful afternoon, John squeezed my hand and said in a whisper, "I'll see you Monday in front of the school, huh?" I smiled and said nothing.

For a full month, John and I saw each other daily, although not always by the school. My infatuation with him grew steadily, and my parents watched worriedly. They told me that I was too young and he was too old, among other things. But before our relationship, if one could call it that, could develop further, earth-shattering news reached us by radio and newspapers.

DEVALUATION AND DESTINY

It was news that destroyed our world for a second time. My father came home from work late one evening. He walked into the house with two regular size suitcases, one in each hand. He walked into the bedroom he shared with my mother and put them into the armoire and locked it with a key, which I found strange, and put the key in his pocket. He had never locked the armoire before. He greeted us as usual after he had refreshed himself, walking briskly into the dining room for a late supper.

It was past nine o'clock and my mother and I had already eaten, but we sat with him to keep him company. He was calm or so it seemed, but his face was drawn and his eyes looked serious and tired. My mother, who knew him well, refrained from asking him questions but watched him silently, with great anxiety. I could not wait any longer and asked him what was wrong. My father put his finger against his lips and glanced quickly at the servant, who was just leaving the dining room to get something out of the kitchen. When she was out of earshot he whispered, I'll tell you later when we are in the bedroom.

I had also noticed that father had not reached for the whiskey bottle that evening, as he usually did, the moment he came home. What was even more odd, his work hours were from seven in the morning to 1:30 pm every day. It was nine in the evening now. So as not to raise any further suspicion, he read the newspaper for a while as usual and asked us to do the same.

There it was, in huge bold letters, "DEVALUATION OF THE DUTCH GUILDER" and the "HANDING OVER" of the Dutch government to the Indonesian government, after more then 350 years. The Dutch wanted to hang on, but the United States pressured them to let go.

I felt sick to my stomach. I knew what this would mean. I scanned the papers, and there it was: people of Dutch-Indonesian heritage were asked to choose between two countries and two citizenships. I couldn't believe this was happening, and with a jolt the premonition I had in the botanical gardens in Buitenzorg came rushing back to me. It had all come true, we would leave our beloved islands, the country of our birth.

We knew that we could not stay. We would be treated as third class citizens, which turned out to be exactly happened to people who chose to stay. I was dizzy with shock, and my parents were white in the face. And that same evening the three of us sat on my parents' bed, cutting the money in half, bills after bills after bills. That was what my father had carried inside the house so secretively, in those two big suitcases: two million guilders worth of it. He had already known for some time that this was going to happen, but he did not know when it would take place. Early the next morning after cutting up money for most of the night, my father left the house, again with the two suitcases still full, but reduced in value by 50 percent. I don't know where he took it—he would not say. Back to work, my mother and I assumed.

It was the end of 1949 and the confusion about the money devaluation was immensely disturbing to all people. Again we lived from day to day, not knowing what the next would bring us. My father was ordered to go back to the financial headquarters in Batavia, now already being called *Jakarta*. We packed up our belongings and returned to the capita, where everyone we knew was highly agitated. All the Dutch flags were removed and the Indonesian Red and White took their place. My parents soon decided, as did so many others, to leave the Dutch East Indies, which were no more, and to move to the Netherlands. For the few months until our departure, we lived in Jakarta with my cousin Eric's parents. In June of 1950 we left for Holland.

Eric, now eighteen years old, had decided to remain in what was now called Indonesia, and his parents decided the same. Eric married three years later, in 1953, when my parents and I were already settled in Holland. It was not until ten years later that he and his family came to The Netherlands, acknowledging that Indonesia was just not the same at all. In 1960, when he and his wife and two children finally arrived in The Netherlands, my family and I had already left for the United States. To this day, we have never seen each other again. Sad to think of how close we were as children and even as teenagers. Distance indeed can destroy a strong bond, and time and different lifestyles will do the rest.

FINAL FAREWELLS

Two weeks before we left for Holland we visited Asim for the last time to say goodbye. We knew where to find him, at his little stand at the Big Market place called Pasar Senen. When he saw us, he removed his sunglasses, sought my hand, and took it between both of his and brought it to his forehead in a gesture of deeply honored greeting. He did the same with my parents. "*Nonnie sudah besar*," he said over and over, meaning "Little miss has grown so much," and, indeed, I was now half a head taller than he was. He was getting gray, I noticed, and had lost some weight. He asked me never to forget him. "How could I," I answered, "You belong to my youth."

Tears welled up in his eyes and, to hide them, he suddenly bent down and grabbed an old black leather attaché case, once belonging to my father. My mother had given it to him a long time ago. He rummaged through it and smiled when he found what he was looking for, showing it to us. It was a picture of my parents and me at age six and our dog, neatly framed. "See," Asim said with a trembling smile, "I will never forget all of you, I've got you always with me." We told him why we had come to see him; he said that he was aware of the situation and understood fully our decision. "It is best for you to go," he said softly. Tears rolled down his cheeks and with bent head he grabbed my father's hand and said a silent goodbye. My father hugged him and thanked him again for everything he had done for my mother and me during the war. My mother did the same. He then grabbed my hand and asked me to send him pictures of us in Holland, which was called Negri Blanda in Indonesian. I tearfully promised him that I would. He should check for them from time to time at Sinjo Eric's house, I told him through sobs. I hugged him, then had to extract my arm from his grip. I then turned around and ran back to the car, not once looking back.

Asim told my father where we could find Ierah, to whom we also wanted to say our farewells. When my parents joined me in the car, they both had tears in their eyes. Asim and Ierah were part of our family. They had risked their lives for us many times during the war, something we would never forget.

The next morning my father drove with us to the little village where Ierah lived. When she saw us from afar, she stood still and just looked, not believing her eyes. Then she threw down her basket with her clean wet clothes, which she just had washed in the stream behind her little house, and ran toward us. She knelt down at my father's feet and grabbed his hand. My father lifted her up by her arms and gave her a hug, and my mother too hugged her. Then, not really recognizing me, looking for the little girl she had raised, she walked toward me with disbelieving eyes. "*Inih Ierah punja nonne ketjil?*" "Is this my little miss?" she asked tremulously.

I just threw my arms around her and, for an instant, I was very small again. I could smell the fresh flower she always wore in her hair, a fragrant flower of a light green and yellow, formed like no other, its fragrance matchless. It was her favorite to wear and was called *tjempaka*. We gave her a gift of money, which she accepted it with trembling hands. I gave her a picture of me to keep, which she pressed to her chest. "I will always keep it," she whispered. After explaining why we had to leave for good, we then said our goodbyes. She understood and as with Asim the separation was heartbreaking. Again I ran blinded by tears to our car and refused to look back. My parents again followed with tearful eyes.

It was a extremely emotional time. I never forgot those two, and even now I still remember Asim, squatting behind my chair at the dining table at supper time, swatting at the mosquitoes. I almost can taste the Indonesian goodies he made for me, sneaking them to me in the kitchen when my mother could not see him. He was also the one who ran beside my first big bike, when the training wheels were removed, and the sweat dripped into his eyes, blinding him in such a way that he almost fell a couple of times.

Ierah, my nanny, slept on a thin mattress by my bedroom door until I was eight. She dressed me and combed my hair and bathed me until I was eight. She fed me and hushed me to sleep when I was very little. She carried me on her hip in a sling for hours on end, while doing other chores, with one hand. They were part of my past as if they were my family, a precious part of our household.

We had accepted my Uncle Ed's decision to stay in Indonesia, with his wife and son Eric, but the worst news for me came when my grandmother announced that she had chosen to stay with them. She was too old to leave behind the place of her heritage. She said that all the ghosts of her past were here in Indonesia, and "Who would tend to the graves?" I could not believe she had chosen to stay behind, but later, when the shock had worn off, I could understand why she had done so. She *was* the colonies. Holland would kill her in a few months. She would have died of a broken heart. She was now 72 years old, not very old from today's perspective, but she was a woman who had gone through so much and lost so much more. She was bone tired. We respected her wish.

The evening before the day of our departure, my parents and I said our goodbyes to Oma, Uncle Jack, and Aunt Helen. Uncle Jack and Aunt Helen, their children, and grandchildren would be leaving for Australia pretty soon. My grandmother would be living with Eric and his parents from then on. All through the evening, I held Oma close, not wanting to let her go. Gazing at her as if to imprint her features and every line of her face into my brain, I thought to myself that she would indeed appear austere and somewhat stern to people who did not know her as her grandchildren and children knew her. But I was also very aware that this autocratic bearing was often softened by a beguiling charm, a great sense of humor, and an easy naturalness. Especially now with her guard down, it was a most vulnerable face, open and fine, full of wisdom.

Our farewell was heartrending and had such a finality to it, something hard to put into words. I knew with a certainty that I never would see my grandmother, nor Eric and his parents, ever again. Our truck would pass the house where my grandmother lived early in the morning, and she promised to stand in front of the entrance, to wave goodbye to us one more time.

She was there just as she had promised, when the trucks with all the emigrating people passed by. I screamed my goodbye to her and yelled that I love her and please to write to me. But she did not hear. She turned her head at the moment we passed her and, hard of hearing as she was, she could not hear my voice, which was drowned out by the noise of the traffic. For the last time I saw her, as tears streamed down my face. She stood there, so small and forlorn, but proud and straight, and that is the way she has stayed in my mind.

Four hours later, we watched the coastline fall away. Steadily the ship carried us away to cold and distant shores. It left the harbor of Tanjung Priok, and with that it left the country of my birth, the backbone of my youth and heritage, my beautiful islands, known to a great many as the Emerald Belt, the Gordel Van Smaragd, as it is called in Dutch.

It was June of 1950.

PART II

THE NETHERLANDS

CHAPTER 4

THE NETHERLANDS

We arrived early one drizzly morning, in the already bustling harbor of Amsterdam, after a voyage of 27 days on the high seas. The weather, especially around the Gulf of Biscaye, near France, was notorious among seafaring people for its treacherous behavior. We got a taste of it, and for several days many of the passengers stood with their heads bent over the ship's railing, feeding the fish, so to speak. My poor mother was included in this sorry group, getting worse by the minute at just the thought or smell of food. She lay miserably for two days in a lounge chair on deck, a greenish pallor covering her usually rosy complexion.

Our ship, the Astorias, was old but huge and had served as a hospital ship during the war. It was completely overhauled into a transport ship. Although registered in Italy, its crew was entirely English. The accommodations were minimal. Men and women had separate sleeping quarters in narrow bunkbed-lined cabins, six people to a cabin, with bath cubicles farther down the hall. The meals were edible but bland, typical of English cuisine. The drinking water tasted brackish, and the bathwater would not lather because of its high salt content. It was clearly not a luxury cruise.

A more pleasurable note was the discovery of many familiar faces on board. Many of the people my parents and I had befriended during our military years in Menado traveled with us on the ship, and I recognized several of my schoolmates from Batavia. With a sharp stab I missed Eric, and looked around in the hope of finding Carla or Frieda among people from Menado, but they were not among them. Groups quickly formed, as on the voyages we'd made four years earlier, going from island to island during our military years. Again an impromptu band was formed, falling into place almost effortlessly. Guitars and saxophones appeared as if from nowhere, and again the ship's piano and drum set completed the little orchestra.

A strong bond developed among the passengers during the twenty-seven days aboard the Astorias. We felt secure and safe, and the atmosphere of the colonies still surrounded us. Every day at midday, the ship's captain played the beautiful tango melody La Colondrina. The lovely sounds issued from the ship's loudspeakers, reverberating over the vast waters, and everyone listened in rapt silence.

One day the crew organized a party, a very traditional one, to celebrate the crossing of the Equator. Old Neptune came aboard, covered with seaweed over most of his head and body. We recognized him as one of the crew members, a jolly fellow who always had a smile and a nice word for everyone. Meanwhile, many of us on board were chased and doused with seawater, according to tradition—although the real meaning of the tradition has eluded me over the years. Toward the end of our voyage, we also attended an informal captain's dinner.

Two days later, we entered the harbor of Amsterdam. Farewells were once again said, and addresses were exchanged among those who already knew their destination. Most people were met by a welcoming committee or organization, steering them into waiting buses that brought them to the reception and housing centers providing temporary quarters. My parents and I were met by friends from Menado, the de Waards, who had arranged temporary accommodations for us. Our final destination was the small but lovely town of Blaricum. From the ship's rail, we spotted our friends among the milling crowd on shore. They had left Indonesia eight months before us and were already settled, not too far from where they found a place for us.

As I looked down at the shore, waiting for our disembarkment, I briefly thought of that time, some four years earlier, when we entered the harbor of Menado, in Celebes. What flashed through my mind was an early morning panoramic view of golden, sandy beaches against a backdrop of sparkling greenery. Now that it was time for us to leave the ship, I realized that it was our final connection with the life we had once known. And as I saw my people go in all different directions, a band of steel gripped my heart. I walked with leaden feet down the gangway, apprehensive about the future in this damp and chilly land. Already I missed the warmth of the colonies. Putting these disconsolate thoughts aside temporarily, I shared a joyful reunion with our dear friends, who hugged us from sheer happiness. They had hired a taxicab and drove with us to our temporary accommodations.

BLARICUM

Blaricum was a small, picturesque town surrounded by fields of many-colored heather, mainly purple, deep rose, and light pink. The town lies in the beautiful province of het Gooi, an hour's drive from Amsterdam. The little town toward which we were heading was exceptionally pretty in summer, the cottages, with their thick thatched roofs and colorful yards, lining the streets. The yards were carefully landscaped and trimmed.

The taxi stopped in front of a house that was a tiny bit larger than the others I had seen so far. The roof was of blue gray slate pitched gently down to touch stone walls the color of eggshell, a soft white with a hint of beige. The many windows were flanked by dark brown shutters, while the double front door was painted a lighter brown and decorated with black nail heads and iron hinges. Every detail added to the charm of the picturesque architecture. Blood red geraniums, snapdragons in all colors, and blue lupines were everywhere in the little yard, its crooked path leading to the front entrance.

We learned that the owners were out of town with their two small children. They were staying with their parents for three months and renting their house to us for the duration. The house, although larger than most in the town, was small in comparison to our colonial ideal, the kind of sprawling houses we had known from birth. But it would certainly do for the moment, we thought—not knowing the extent of housing crisis that gripped Holland with the steady influx of Dutch-Indonesian families.

Tentatively we inspected the house and to our relief found a tiny bathroom with a shower. Considering the fact that most houses did not have bathing facilities in those times, we felt fortunate indeed. Secure in having a good place to stay for three months, we began house-hunting immediately and discovered, to our dismay, how serious was the lack of housing, especially in the large cities of Amsterdam, The Hague, and Rotterdam, where we eventually wanted to live. Large cities presumably would have more job opportunities for my father and me than the small towns.

In the meantime, more and more people were traveling from the former Dutch East Indies to the little country of Holland, upsetting its balance. The country was ill-equipped with either housing or job opportunities for such in influx, and the situation created discontent on both sides and discord between the Dutch and the Dutch-Indonesians.

Four more Dutch-Indonesian families soon arrived in Blaricum from Indonesia, increasing the total to six. One of them was the van Laren family, who arrived exactly a month after my parents and I did. They had four children, three boys and a girl. I soon befriended the girl, Letty, who was sixteen years old, a year younger than me. Her older brother, Luke, was eighteen. Three years later, in the city of The Hague, he was the man I married.

In September of 1950, Letty van Laren, my new friend, and I registered in Hilversum to continue our education. Letty entered the H.B.S. (Hoger Burgelijke School) for two more years and I, with my H.B.S. certificate tucked in my purse, entered a two-year business college. We rode our bikes to school every day that autumn, through blasts of wind and sheets of pelting rain. As the weather turned colder, our freedom was restricted by the unaccustomed clothing we needed to wear, from raincoats in the fall, to heavy woolen coats in the winter, with heavy boots. Feeling stifled and dismayed, we plodded to school each day and home again, hating the routine yet compelled to persevere, longing for the warmth and sunshine we had once known.

Around that time, as my family was urgently seeking other quarters, we found out that the owners of our cottage planned to stay in Amsterdam for another two years. The young man had found a well-paying job in construction and, with the extra income from the house he had rented to us, he and his small family could save money by living with his wife's mother for that time. We were elated, for it solved our housing problem for at least two years, and Blaricum was a lovely town, with more and more Dutch-Indonesians arriving each week. In the nearby town of Laren, a reception center was opened to provide temporary housing for the incoming stream of immigrants. Since the two towns were only fifteen minutes apart, we came into frequent contact with many of our people; old friendships were reestablished and new ones flourished.

MY FIRST SNOWSTORM

One afternoon in early December, when Letty and I were on our way home from school, we experienced our first real snowstorm. At first the snow was light, so we sort of enjoyed it, but within minutes the wind had picked up and the flakes became bigger and came down faster. It was very wet snow and soon, with the wind blowing at our backs, we weren't having fun any more. We also had taken a shortcut through an open field, where heather bloomed in the summer. The wetness and the icy wind chilled us to the bone. I can remember the misery perfectly when I think about those moments, even after all these years.

The bikes slipped and slithered. The bike trail was narrow, and we rode in single file. We did not speak, concentrating on making our way along the trail. Also, the trail itself was rough, with rocks and gnarled roots embedded in the frozen ground. Once the snow stopped falling, it began to freeze, and the trail became even more slippery and treacherous. We might have gone a different way if we'd known the danger, but this was our very first experience with such difficult weather conditions.

Blue from the cold, we finally came to the main road. Fog, which had hovered over the open fields, was blown away by the roaring wind. Now that the snow had stopped and the fog was gone, the late afternoon air was tinged with opal, and the grayish sky filled with incandescent light. The light seemed to emanate from some hidden source right below the horizon, most peculiar in these northern climates. Suddenly blazing with intense clarity, the light lasted just a few moments, but I caught it, even in my cold and misery. Letty and I stopped and got off our bikes, panting for breath. The town we lived in was now straight ahead of us.

A tall young man came toward us, also on a bike. Later we got to know him as Rob Hagen, son of the baker who supplied the town of Blaricum with fresh bread early in the morning. The young man lived above his father's bakery, in the same street as me. I had talked briefly to him several times, when he was delivering his father's bread. He was eighteen and had just finished high school. He was extremely good looking, with dark, wavy hair and deep-set eyes, tall with a well-built, sturdy frame. In spite of his rough workman's clothes, there was something gentle and fine about him, both in his expression and in his demeanor. His face was open and friendly, and his wide smile, with dazzling white teeth, was warm and mischievous. His blue eyes were kind and full of understanding.

"What on earth are two girls from the tropics doing in miserable weather like this?" he cried. "We'll be damned if we know," I snapped. He ignored my crabbiness and eyed us with concern. "Come on, I'll help you get home," he said, wheeling around. After we stiffly climbed back on our bikes, he pushed us in turns toward home.

My house was closest. Shivering all over, we slipped down the icy path into the yard. Letty and Rob came into the house with me. My parents helped us out of our soaked coats and boots, and Rob suggested that we take a quick very warm bath (or, in our house, a hot shower) and then put on warm, dry clothes. My mother made hot cocoa, and by the time we came into the sitting room, Rob had arranged our chairs near the stove and my mother pressed cups of hot cocoa in our hands. We were bundled up in warm pajamas and robes; I lent Letty mine and I wore my mother's. We had warm, fluffy slippers on our feet. Slowly the color came back in our faces and the numbness in our hands and feet disappeared.

After a while Rob left. My parents, Letty, and I thanked him profusely for his help in getting us over the last icy couple of miles. When he encountered us, we both were at the end of our ropes. Someone called Letty's parents on the phone, to let them know that their daughter was safe at our house. They agreed to let her spend the night. Since we both wore the same size dress, I would lend her some of my clothes to wear to school in the morning—but only if the weather improved. By the next morning, a sheet of ice had formed over the cobblestone side streets and the main roads.

Rob had explained before he left, that, if it did freeze, the roads would be impassable. Traffic would be stopped for hours, until a mixture of brine, sand, and salt could be scattered over the streets. Dreading more cold and wetness, we decided to stay home the next day after our experience in the storm. Perhaps later in the day we could go out for a slippery walk through the woodsy parts of Blaricum, which led to the little shopping area in the village itself.

In the meantime we crouched around the warmth of the old-fashioned stove. What a miserable existence, we thought, to be prisoners of the weather and its conditions, unable to make plans or to go when and where we wanted. We had never been restricted in this way before. For us, coming straight from the sunny tropics, this kind of inconvenience was unthinkable. Indeed, there were heavy monsoon rains in the wet season. But even then, the rains were intermittent, and we could outwait them and continue our activities unhindered for the rest of the day. So many times that first winter, when walking and when riding my bike, I slipped and fell, wearing black and blue bruises for months. And looking around me, I could see that I was not the only one.

LIFE AMONG THE DUTCH

Another difficult adjustment for my mother and me was life without the help of servants. Accustomed to their services all our lives, we had been enormously dependent and were suddenly in great distress. Neither of us had ever done any kind of housework. We had never had made a bed or set a table or scrubbed the floors or washed the windows to keep a house tidy. Our Dutch neighbors were not aware of the sheltered lives we lived in the colonies and quickly labeled us lazy and untidy.

For the first two months, I was miserable, trying to figure out how to cope with what was for us a strange and middle-class way of life. Self-pity assaulted me, and tears were frequent. I felt helpless, and my mother even more so. Even life in the concentration camp during the war, struggling to stay alive, had not taught us how to cope without servants.

Knowing how the Dutch thought and spoke of us, many of the younger people among us took the initiative, determined to learn everything there was to learn about this new lifestyle. Within six months, I had it all under control, cleaning the house, washing the windows until they squeaked, and doing the laundry, while my mother took care of the meals. I did all this energetically but with enormous distaste.

There were differences as well in attitudes toward personal hygiene between people in the tropics and those in a cold climate. Although the Dutch were scrupulous in their housekeeping, they were less so about keeping their bodies fresh and clean. Many houses lacked bathing facilities, so people had to limit themselves to a quick sponge bath in the kitchen—or not at all, I imagine. And perhaps they would have the luxury of a visit, once or twice every two weeks, to the public bathing houses for a warm bath or shower, with a time-clock set by a bathing-house attendant, ticking off the minutes. This lack of hygienic facilities in Holland was very repellent to a people accustomed to a very different way of life. We, who were used to two daily baths in the tropics, and always with a change of clothes at hand, shuddered at the thought of not bathing for days.

My early impressions of these inconveniences left a lasting mark, and a dislike for Holland that I never seemed able to shake. Oh certainly, I met some lovely, warmhearted people there—Rob and his parents, for example. But in general I found people in Holland argumentative, opinionated, and very much out for themselves. And many appeared aggressive, their attitude bordering on rudeness, which appalled me. They spoke harshly and with great impetuosity, even when making a simple point in their conversations. In the world in which I had been raised, communication was much more refined.

A BOY NAMED LUKE

Spring came, and our first year's battle with the cold had almost ended, although the dampness remained for quite some time, with rain and more rain every day. My heart longed for the warmth of a sunlit land, filled with people with sunny dispositions and friendly smiles. I longed for my grandmother and Eric and all I had left behind. It took two grueling years for me to accept our situation in a land where we spoke the same language, but where our lifestyles were so different. We spoke Dutch with a certain lilt and with a dialect typical of the colonies. To my ears it sounded softer than the guttural sounds produced by the people in Holland in their speech. Of course, they in turn thought our speech to be coarse and uneducated. The contrast might be akin to that between British and American English, with certain differences in terminology and expressions, as develops in all colonies.

In the meantime, Letty, her brother Luke, Rob, and I had registered for dancing lessons in a dance club in the nearby town of Hilversum, which we attended faithfully every Saturday evening from seven to ten. Luke and I became dance partners, to the intense displeasure of Rob. He was attracted to me and a little jealous of Luke. I liked Rob very much but I was not in love with him. It was hard to make him understand. Now more then ever, Luke and I sought each other out. We went to the movie theatre together and took endless bike trips to all kinds of sights of interest. Although we always went with other people in a group, the two of us usually paired off together.

Poor Rob was miserable, yet he preferred to be with me in a group that included Luke and Letty than not to be with me at all. And, as time passed, John Huizinga, my motorcycle police officer from Semarang, became more and more someone from my past that I had to leave behind. Our letter writing dwindled, and finally it stopped. Something similar occurred in Luke's life. He had corresponded with an American girl he had known in Indonesia. Her father was an American missionary in Borneo, where Luke's father operated a huge sawmill as the head of Forestry. As is so often the case, distance and different lifestyles in different parts of the world can be the killers of young and newly blossoming romances. These circumstances affected Luke in his relationship, too.

After we had known the van Laren family a few months, my mother came to the conclusion that as a young girl she had known Luke's grandfather, Tom, and his sweet and kind Javanese wife, Satima. My mother visited them the first time with a niece of the family whom she had befriended, came to visit them regularly, and got to know them very well. Opa Tom, as Luke's grandfather was known, also had Dutch parents, but like my grandfather, had been born and raised in the Dutch East Indies. He also owned a plantation, although on a smaller scale than my grandfather's coconut plantation. His was a plantation full of fruit trees, bearing a special type of citrus fruit with thick, aromatic rinds, called citron. The fruits were peeled and then sugar-coated to transform them into candied confections, which he exported to Europe and other parts of the world. Candied citron is favored especially by the English for making their famous fruitcakes. Candied citron peel is called *sukade* in Dutch. Opa Tom also had acres of a type of dwarf coconut. The trees were about half the height of their tall and graceful green cousins, sturdy and pretty looking, yellowish in color. Their fruits were smaller in size than the regular coconut, also yellow tinted, and as good to eat as any.

The van Laren plantation house was idyllically situated high up in the hills and mountain region of Sedaju, in a beautiful part of central Java. The family also had hundreds and hundreds of chickens. They kept for breeding and for the eggs, which they distributed to the surrounding marketplaces. Their stalls were full of horses, which they raised for the family's own use.

BARONGAN

The van Larens were descendants of nobility from The Netherlands, as their double name indicated. Their full family name, van Laren-van Palls, and their family crest dated all the way to the year 1353, and Opa Tom was enormously proud of his ancestral history. Luke's father carried the official baronial title until his death in 1979, but he did not use it in public, since a title in the Dutch-Indonesian community was often subject to ridicule. The ignorant and less educated probably never heard of genealogy, or perhaps they assumed that nobility was always associated with being haughty. Time and time again, after we were married, we heard people say, when they heard of the double name and the actual title, "Oh Baron—*Barongan.*" *Barongan* is an Indonesian word that refers to gigantic dolls made of bamboo and paper mache. Dressed in outrageous clothes of all colors, they dance through the streets of Indonesia on special occasions, fending off bad spirits. And so it was that the lineage we should be proud of became a subject to avoid. It was only here in America that we found a healthy interest in one's family roots, perhaps because of the close connection this country has with England and its nobility.

After we were married and living in The Hague, Luke and I were invited annually—or summoned is a better word for it—to a large formal event that was held annually in the small palace of *het Kneuterdijk*. Although a wonderful experience the first time, this party for the nobility was an affair that the two of us began to dread, since it entailed obligatory expenses that we couldn't afford at the time. Luke needed a tuxedo and I needed an evening gown, as well as all the accessories, plus the taxi-cab. We would rent most of what we needed. After the initial thrill, the event meant nothing more than monetary inconveniences for us. As soon as the gold-edged envelope with the annual invitation arrived, we began to worry. Finally, after the third year, we decided to put a stop to something we actually could not afford and completely ignored the invitation. Now, even after forty-two years of living in the United States, since 1945 we still get yearly calls from the Central Bureau for Genealogy and have to report changes to our family during the past year, since all the information is recorded in the book of Dutch nobility.

THE HAGUE

In 1952, after living for two years in Blaricum, and two years into my father's retirement, he suddenly wanted to return to a more productive life than endless walks in the Blaricum woods and heather fields. Only 54 years old, he became increasingly restless and impatient. My family decided to move to The Hague, which thrilled me, since Luke had moved there just three months earlier with his family, to finish his technical education in electronics, a field he had chosen just a short while earlier. In The Hague our families continued their friendship, and the relationship between Luke and me was blooming nicely. I found a job at the Embassy of Indonesia in The Hague, working as one of two secretaries for the ambassador himself. My father following suit shortly after I was hired, landing in the financial department of the embassy, his field of expertise.

The house we had occupied in The Hague was old but stately and in sound condition. Once a gentlemen's home, with high, elaborately carved ceilings edged with grapevine designs, one could easily imagine the quality and elegance it had projected in its prime. It had three stories with a main staircase, situated directly across the main entrance door, serving the three floors on the left side within the building. My aunt Gina, my mother's younger sister, and her husband Gerry, who had followed us to Holland, occupied the ground floor. My parents and I lived on the second, and the owners resided on the third. We considered ourselves extremely lucky to have found a place like this in such a short time, considering the acute housing shortage.

Our apartment consisted of two bedrooms, a sitting-dining room, and a large kitchen that spanned the width of the apartment in the back. One could easily see that the original sitting room had been converted into two bedrooms we now occupied and the sitting-dining had at one time been a large living room, with our kitchen a sunroom of sorts. We were deeply disappointed to see that the house lacked a shower or a tub. It had only a toilet cubicle and a cold water sink right off the always-shadowy staircase landing. The kitchen was the only place with a small but adequately hot water boiler, attached to the wall directly over the sink, providing the only opportunity for a daily sponge bath. With great longing the wonderful facilities in the colonies sprang to mind, and even the warm water shower we enjoyed in Blaricum was a remembered luxury. I put up with this unsanitary situation grudgingly and made my weekly trip to the public bathing houses with great aversion.

Our neighborhood, at least, was clean and nicely kept. Considering the apparent Dutch tendency to outward and external cleanliness only, this was easy to understand. Also, the shopping areas were close by, and since the main form of transportation in this country was your own two legs, either on foot or on a bike, this convenience was a big plus. Like most large cities in the world, the city of The Hague had ample public transportation, but walking was involved in getting to it, through snow, rain, and wind. This was another situation to which I adapted with difficulty, spoiled as I was by the perquisites my father's job provided for him and his family in the colonies. Longingly I thought of the shiny Chevrolet that provided us with a steady means of transportation, up to our very last day.

Chapter 5

MARRIAGE AND FAMILY

In July 1953, Luke graduated, and we were married exactly a year later. I kept my job at the embassy, and my father continued to work in its financial department. Luke found work quickly at the Department of Buildings and Road Works, as a draftsman. On the surface, it seemed that we had adapted to living in the Netherlands. We were happily married and soon were expecting our first child. And sometimes, as I looked at my young husband, I was amazed by how much he resembled my own father.

Was it that, I mused, that had attracted me to him? A familiarity, perhaps, that I was looking for? Luke resembled my father, not in his features, of course, but in his character and mannerisms. He was quiet, just like my father, and on many occasions kept himself in the background. Like my father, Luke had a gentle nature and was somewhat shy in public, an attribute he disguised with an air of aloofness and reserve. He preferred cozy bridge parties at home over "doing the rounds" in the city on Saturday nights, for instance, as most young couples did. It was always I who prodded him to go places with me.

But he loved to dance, and we often did that. He also loved the outdoors and had a keen eye for nature's beauty. He enjoyed long walks through forested areas. Both as a small boy and later as a teenager, on warm, sunny days near his house in Borneo, he often swam in the rivers as his friends paddled their wooden canoes. Like my father, he was musically inclined and played the guitar and piano very well. He also had a capacity for completing huge amounts of work, persisting until it was finished. And in whatever he undertook, he always looked fit and brimming with health.

I remember one day he wore a pale blue, long-sleeved shirt and dark blue slacks that I had recently bought for him. They looked good against his lightly tanned skin and well-muscled body. Looking at his dark head and arresting profile, while walking hand in hand in the summer brightness of a park near our house, I found my husband quite handsome. His eyes were warm dark brown, deep-set under well-shaped eyebrows. His mouth was generously shaped and his lips were full. His straight nose with a highly shaped bridge is not at all like the pudgier noses of many Dutch-Indonesian people, which most of us have inherited from our Indonesian ancestors.

Luke has also a very low tolerance of alcohol and abhors the taste of all spirits. He drinks sparingly—just to join me, perhaps, in a glass of wine when we go out to dinner. In this he was certainly not like my father, but then my father drank to ease his inner pain.

SCHWARTZE CAT

A humorous episode occurred when Luke and I were on our honeymoon in Germany alongside the Rhine. I wanted to visit one of the famous German wine cellars and taste the renowned Rhine wine with the brand name *Schwartze Cat*. We were staying in an idyllic little town, wedged in the Sieben Gebirgte, the seven-mountain area, alongside the Rhine River, a beautiful area, romantically situated. Luke agreed to the plan, and after dinner we leisurely walked to one of the many cellars. The place was already crowded with customers, Germans drinking the wine like water, and because of the poor ventilation the smoke of cigarettes, cigars, and pipes, as well as the alcoholic fumes of beer and all sorts of wines, hung thickly in the air. We sat down and an *ober*, German for waiter, came to take our order. I ordered a big glass of *Schwartze Cat* and, to my surprise Luke ordered a big glass of Coca-Cola. I could not believe my ears: here we were in Germany, in its famous wine region, and he ordered Coca-Cola. When the *ober* brought our drinks and the pieces of sharp cheese that came with them, Luke fumbled with the money he had to pay the *ober*. I found it odd, he never was that sluggish. He paid and we began to sip our drinks.

Suddenly Luke looked straight at me. I noticed a glassiness in his gaze, of the kind mostly found in someone who is intoxicated. Then his head went down with a bang on the wooden table, and Luke was completely out. I thought he had been poisoned and started to scream. *Obers* came running from all directions. Our *ober* asked me if Luke had eaten dinner, and I answered that we had. "There's one more possibility," the *ober* volunteered. "For a person who does not drink, atmosphere in here, with its heavy fumes and smoke, can cause intoxication." That is of course exactly what had happened to Luke. Looking back at that evening, as I strolled along in the park, I grinned inwardly, thinking about what happened in the wine cellar in Germany.

FAMILY CHANGES

A few months later, our first child was born—a strong, robust baby boy, 9 pounds, 6 ounces, brimming with good health. Luke and I could not get enough of watching his perfectly formed, sturdy little body. He had the biggest eyes, dark and fully lashed, a button nose, and lips that were somewhat pouting. He came into this world with a shock of dark brown hair. We named him Peter.

Our happiness at this time was darkened by only one incident. My grandmother passed away quite suddenly of a heart attack at the age of 76. She died peacefully in her sleep. Her favorite and devoted maid servant Siti found her in the early morning hours while bringing her mistress a cup of hot tea. Although my grandmother had known that I was expecting my first baby, she died just three months short of the birth. We were in steady contact with each other by correspondence, and she couldn't wait to see the first pictures of the baby. Crushed and feeling the loss acutely, I sat for days in the corner of my room, wishing with all my heart I could have been with her at the moment of her death. Even attending her funeral was an impossibility for us to afford at the time. In my misery, I suddenly heard her voice softly but firmly in my ear, saying in her calm, strong way, "I'm happy where I am. You are my granddaughter and always will be. Take care of your son, and be strong." The misery lifted from my soul, like the lifting of a dark and pressing cloth. For the first time I also knew with certainty that the child I was carrying was a boy.

The early years of our marriage passed quickly. In 1956 our daughter, Lisa, was born. She, too, was a sturdy, healthy baby. At ten pounds, she was my biggest baby of my three children. She was such a beautiful little girl, with her abundant dark brown hair, dark brown eyes, and a round little nose and mouth. She was such a good and happy baby, until well into her second year when, playing with a neighbor's little son who had whooping cough, she contracted the disease herself. I will never forget that time, when Luke and I stood helplessly by as she was seized by horrible coughing spells so severe that she would turn purple in the face. We could help only with lifting her little arms over her head to expand her rib cage so she could breath more easily, trying to make the coughing spurts stop. Lisa's physical discomfort lasted well over a month, then finally subsided and eventually disappeared. She was healthy again, but the disease had left her with asthmatic bronchitis, which she had to battle with after each cold. I remember many a night, sitting up with her until the early morning hours.

Luke had by now enlisted in the Dutch Air Force, right after Lisa celebrated her first birthday. He enlisted voluntarily, although his motive for doing so was a three-year course in more advanced electronics, something we could not have afforded on our own. He signed up for six years. The base was located three hours by train in the northern part of Holland, which meant, a half day spent on travel time in those years.

Right after Lisa was born, my parents, Luke and I, and our two children moved to a larger house, with a small yard in the back for the children, right across from a cozy little park with a pond in the center of it and a tram, a kind of cable car stop, right in front of our house. In summertime, the children and I took little walks around the pond, feeding the many ducks and geese with bread crusts. Luke came home only on weekends and sometimes not even then, if he had guard duty to perform; after such duty he would have four consecutive days home.

My parents, especially my mother, did everything possible to lighten the burdens of my daily life. She baby-sat often in the evening to give me the opportunity to unwind. Of course, I gave up my job at the embassy after Lisa was born, with Luke away most of the time. My father still continued his job at the embassy, which made me happy. It kept him busy and occupied his mind. Grandchildren gave them both a reason for living, enjoying every moment with them. I enrolled myself in the Tennis and Badminton Club organized by the Department of War in The Hague, where the games were seriously played and the members seriously trained. At first I was not looking for that sort of exercise, but after a while I began to enjoy the competitiveness of it.

TENNIS AND BADMINTON CLUB

Tournaments were put together, and we began to travel all over the country to play other teams. Tough training was called for, and my evenings were spent frequently at the club, after the children were made ready for bed. My parents encouraged me to do so at first, knowing that it would give me needed exercise and diversion from the rigors of daily life raising children. Mostly I played singles, but I did have a steady partner to play mixed doubles with, who also was my trainer and my coach.

His name was Dave van Dam and he was a captain in the Dutch Army, and also of Dutch-Indonesian descent. Because of the coaching involvement, Dave and I did see each other almost daily, in the evening. He would come to our house to pick me up in his car, so I did not have to go on my motor scooter, especially in rain, wind, and snow in the winter months. My mother, who had encouraged me to join the club, now began to have a change of heart. She thought I saw too much of Dave and not enough of my husband. She started to treat Dave quite shabbily when he came to our door, stopped inviting him inside, as she used to do.

Uneasily and nervously, I tried to explain to Dave her odd behavior as carefully as I could. He listened to me quietly, then said, "Well, maybe she is right to worry." He said it so softly, which made me glance over at him. He was watching the road. Suddenly he reach for my hand and gave it a warm squeeze, but let go of it almost immediately, as if to reassure me not to worry for whatever reason.

Since he was twelve years older than I, I always saw him as playing the part of a big brother. His usual behavior toward me could only be construed as fraternal, as he always had kept everything light and jocular, from the very first day we met. But now, I wasn't so sure anymore. We rode in an uneasiness that was new to us. I remembered certain moments when Dave had done things for me that were entirely out of his usual way. He had always given me extra attention and consideration, which he did not seem to have given to others. Perhaps my mother was right and should I withdraw a bit. After all, I was married to a good man and had two children. Dave was married too, although his marriage had stayed childless.

MOVE TO HALSTEREN

Shortly after this unsettling episode, in June of 1959, Luke came home with the news that we had been assigned to a brand new housing development specially constructed for military men and their families, close to the Air Force Base. The building was coming to an end and the finishing touches were being applied to the houses. We would be moving within two or three months. I looked at Luke in confused surprise.

The Air Force Base was located in Woensdrecht, which was in North Brabant, an area that was extremely quiet and rural. The neighborhood, newly built, was in a very small town, not too far removed from the base. The town was called Halsteren and the nearest fairly big town, Bergen op Zoom, was an hour by bus away—a bus that came only once every two hours.

I was only 26 at the time, and Halsteren, encircled by farmland and farm houses, was really not my cup of tea. I was certainly happy to be with Luke again every evening, but what else was there to do in such a small village during the day when he was at the base and our son Peter in kindergarten? I still had Lisa, now three years old, to care for and the house to keep clean, but one could clean only so much, I thought fretfully. I would miss my friends, the movie theatres and the dance parties that Luke and I occasionally attended when he was home on the weekends, mostly together with a large group of friends. I would have to say goodbye to the sports club and to Dave, I realized with a spurt of regret and a feeling of loss. And most of all, I would miss my parents, since I had actually never left them before. For Luke I feigned happiness and enthusiasm, and I did in a way look forward to our first home, alone at last and together as a young family should. This home would really be our first real one. "We could refuse the offer," Luke suggested, with disappointment in his voice. He knew me so well and had detected the hesitation and the bewilderment within me immediately. "But that means going back to the very bottom of the housing list, a risk we shouldn't take," he explained and a fact I understood fully. Damn, I muttered to myself, and then I grimaced wryly, baffled by my own inconsistencies.

Sooner than we thought possible we moved to Halsteren and away from The Hague. We bought new furniture and shopped for curtains and draperies and could finally use the pot and pans and all the other household knickknacks we got as wedding presents five years earlier. The beautiful china service and silverware for eight given to us by my parents and Luke's parents came now into good use. It was fun as long as it lasted to decorate our home. I was ready to learn to entertain on my own, away from my parents.

HOUSEWARMING

We wanted to give a housewarming party, except that in Holland one did not called it that. There was no word for it in Dutch, to my knowledge. The group of people in our new neighborhood were mostly of our age group, and many were of Dutch-Indonesian descent, we quickly noticed. Since it was approaching the end of August and nearing Luke's birthday we decided to celebrate these two together.

Our new house was a typical townhouse, seen all over Holland, situated in a row of identical houses, tall and narrow with a relatively simple architectural facade. The exterior appearance, however, belied the interiors, with rooms considerably larger and more generously proportioned than the narrowness of the house suggested. It had three bedrooms and—hallelujah yes!—finally a real bathroom, with a separate shower and a sit-down bath, all on the second floor. The first floor had a large living-dining room, an entrance hall, a half bath, and, next to the dining area, a large, airy kitchen. The staircase with its wooden banister rose to the upper floor and landing, where a pull-down ladder hidden in the ceiling gave entrance to the attic.

There also was a small backyard—actually tiny was a more precise a word for what I was accustomed to in the land of my birth—but at least it was a yard, with a roomy shed for our motor scooters and, attached to it, a smaller area to keep the black and dusty coals that were already stocked for winter's use. Looking at the coals gave me a shiver, thinking about the winter cold and the messy slush it created on the roads and sidewalks, dousing my enthusiasm for a moment. After nine long years in Holland, I still disliked being here. A plan had slowly begun to form in my mind, that we would move away from all this and go to America.

But for now this would do, and I concentrated on the upcoming party. I had to learn to be creative with very little. Since I was not brought up to appreciate the tricky game of financial wheeling and dealing before spending even just a few dimes, this was extremely hard for me to do. From my grandparents' holdings that were lost during the war, each of their children and grandchildren received a miserly pittance of a compensation payment, and I was very careful with my part for a while, although it was quite difficult for me. Scrimping, saving, and making do were not part of my upbringing, even after the war in the colonies, when there was rarely any spare money available for luxuries. I struggled with the conflict of wanting and having, particularly with the somewhat extravagant décor, at least for our budget, of our Halsteren home. As I stood in the doorway of the living room on the Friday evening in August a day before the party and just a couple of months after we moved in, I smiled with satisfaction and pleasure. I had turned on the two soft jade Chinese lamps with their creamy shades. The atmosphere was inviting, and the new furniture gleamed in the light. One long wall I had painted soft peach, and it made a perfect backdrop for the two large oriental landscapes beautifully brush-stroked in a variety of greens and peach in simple gilded wooden frames. Rafts of soft green draperies rippled at the two picture windows located at each end of the long room, front and back, and also covered two long sofas and two armchairs. This soft, verdant color added to the richness of the scheme. The soft green sofas were enlivened with cream and peach silken cushions that I had bought just the day before. I hoped that I could find plastic covers to protect them from smudges caused by dirty little fingers. The entire scheme was chosen well but not wisely for a family with two small children.

After a final admiring glance, I moved briskly across the champagne colored carpet, plumping the cushions and checking the cigarette box on the coffee table. I then turned and hurried back to the dining area to finish setting the table I had started earlier in the evening, for the next day. We ate our daily meals in our eat-in kitchen and the dining area was used only for more formal occasions, like the one tomorrow.

The menu I made up was simple. It was going to be a buffet style dinner, with the guests serving themselves. I put out several silver-plated ashtrays and a silver condiment set. Then I added wine and water glasses, grouping them together as I moved around the long, oval table. As I went along, I remembered my grandmother's parties and entertaining skills, seeing her and the servants moving gracefully and rapidly through the huge rooms, the layout of silver, glasses, and dishes clear in my memory. My room was not huge and there were no servants to assist me, but my grandmother's refined ways and teachings had taken deep root within me.

When I stood back to regard my handiwork, I suddenly wished I had some flowers for a centerpiece. I could see in my mind's eye the many vases of fresh tropical flowers adorning each table in my grandmother's hotel, plantation, and private quarters. But flowers here in Holland were expensive, at least for our budget, and died so quickly. The four-armed silver candelabrum were certainly pretty enough with its tall, white candles. I decided the table looked quite pretty and did not need any further embellishment.

Saturday evening arrived. The guests, six couples, were expected around 7:30. It was a quarter past six at the moment. Peetie and Lisa were at a neighbor's, Jack and Dora van Wagen, two houses down the street. I had invited the van Wagens too, but Jack was on duty that weekend and Dora volunteered to keep the children for a night to give her four-year-old son Maxi company.

I turned to go into the kitchen just as Luke walked in, softly humming a tune. He stopped and let out a long whistle of surprise, grabbed my hand, and twirled me around, continuing to whistle in an admiring way. "You look positively beautiful," he said, stepping away from me, his eyes bright with approval. I smiled at him tentatively and twirled around again. I was wearing my favorite shoes, a pair of black silk evening pumps in a new Italian style, with thin high heels and extremely pointed toes. They were exactly right with the outfit I had chosen for the evening, a long-sleeved gray silken top with a boatneck and a silver gray taffeta skirt. The skirt puffed out like a bell flower over a stiff tulle petticoat I had bought just the other day. This type of petticoat was the fashion at the time, and the bouffant effect it created was flattering to my legs, which I considered too skinny. As a finishing touch, I put on black drop earrings and a bright red shade of lipstick. I was ready for my guests at last. They were all young lieutenants, like Luke, who came with their wives. Most of them I had met at the welcome party for couples that the military had hosted a month ago. And one couple lived on the same street we did.

I had made up a menu and prepared the food myself, and now everything was in pretty dishes waiting on the kitchen table, ready to be brought into the dining area and to be served. There was a large platter of Melba toasts decorated with small heaps of pâté and chopped deviled eggs. I planned to serve those first with the white wine before the main dish. I also had made a refreshing Dutch-Indonesian potato salad, called *Huszarensla*, a mixture of potatoes, diced red beets, chopped onions, pineapple chunks, diced cold meats from the day before, and small baby green peas, and chopped hard boiled eggs. My grandmother always made it the best, and I had her recipe. The main course should be filling, rich, but inexpensive to make, since I was running low on cash as it was. I decided on a macaroni dish, made with lots of beaten eggs, milk, diced ham, and cheese, with a crunchy topping of buttered bread crumbs with a touch of garlic. I made two trays of that and cut them into squares. For dessert I offered preserved brandied fruits in a sweet, creamy sauce. That would top it off nicely.

The people started to arrive shortly after Luke and I transferred the dishes from the kitchen to the dining table, with only the main course kept in the warm oven for later. There they were: the van Dorens, the Ackermans, the van der Veldens, the Willingas, the Huizens, and the van den Bergens. Everyone came whom I had invited. They admired the room's décor, which tonight was somewhat dimly lit, but attractively so, lit by the two Chinese lamps in the living room, and two small wall-mounted lamps on either end of the sideboard, and the flickering candles in the center of the dining table. In this warm, golden light, the mahogany table, with its highly polished surface, gleamed darkly with the glassy sheen of a mirror. Reflecting against it were the glitter of glass and silverware and the sparkle of white china plates, rimmed with silver.

The light green of the curtains and sofas gave the room its restful tranquility, the soft peach-colored wall made a pretty and refreshing backdrop, and the candlelight suffused the room with mellowness. There was no awkwardness amongst the guests, in spite of our short period of acquaintance. The atmosphere was jovial, as joke after joke was cracked. The appetizers disappeared quickly, and the wine loosened people's tongues even more. It gave me great satisfaction to see that people were enjoying themselves so much. All the work and effort was well spent after all. The *Huszarensla* vanished rapidly, as did the macaroni main dish. Even the dessert was a smashing success, and compliments to the cook were generously given. I accepted gracefully, blushing with pure delight and pleasure.

Luke had the record player on, and soft music filled the house. It was an August evening, and the two bay windows in front and back were open. The house was cool in the evening air, and a light breeze relieved us from the cigarette smoke and freshened the air. With the windows open, we had to extinguish the candles, which in addition to lending atmosphere were also used to fight the smoke, as were some wet sponges in small bowls hidden out of sight behind vases and picture frames. It was well after midnight before the last guests left.

As we washed the dishes together—by hand as it was done in those days in Holland—wiped clean the dining table, put away the clean dishes, and emptied and washed the ashtrays, Luke and I congratulated each other on the success of the evening. Buoyed by our success as hosts, we played with the idea of another party, this time including the children and their parents. December 5th is the celebration of the birthday of *Sinter Klaas* or *Sint Nicolaas,* treasured by the Dutch and Dutch-Indonesians alike. Happily we thought about opening our home for this celebration for the children and their parents of the neighborhood. December was still months away, and there was still plenty of time to plan. Tired but satisfied with the course of our first party, Luke and I turned off the lights and ascended the stairs to our bedroom.

CALIFORNIA DREAMING

The morning following the party, I received a long letter from a dear old friend of mine, Hanny Miller, who had emigrated to the United States a few months earlier with her husband Henk and their two young children, Ronny, a boy of five, and Pammy, who was four years old. The letter was full of enthusiasm for their chosen new country. Their sponsors were Californians, and so California was where the Millers were to reside for the first five years, close to their sponsors, until they became U.S. citizens or became financially independent. In any case, it would take five years. Hanny wrote that Henk had found a job in a large supermarket chain (he had been a high school teacher in Holland) and liked the people and his new environment very much. Most of all, they liked the California weather, full of sunshine and warm days.

Dreamily, I tried to visualize the Californian surroundings. My imagination was influenced by the Hollywood movies I had seen, so the jumble of images was probably quite distorted. Over the past two years, we had seen one after another of our friends leave Holland. I kept in close contact with all who had left. Not all of them landed in California. Some, as we did later, settled in New England, some in New York, Florida, Oregon, Washington, and Arizona. But most congregated in California—if not right away, then later in their years in the United States. In California, they found a warm climate, which was such an important part of their home that they missed. Although it was not quite the same climate of the tropics, it was at least warm and sunny most of the year.

The seed that led to our emigration was planted two years earlier in 1957, when President Dwight Eisenhower opened a special immigration quota for the Dutch-Indonesians who had lost their homeland. The American president gave us the chance to make a new life in the United States, starting over again out of our free will. Luke and I had talked about emigration many times, but my parents, who were now both in their sixties, were uppermost in our minds. I was their only child, and they had no one else to cushion them in their old age, which was approaching.

One other obstacle prevented us from going. Luke had signed up for six years in the Air Force, and still had two and a half to serve. He had finished the electronics training that had been a decisive factor in his joining the Air Force in the first place. We had heard that exceptions were sometimes made to the service obligation rule to allow for emigration, but no one was sure. Luke promised to make serious enquiries about the possibility, for the thought of emigration was now firmly and foremost in our minds.

In the middle of September, on a blustery day, Luke came home from work and impetuously pulled me up from the chair in the kitchen, where I was sitting at the small table, cleaning green beans for dinner. He twirled me around and around in a wild dance of some sort. Breathlessly he communicated to me the good news of the possibility of an early discharge from the Air Force. After he'd released me and my equilibrium was somewhat restored, I could only gape at him in complete but pleased surprise. Luke kept saying, "We can go if you want to go, Nora."

I ran past him to the phone and called my parents immediately to share the news with them. Both were very enthusiastic for us, but I detected a sad note in my father's voice. My mother told me frankly and happily, "Good. You go first and we'll follow whenever you are settled. Look for a sponsor for us." She was determined to follow us to the United States, if we decided to emigrate. My father, however, was tired of being uprooted and not at all interested in leaving his home again. It was that thought that had created the sad note when I spoke to him. He was letting us go, so to speak, not knowing what the future would hold with a great ocean separating us. In those days, travel was still not as easy as it is at the present time. And of course the money factor played an enormous role. But I knew if my mother wanted to follow us, then that is exactly what would happen. I related both their reactions to Luke, who just smiled. He too knew my mother all too well.

We pushed the thought of emigration away for a while, storing it in the back of our minds for now. There was a lot of serious checking to be done before putting the wheels into motion for such an important decision. It meant another uprooting, although it made an enormous difference to us that this time it would be done by our free choice. That was not the case when we left Indonesia, knowing that if we chose to stay, we would be reduced to second class citizens with not much say about our future. That was not a fair choice to me.

SEEING THE COUNTRYSIDE

Knowing that we might not be living forever in The Netherlands, Luke and I planned a short holiday trip to see some of the country's many castles, together with our children. We planned to rent a car and carefully plotted our route. As a history buff, I was very much looking forward to this trip. When we told the children, they were elated. Peetie's round dark eyes sparkled with anticipation. He had just returned from kindergarten, and was still dressed for school: short gray wool pants, white long-sleeved dress shirt, and a blue and gray striped tie. A tiny woolen gray sports jacket, a gray cap, white knee-socks, and leather black laced shoes completed his school attire. He looked like a miniature adult male.

Peetie was now a sturdy little boy of four, who loved to play cowboys and Indians with his sister Lisa and his little friends in the neighborhood. He was inspired by the American TV programs The Lone Ranger and The Texas Rangers, which he watched faithfully at five p.m. every Friday. His little sister was usually the Indian, whom Peetie would lasso several times a week. Meekly Lisa would let him have his fun, while her big dark eyes implored me to get him to stop and leave her alone.

At three, Lisa was still too young to get excited about going to see the castles, but the promise to be driven in a car spurred her on to do a wild hippety-hop sort of dance on her chubby little legs. In fact, riding in a car was a relative novelty for all of us. She was an adorable child, with a smile for everyone, even after she had just awakened from her afternoon nap. Peetie and Lisa were not wild or nervous children, but they were constantly exploring and learning—two activities that sometimes got them into trouble. They were into every thing in a quiet way and, when caught in their games of exploration, would look up at Luke and me with the eyes of such innocence that they were hard to resist.

On a beautiful sunny morning in late September, we drove to Gelderland to see our first castle. Dating from the fourteenth century, Loevestein is one of the oldest in The Netherlands open to the public. It was famous as the castle from which Hugo De Groot, a seventeenth-century Dutch philosopher, made a daring escape in March 1621, after becoming involved in disputes with the Calvinists. De Groot attended the University of Leyden at the very young age of eleven and graduated when he was only fifteen years old. We saw the book-chest in which he escaped, which was specially made for him with a double bottom and used to bring him books while he was captive. He crouched inside as he was smuggled out of the country, to Antwerp and later to Paris.

This castle, typical of those we saw, was surrounded by a moat. It was centuries old and stood in the old town of Poederoyen in Gelderland, in the east of Holland. An ancient drawbridge was lowered, and we joined a small group of people already waiting for the castle doors to open. The iron grate rattled noisily as it rose, and slowly we walked toward the huge castle door, solid wood and encased in iron. Our children were impressed by all the noise and the hollow-sounding courtyard. One could imagine how it must have been in those ancient times, with the clatter of the horseshoes on the cobblestoned inner courtyard and the men mounting their horses in heavy armor, their swords clattering against the horses' stirrups.

The heavy doors swung open, and bright sunlight poured in through the ancient portal, changing everything to pure gold, diminishing the austerity of the great hall, built entirely of dark gray stone. As we stood in this ancient castle, I was gripped for an instant by a sense of the past, which often invaded me at unexpected moments when I was in old places such as this. The castle Loevestein had remained relatively unchanged since the fourteenth century. Suits of armor glinted in the dappled sunlight, crossed swords were mounted over the huge doorway, and many shields and silken banners of the castle's armorial bearings spilled color onto the somber walls. A huge pewter bowl rested at the center of the long oak table. Two chairs stood at either end of the table yet, curiously enough, there were eight little footstools, four on each side, for the family's eight children. Apparently, only the adults sat while eating; the children stood to avoid lingering over their meal—or so the castle guide told us. The tranquility in this austere, ancient building was a palpable thing, which made me catch my breath in awe.

We were now directed to the far corner at the back of the great hall, where narrow stone steps led to the second floor. The steps were so narrowly built that we had to ascend in a single file. Later we were told by the guide that there was a purpose to it all. The narrow steps prevented a mass invasion of enemy soldiers from running up the stairs. In that way, a single man at the top of the stairs could hold off invaders by striking down the first one in line with his sword or lance. The man at the top of the stairs would be assisted by another, who would hand him a steady supply of weapons.

The ramparts on the castle roof held rows of small barrels with handles on them, lined up near the ramparts' edge. Not too far away, one could see a huge iron pot in which hot oil was kept boiling. In case of attack, the small barrels were rapidly filled with hot oil and poured quickly over whoever was climbing the castle walls, their ladders were toppled, and the scalded invaders would come crashing down to the ground. Quite a neat trick of defense in those days.

The smallish stature of the people in medieval times was quite notable. The beds were so short that Luke's and my feet stuck out quite a bit at the foot end, when we tried them for size. We also tried on the suits of armor, which did not close over our chests. And the adult size boots, for a full grown man, were comparable to a woman's size seven (American) today. We wondered how the men could swing those heavy swords for any length of time. They must have been physically quite strong, in spite of their small size, to be able to fight in those suits of armor. The visors were also quite heavy and suffocating, restricting their movements.

The children watched everything with great interest, especially in the children's chambers There were many carved wooden toys and dolls, and many examples of the children's clothes of the time. Small suits of armor, miniature copies of the adult sizes, seemed just made for play. The armor of a nine-year-old boy fit perfectly on Peetie, which he modeled proudly for everyone to admire. Lisa tried on a little girl's dress, that of an eight-year-old, that also barely fit over her chubby but sturdy little frame.

Finally we came to the book chest with the double bottom in which Hugo de Groot was smuggled out of the region. Again we wondered how he could have squeezed himself into that narrow space for hours on end, with just a few holes on either side of the chest and on the bottom to supply him with fresh air. All and all, it was an interesting day.

The tour ended soon after that and we sauntered out of the castle with the rest of the visitors, crossing the huge inner court and walking over the drawbridge, out onto the castle grounds. The four of us had worked up an appetite after the tour and we lunched at the cafe-terrace near the castle grounds. We decided against viewing another castle, since that would be more than the children could absorb. We had seen the oldest and most interesting of them all, and the others would only pale in comparison.

Instead we decided to tour the country a little and stop on our way back home at an amusement park and storybook town especially built for children, named Efteling, in the town of Tilburg in North Brabant. It was in the same province where we lived.

Efteling and the area surrounding it were colorfully and beautifully arranged and constructed. Talking elves sat beneath brightly painted wooden mushrooms, and sitting upon the mushrooms were all kinds of storybook figures. We saw the gingerbread house of Hansel and Gretel and the house of the Old Woman Who Lives In A Shoe, each giving the children a chance to examine every little detail inside, seeing their fantasies come to life. Peals of laughter rang out from the small constructions as they recognized certain characteristics from their storybooks at home.

Luke and I sat outside on one of the benches conveniently arranged for tired parents, admiring the surroundings, which included beautiful gardens. Shade trees were slowly turning colors, although the temperatures were still in the low seventies on this exceptionally beautiful day at the end of September. We had chosen a good time for our travels. The children came running out of the old woman's shoe, squealing with pleasure, their faces flushed. Luke bought lemonade for the children and coffee for us and, for us all, bags of piping hot *patat frites*, served with a creamy rich mayonnaise. This is one of the specialties of Holland; *patat frites* are sold on street corners and in parks, just as hotdogs are sold in America. They are just french fries, served in large strips, country style, but the sauce is exceptional—a specialty craved by adults and children alike.

After our snack, Peetie and Lisa wanted to see the house of Little Red Riding Hood's grandmother and the Wicked Wolf, but for that one they both wanted us right next to them. Lisa's little hand was reaching for mine even before we entered the cottage. Peetie caught hold of Luke's hand and hesitantly entered the doorway. Lisa wanted to be carried and Peetie hid behind Luke when they discovered the life-sized wolf with grandmother's sleeping cap on its head lying in the bed. Mechanically the wolf opened his mouth to talk to Red Riding Hood, who stood at a safe distance away from the bed listening to her grandmother's voice from the ferocious looking wolf. Little Red Riding Hood was a clever and masterful simulacrum. Even I had to look twice to assure myself it wasn't a real live person standing in the room looking at the wolf.

After Grandma's house, we visited Sleeping Beauty's Castle, an almost perfect replica of the real castle we had seen earlier in the day. The children recognized the likeness. "Oh look, it's the castle but smaller, for children," Peetie said. "Let's go inside," Lisa suggested, pulling on my hand. Peetie let go of Luke's hand and ran toward the entrance with Lisa closely behind him. They had such a good time, our little ones. People watched them play, smiling tenderly. They were an adorable twosome, extremely protective and considerate toward each other—but that was to change later in their lives, most unfortunately.

Luke and the children then went for ice cream, while I sat quietly on one of the benches and took in the beauty around me. It was one of those rare and beautiful afternoons at the beginning of fall that occur quite seldom in North Brabant. The sky was light blue, clear and radiant, with a few scattered cotton-ball clouds scudding intermittently across the sun. The surrounding gardens of Efteling were riotous with late summer color, and the air was filled with the scents of flowers and shrubs. The flower beds were a little too rigidly manicured for my taste; I like their natural abundance, gently curbed when needed.

The day was drawing to an end. Luke got the car from the parking lot and picked us up at the entrance of the park. They children were exhausted from all their activity and quickly settled themselves on the backseat for the ride home. It had been a wonderful day for all of us, one we would always remember with pleasure.

ST. NICOLAS DAY PARTY

Toward the end of November, the party Luke and I wanted to have for the children of the neighborhood and their parents, which had been just a vague idea, began to take real shape. *Sinter Klaas* or *Sint Nicolaas* is a Dutch tradition that could be compared with Saint Nick or Santa Claus in the United States. The celebration, however, has nothing to do with Christmas. The legend is that, each year on December 5th, Saint Nicolas comes all the way from Spain to Holland to give presents and cookies to children at night. He is a bishop, and he rides a white horse through the streets in a wine-red robe and a bishop's miter, flanked by six black men, called blackamoors, on foot. Dressed in medieval attire, short balloon-like striped pants and plumed berets, they carry gunnysacks slung over their shoulders. Three sacks are full of presents for well-behaved children, and three of them are empty. The empty sacks are to carry naughty children back to Spain, where the bishop and his helpers came from, where according to the legend the children never see their parents again.

Although when the legend was young, the bishop visited only the very poor, now on this celebrated day he gives toys and handfuls of candy to all the little ones, bringing smiles to their faces. When we lived in The Netherlands, some families would hire men to play the roles of the good bishop and his helpers, and others had friends or relatives play the part of *Sinter Klaas* and *Zwarte Piet*, the latter meaning Black Pete in Dutch.

By the first of December, our preparations were set in motion. We invited six couples with their children and hired the Saint and three of his helpers. The party was to be given at our house. We would provide all the refreshments, including plenty of candies and cookies for the children. The cost of hiring Saint Nicolas and his helpers was divided among the other six families.

On the night before the party, when the children were sound asleep, Luke and I took out all the presents, both for our children and the others, from their hiding place in the little shed behind our house. Peetie and Lisa both wanted scooters. We had a red one for Peetie and a pink and blue one for Lisa. Storybooks and all sorts of board games were also among the gifts. And from Albert and Molly, their Opa and Oma in The Hague, for Lisa there was a beautiful big doll and a silver necklace with a silver heart and her name engraved on it. I would have to keep an eye on such a precious gift for such a small child, I worried. And for Peetie they bought a child's watch and a set of toy cowboy guns, which he had admired and desired for quite some time. From Carl and Lena, Luke's parents, Lisa got a doll stroller and Peetie, a fancy cowboy leather vest to add to his cowboy paraphernalia. He already possessed a cowboy hat, a lasso, and a red bandana he wore over his nose and mouth. He had seen men do this on television on his favorite TV series "The Lone Ranger."

The evening before, the man who would play the good old Saint came to our house for a run-through. He was instructed how to get into our tiny back yard from the walk that leads around the house. The shed door would be unlocked and our living room drapes drawn before his arrival, to avoid his being seen by the children. Since it was winter, no one would find it odd that the drapes were closed early, since it was nearly dark outside in early afternoon. Luke showed "Saint Nicolas" into the living room, where a specially decorated chair was set in the center. That was where he would sit the next day, with his helpers standing behind him.

On December fifth, St. Nicolas Day, everyone in our house awoke early. The children, much too excited to sleep any longer, jumped onto our bed. "Come downstairs with us," Peetie exclaimed excitedly, and Lisa imitated her brother immediately. "Yes, yes come downstairs with us." Before we could get up, they flew down the stairs, which made Luke and I shout in unison, "Slow down before you fall!" Shrieks and exclamations now reached our ears in the bedroom. Saint Nicolas's horse had eaten all the grass and carrots they had stuffed into their shoes and placed near the stairs before they went to bed. The bowl of water they had put next to their shoes was also empty. In their place were chocolate letters, marzipan piglets, and storybooks. They bolted back up the stairs, a beheaded piglet in one hand, a chocolate letter in the other, a mouth full of marzipan, and under their arms a storybook each. Their faces were rosy with excitement and their dark eyes gleamed with pleasure. So often I reflect on those years when my children were young. What a pleasure they were then, and such a blessing for us. I will cherish those moments as long as I live.

At 3:30 in the afternoon, the guests began to arrive, their children trailing behind them hesitantly, eyes darting to and fro. Who knows, the *Zwarte Pieten* could be lurking in the corners of the living room, and none of the children was sure if they would be carried off to Spain in an old gunnysack or would be given a present. They could certainly remember being naughty in the past year. What if their parents had written to the Saint to complain, as they had often threatened to do?

We gave the children cookies and hot chocolate in little cups. Although they accepted the cookies quickly, they seemed too excited to eat, but all drank their hot drink eagerly. Luke and I had arranged a semicircle of folding chairs around the "throne." The adults sat down while chatting with each other, and the children, including ours, were quiet as mice. When everyone had arrived and had been seated, Luke disappeared to give the men the sign to come in with all the presents. Only the presents too large for the gunnysacks were not brought in. They would be found "accidentally" later, after the guests left. In the other children's houses, the larger presents would also mysteriously appear when they got home, since it was impossible for the helpers to put everything in the gunnysacks.

The doorbell rang, and the children crawled into their parent's laps, ours included. I had two who were crowding in on me, since Luke was at the door. Saint Nicolas came in first. Stately and professional, he walked to the center of the room led by Luke, who then seated the holy man. The three *Zwarte Pieten* followed. Two had bulging sacks with them, but one had an empty one slung over his shoulder. He also had a rod or birch in his hand. This was the *Zwarte Piet* all the children feared and dreaded most of all. Some shrieked and hid their faces against their parents' shoulders. Even the adults were impressed. The whole performance was indeed intimidating.

After the blackamoors had positioned themselves behind their master, one of them handed the Saint a list with the names of the children, their ages, and their parent's complaints. The first name called was that of a boy of six, Reggie Slager. He was the bully of our little group of children. Now extremely subdued, he clung to his mother fiercely. She coaxed him over to where the Saint was sitting. Saint Nicolas stuck out his hand reassuringly and pulled the trembling boy toward him. He spoke to Reggie in a gentle manner, asking him not to be so aggressive and bossy to others and telling him to share more often. Reggie nodded vehemently several times. His eyes never left the *Zwarte Piet* with the rod and the empty sack over his shoulder, who made comically threatening gestures at him all the time the Saint was talking to him. Reggie shivered in fear, poor little guy.

Two more children were called forward before our children's turns came. When Peetie's and Lisa's names were called, they reached for each other's hand and Lisa grabbed mine firmly. Bravely they faced Saint Nicolas, but both avoided looking at *Zwarte Piet*. Luke, who stood aside to take pictures, stifled his laughter—but I had tears in my eyes. My two little babies were scared but so very, very brave! After Lisa had been given her doll and Peetie his toy gun set and after numerous promises to be good for a year, they finally lifted their eyes to *Zwarte Piet*. He winked at them, after which they tremulously smiled and ran back to their places, clutching their hard-earned presents, soon to forget their ordeal of just a moment ago.

After all the children received first a lecture and then their presents, they showed off their toys to each other proudly. Now the time had arrived for the Saint and his helpers to make their departure. With great relief, the children waved to the Saint and his helpers and sang the traditional farewell song, *"Dag Sinterklaasje, Dag, Dag!"* meaning "Goodbye, St. Nicolas, goodbye, goodbye." They all reached for their drinks and their cookies and candies, gobbling up the treats and noisily chatting about all sorts of things of importance to children alone.

Around seven o'clock people started to leave, but some stayed a while longer to help to straighten up the house. They all thanked us at the door for a successful afternoon and evening, cracking jokes as they left. Soon Luke, Peetie, Lisa, and I were alone in our living room. The children were surrounded by all their new treasures, in which they were totally absorbed. Luke and I watched them, relaxed, as they played. We were all still too full with party food to be interested in supper. The party was fun, and it was well worth the trouble to see everyone having such a good time.

CHRISTMAS AND THE NEW YEAR

Christmas 1959 came and went. It was more a religious event in our family than anything else. My parents came from The Hague to spend the holidays with us, returning home right after New Year. Our children were delighted to see them and were never far away from their sides, at least for the first two days. After that they returned to their group of friends and games, playing outside if weather permitted. On Christmas Day, a small but very pretty tree graced the corner of our living room. It was beautifully decorated in plenty of red and silver, and underneath it were small presents of love and appreciation addressed to one another, to be opened after dinner.

Molly, my mother, promised to create her Indonesian specialties, traditional holiday dishes. *Zwartzuur* is made from duck or chicken. *Ayam Kodok* is an absolute masterpiece. Let me elaborate on these two dishes, which are totally foreign to American tastes.

The name *Zwartzuur*, which means "black and sour," derives from the taste and color of the dish, which is somewhat sweet and sour and dark from all the wine, spices, and onions in which it has been simmered.

The name *Ayam Kodok* derives from the form the chicken takes when it leaves the oven, so plump looking that a huge frog comes to mind. *Ayam* is chicken in Indonesian and *Kodok* is frog. My mother would buy a large chicken or capon and, after preliminary preparations, she would make a slit in its back. With the utmost care so as not to damage the skin, she would remove the entire chicken from its skin, in one piece. She then ground the meat, by hand in those days before food processors, and mixed it with chopped red beets, green olives and pickled cucumbers, and spices. Mom also made hard boiled eggs, which were arranged in the skin after the chicken was stuffed. When it was sliced, the eggs appeared neatly in the center of the slices. To me, it is a masterpiece that requires the utmost in patience and dexterity to accomplish. Not many home cooks would even attempt to do such a fine dish in the busy world of today. The end result, looked, smelled, and tasted heavenly—not like a frog at all.

The meals prepared by my mother with care were real family feasts, served with joy and all the trimmings. For dessert there was a beautifully made and delicious cake from a local baker, for my mother, although a gifted cook, was never much of a baker herself. That was just not her cup of tea.

And so we celebrated Christmas quietly with our immediate family, as most families in Holland did in those times. It was something of a contrast to the lavish Christmas celebrations held on the plantation of Alfred and Tina Rozen, my paternal grandparents, before the war, in Indonesia. We celebrated gloriously, yet serenely so. I can still smell the black rice porridge boiling in the great plantation kitchen, served with the thick coconut milk cooked with the leaves of a family of the pandanus plant. This specialty was made especially for the field hands and their families, although of course the Rozen family enjoyed it as well.

For the children of all the field hands, there were inexpensive little gifts, purchased by Siti the plantation housekeeper at the numerous little Japanese stores in downtown Batavia. A week prior to the celebration, they were wrapped in red and green paper by all the servants of the house and placed in huge baskets, ready to be brought to the families with children by the overseers and their helpers. A horse-drawn carriage carried the steaming porridge in big kettles and big pots from the plantation, stopping near the area where the field hands and their families lived. People surrounded the cart in no time with containers in hand, waiting for the treat.

Just like my children in The Netherlands, the children received their toys with starry eyes and smiling faces. There was also an enormous juniper tree, full of painted wood and glass ornaments and candles, in the large living room of my grandparents' house. The tree could be lighted for only a short period of time, right after Christmas dinner, and two servants were stationed near by with candle extinguishers on long rods in their hands in case of a wobbly candle ready to tip over. My grandmother would play Christmas tunes on the piano, with the entire extended Rozen family, with all the children and grandchildren, surrounding her and my father playing the violin or guitar, all singing beautiful Christmas songs together. Those memories are still extremely dear to me, those memories from my childhood time. They are my most precious possessions from that long ago time, since pictures are long lost due to war and the many uprootings the family endured.

Recognizing the faraway look in my eyes, Luke understood the reason. "Thinking back of other Christmases?" he asked softly. I nodded. My father, who observed me quietly from across the sitting area, murmured, "Those were glorious times, huh? I know, I still think about them too, once in a while," he added softly.

New Year's Day arrived, and my parents were ready to return to their home. We brought them to the station in Bergen op Zoom, missing them already. The children clung to Opa and Oma's hands, not wanting to let them go. We promised to be in The Hague in April with Easter, or *Pasen* in Dutch, and planned a trip to the famous tulip fields and flower park called Keukenhof, which is in Lisse, a town between The Hague and Amsterdam, near Haarlem. This park has been called the greatest flower show and exhibition on earth. And people from all over the world come to visit its gorgeous panoramic views.

After my parents had left on the train, Peetie and Lisa were quite subdued, and to take the sharp edge off the farewell, Luke and I decided to take them to see a matinee showing of the movie Snow White and the Seven Dwarfs. It was the second day of 1960 and Luke had the day off. We had time to grab a bite to eat before the show started, and Peetie and Lisa, their sadness forgotten, ran hand in hand to the little eatery. Luke and I shook our heads—how quickly children forget, and what a blessing it sometimes is. We were seated immediately and ate quickly. Lisa normally a very slow eater, ate hurriedly with the prospect of going to the movie. Peetie never had any problem with food. Luke paid the bill and we all walked to the theater a couple of buildings down the street.

The theaters in Holland were quite different from American movie theaters, not so much in terms of structure, but more in how they are operated and organized. At that time, most theaters were beautiful inside, and food and drinks were not permitted to be brought in. People dressed up to go to the theater, and there were long intermissions during which one could buy refreshments. With children in tow, we usually kept a couple of candies in our pockets for them to munch on, using the intermissions to get drinks and to usher them to the restrooms. Peetie and Lisa loved the movie and were totally engrossed in it. Luke and I smiled at each other— they had a great day after all. We took the bus home, catching it directly in front of the theater, and had a peaceful ride in which the children talked nonstop about what they had just seen. We arrived at our stop almost too soon, a short walk from our home. What started out to be a bit of a sad day turned out to be pleasant after all.

Chapter 6

EMIGRATION PLANS

Our inquiries about emigration to the United States soon took concrete form. On January 15, we received a notice from the Wereld Raad Van Kerken, which is the World Council of Churches, which at that time was located in Rotterdam. At that time, this organization had among its missions assistance to candidates for emigration to the United States. The notice urged us to apply swiftly if we planned to emigrate. Luke and I had talked again and again about the possibility of emigration, and now the time had come to make the important decision. Early one Friday morning at the end of January, we left for Rotterdam, having dropped off the children at a neighbor's house down the street. Bert and Stella Mulder had two children of their own about the same age as Peetie and Lisa, and all the children were delighted to be together.

It was 9:30 in the morning when we arrived at the appointed building. After a lengthy conversation with an American official and his interpreter, we were led to an area with long tables placed in rows, one after another. Each table was labeled with the name of a religion and the church it represented. We automatically turned to the Catholic table and sat down to speak to the church official, who greeted us with a handshake. He asked us to name three states in which we were interested in living. In a mixture of Dutch and halting English, we right away chose Arizona, Florida, and

California, although we had not the slightest idea what these regions were like, other than the images we had seen in pictures and movies. The one thing we knew was that, in the three states we picked, the winters were very mild. We had enough of snow and cold, miserable weather.

With our preferences firmly stated, we waited for more questions. The official looked at our application papers, scratched behind his ear and then said, "You have two children?" Luke and I nodded. The official then told us that we would be put on a waiting list, since families with four or more children had priority. I stood up, thanking him curtly but politely. Luke gaped at me uncomprehending, but followed me quickly to the next table, which represented the Episcopal Church. I sat down with Luke beside me, and again we testified to our wish to emigrate. Again we were asked our choice of state. We repeated to the clerk the same answers as we had given to the Catholics behind us, but this time added "It doesn't matter where." Our thinking was that once we got into the United States we could always move to wherever we wanted to be. The Episcopalians had no questions about how many children we had and the waiting list it was not an issue. The gentleman registered us and sent us off with a promise that we would hear from them as soon as they had found us a sponsor. We thanked him profusely and left his table.

With the decision made and initial step finally taken, we felt enormously relieved. Now it was up to the authorities, Dutch and American alike, to determine where and when and how we would leave Holland and go to America. The wheels had been set in motion. Before we left the building, however, we were led to a separate area to be fingerprinted. We waited in line and had numerous discussions with people with the same ideas and the same frame of mind as we. No one minded the waiting. Before we were called into the office for our fingerprints, we had made friends and had exchanged addresses and phone numbers with the ones who had a phone. Coffee and sandwiches were available downstairs, and someone had volunteered to get some for the people who were hungry. It was way past lunchtime by now. Luke offered to help carry the sandwiches and drinks. Many ordered. The men returned with the food, the money matters were settled, and we ate ravenously.

Not long after it was our turn to be fingerprinted. Then we were done and could go home. We promised our new friends to stay in touch and to let each other know where we would be sent as soon as we knew. Luke and I skipped out of the building like two children, light of heart and relieved that the momentous decision was behind us. We immediately planned a trip through Holland and Belgium to see the places we had never had the time to visit before. Luke had a week's vacation coming up, which we decided to use in conjunction with the Easter holidays. It would be some time before we would get word from the emigration authorities anyway, we thought. It was nearing five o'clock in the afternoon when we arrived at the Mulders to pick up Peetie and Lisa.

In early March we received a summons from the Emigration Bureau for all four of us to undergo a physical at the Health Department in The Hague, where most emigrant applicants were handled. We picked a day that Luke had off and arranged to stay with my parents for the night. We explained to Peetie and Lisa what was expected of them; the only question they had was, "Does it hurt and are we all going to be together?" When we assured them that at least they would be with me, they concentrated on the upcoming train trip and staying with Opa and Oma for a night. They loved the tiny little park with the pond and the many ducks right in front of my parents' house, where we used to live before we moved to Halsteren. Lisa cried a bit when her blood sample was drawn, but Peetie closed his eyes and bit his lip bravely. An ice cream later on made them forget their ordeal in the clinic.

A week later back home in Halsteren, we received the news that everybody was found healthy, so now we just waited for news that a sponsor had been found for us. After that we could then plan the date of our departure. We were encouraged by the authorities to correspond with our sponsors. We had pieces of our furniture already "sold" to friends in our neighborhood, contingent upon our departure. So far everything seemed to progress smoothly. We were also still were in contact with our friends who had left months ago for the United States, as well as with the new ones we made at the Emigration Department in Rotterdam.

DESTINATION: NEW ENGLAND

The weeks went by at their normal pace. Peetie told everybody who would listen that he was going to America, the land of the Lone Ranger. Lisa wasn't quite sure what all the commotion was all about, but she happily shared in the enthusiasm created by the idea of starting a new life in a new place. From our many connections we knew that it was not a land of milk and honey, but it was one in which we could create a reasonable and comfortable existence. All we needed was hard work, flexibility of mind, and a willingness to follow the rules and customs of the country we had chosen for ourselves and our children, to the point of ultimately become U.S. citizens. From the start that was our attitude, and with all that we encountered in later years, in this land that is so beautiful but so different from what we knew, we were never disappointed in our decision to make it ours.

Shortly before Easter, we got the letter we were waiting for. Our sponsor was to be an entire church group, in this case the Episcopal guild in Hamilton, Massachusetts, in New England. After swallowing the disappointment of not heading for the sunshine of California, Arizona, or Florida, Luke and I danced through the house in our enthusiasm, with the children jumping up and down between us. We could always move later, after the five-year period during which we would be under the close supervision of our sponsors. We were now their responsibility, both financially and otherwise. If anything happened to us, the authorities would turn to them during those five years.

Sometimes I wonder if many emigrants realize how difficult it is to be the sponsor. It is a responsibility that not many people are willing to take. And for that Luke and I will always be grateful to the Americans who were willing to give us a chance to better our future and that of our children. Like our friends before us, we were advised to correspond with our sponsors, in order to get acquainted even before we met. We did this, writing in the best English we could. The Reverend Robert Snyder was the person with whom we corresponded in the time before we left Holland. He was an extremely warmhearted and jovial gentleman, as we later discovered when we met him. He put the lie to the cliché reserved New Englander, proving to be entirely the opposite.

WHIRLWIND TOUR

Easter arrived, and with it Easter vacation. When my parents learned about our intention to tour Belgium and Holland before we left for the USA, they suggested that they keep the children while we traveled. They had already seen Keukenhof twice, and preferred the idea of staying home with their grandchildren, who were about to leave them for a very long time, if not forever.

As a farewell present, they also offered to pay for a motor coach tour for us, and since Luke had a week's vacation, the idea was perfect. It was a way of seeing a lot in a short period of time, since we did not have much time left. From the Bureau of Emigration we'd received the news of our official departure date, which was set for July 13. We were to travel on the Dutch ship the M.S. Grote Bear, and the transatlantic voyage would take nine days.

We balked a little at the idea of our Easter motor coach tour at first, since we pictured such a trip as being only for the elderly. But that was not the case in those days. It was an interesting group that came together for this tour, and many were in our age group. The planning and organization was excellently put together, and we enjoyed the entire trip, grateful to my parents for the opportunity to see important sights and enjoy so much beauty.

In the springtime, northern Europe comes alive, as people gather in the squares and cafes, and all the trees and flowers burst into bloom. There's no better time to explore Holland and Belgium through the streets of the towns and countryside than in spring. Our journey began in The Hague, where we got on the tour bus near the train station. We were driven straight to Brussels, a favorite destination among travelers for its grand and beautiful architecture. Our hotel was very nice, although not elaborate. That evening we got acquainted with our fellow travelers at a simple welcome reception, then had dinner on our own.

The next morning we got acquainted with the Old World capital. Since the postwar years, Brussels had become a bustling cosmopolitan cultural center, famed for its range of classic European architectural styles. We saw the sleek glass European Union Parliament building and the Parc de Bruxelles, an oasis with classic, manicured gardens that especially impressed Luke. We then toured the city's greatest attraction: the Grand Place, now a World Heritage site. Historic seventeenth-century guild houses and the sixteenth-century Hotel the Ville (Town Hall) flanked the lively square. After the tour, the remainder of the day was ours to spend.

During the evening we gathered in the hotel lobby and shared our explorations with our travel companions during dinner at a local restaurant. We made plans for the next morning to see two famed Belgian specialties: lace and chocolate. It was exceedingly interesting to learn about the painstaking craft of lace making at a local lace factory. Intricate hand-knotted lace making endures as a cottage industry, employing about 1,000 workers, most between the ages of 50 and 90. The tour bus then drove us to see the second Belgium specialty being made: chocolate. Chocolate arrived in Belgium in the 1870s, following its colonization of the Congo and its huge cocoa plantations. Traditional Belgian chocolates are mostly filled with cream, liqueurs, nuts, or dark chocolate ganache. Today the finest chocolates are produced in Brussels, achieving a smooth, velvety quality and a rich flavor. I consumed more than I could handle and had to pay dearly a few hours later. That same afternoon, after I felt better from all the chocolate, we were free to explore on our own and decided to take a taxi to Lier, a Flemish town dating from the thirteenth century. We admired Zimmer Tower, once part of the town's medieval fortifications, which now houses an elaborate clock with thirteen faces. We also visited the Beguinage, a former refuge for women who lost their husbands in the Crusades.

The following day the tour bus drove us to Antwerp, and we got acquainted with Belgium's second largest city, which reached its height as an international trading center in the 1600s. We saw the historic Old City and visited landmarks such as the Grote Mark (big market), a central square surrounded by sixteenth-century guild houses: the Old Globe Market was the location of Antwerp's notable Gothic Cathedral; and St. Paul's, a mix of Gothic, Renaissance, and Baroque styles, it seemed. We also explored the restored Schelt waterfront, lined with popular clubs and restaurants.

The next was Dordrecht, back in Holland, located at the confluence of the Rivers Maas, Noorde, and Dordse. Dordrecht is an old river port steeped in history. As we strolled through the town we encountered the seventeenth-century city gate and the waterfront lined with unusual shops and the Gothic Grote Kerk (big church). Next we viewed the historic Kinderdijk windmills, which have a legend attached worthy of elaboration.

The story goes that for centuries, Holland's residents had been at the mercy of frequent floods. (How well we know this, I will relate to you somewhat later in the book). For this reason, the country developed a unique bond with and affection for its many windmills. These innovative structures help to evenly distribute water levels, lessening the threats of devastating floods. The windmills of Kinderdijk village take their name from a sixteenth-century legend involving a baby, a cradle, and a cat surviving being tossed in raging waters. (Kinderdijk means child's dyke). Although modern windmills rely less on wind than on pumping engines, these historic windmills illustrate how the forces of nature served both to threaten and ultimately to rescue settlers in this region.

(A quick note to the readers of this book. There are two different types of windmills. The ones I had just described, the water-mills and the ones which are used to mill the grains. These are structured somewhat differently.)

After Kinderdijk, we went on our way to the George Marshall World War II Museum in Zweindrecht. After which we returned to our hotel in Dordrecht.

The next day we left for Schoonhoven and learned en route about the key role that seafaring has played in Dutch culture and history. In Schoonhoven, a town known for its many silversmiths, an artisan demonstrated the creation of exquisite silver jewelry. It was a wonderful experience to see this, so very different from how the silversmiths in Bali, Indonesia, create their masterpieces. And yet each kind of work is exquisitely beautiful.

The next day we visited Arnhem, remembered as the site of one of the most important and destructive battles of World War II. We saw how the city had been totally rebuilt and was now a magnet for history buffs like myself. We got acquainted with the town's historic district surrounding the Koren Markt (the grain market) and also enjoyed a visit to the Kröller-

Müller Museum, one of Europe's finest museums. And again somewhat later in the day we visited the National Liberation Museum in nearby Groesbeek.

Early the next morning, the bus brought us to the Aalsmeer Flower Auction, where today almost 20 million flowers change hands on a daily basis. We watched the frantic trading from a specially designed gallery, taking in the heady atmosphere.

Later that day we arrived in Amsterdam. It is a captivating city of canals, known for its independent nature and spirit and world-class museums. We explored Holland's capital, admiring its classic brick and stone canal houses adorned with gabled roofs and flowering window boxes. We also saw the seventeenth-century Royal Palace and the Mint Tower with its wooden drawbridge. We visited the renowned Rijksmuseum and admired the masterpieces by Franz Hals, Jan Vermeer, and in particular Rembrandt van Rijn. In that same afternoon we were driven to a diamond factory. Since the sixteenth century, Amsterdam has been a center for diamond cutting. At the factory we saw skilled diamond cutters transform the raw stones into sparkling gems, after which we learned the fascinating history of the diamond industry in this city, in which many Jewish people are involved.

Our next stop was Hoorn, home to some of Holland's greatest mariners, including Abel Tasman, the discoverer of Tasmania, and William Schouten, who navigated a passage around South America and named it Cape Horn (Hoorn) for his hometown. The town was also a center for the legendary Dutch East Indies Company, which rang a familiar bell for Luke and me, of course. On a stroll through Hoorn, we saw glimpses of the town's seventeenth-century heyday in its elegant architecture. On our way back to the hotel, we learned about the complex and contradictory aspects of Dutch culture and society—from the popular royal family to the Dutch social system.

The next day we rode to Enkhuizen, once home to the largest herring fleet in the country. And on a walking tour we strolled down canals and crossed on white-painted footbridges to visit the Zuider Zee Museum, which recreated neighborhoods and a way of life that existed before the enclosure dam was built in 1932 to rein in the devastating North Sea flooding.

The next day around ten o'clock, we finally arrived at Keukenhof. It was a gorgeous day and the sun shone brilliantly. For us Keukenhof Park, the "Greatest Flower Show on Earth," was one of the high points of the trip. Located in Lisse, the heart of the tulip-growing district in western Netherlands, Keukenhof is the former estate of a fifteenth-century countess who grew herbs and vegetables for her dining table, hence the name Keukenhof, which means kitchen garden. We meandered through displays of more than 6 million tulips, lilies, azaleas, daffodils, and all kinds of other flowers, covering some 70 acres. Our senses could scarcely take in the profusion of color and fragrances. We were also impressed with the artistry of the Dutch gardening style. The area's scenic beauty is enhanced by canals and both indoor and outdoor exhibitions, which make exploring very easy. At lunch time we enjoyed making the most of our time in one of the park's eateries.

We were now nearing the end of our journey, but I want to elaborate on two sights we saw that really touched our hearts. One is the Delta Works Flood Control Project, in Veere/Middelburg, set up following the horrendous flood that claimed the lives of almost 2,000 people in 1953. Luke and many of his friends had volunteered to help with the cleanup, which was an immense undertaking. It was a system of giant dams to provide more technologically advanced flood control along the coast of the province of Zeeland. It was an enormous and innovative engineering feat that took 32 years to complete at a cost of nearly $6.5 billion. When we were there in 1960, the project was already impressive. They had started to build a series of sophisticated dams and barriers to close off the coastline, so that the Delta Works would also complement the ecosystem and protect a vast area of vulnerable lowlands. Already we could see the potential benefits of this life—and property-saving wonder. Today, people from all over the world come to see it.

The second sight that greatly impressed us was the effect that World War II had on the Dutch during 1940 and 1945. In May 1940 the Germans invaded small, lowland Holland easily, since it was unprotected by natural barriers. The Germans gained control and thus began five horrible years of misery and deprivation for the Dutch. The war brought food shortages, curfews, and censorship, and the people endured the long, cold winters with no fuel to warm them. Also, many of the men were sent to the labor camps in Germany. Most affected by all this were the Dutch Jews, who were persecuted and sent to concentration camps.

Perhaps the most famous of Jewish victims of Nazi genocide was the young Jewish girl from Amsterdam, Anne Frank. Although she and her family, like many other Dutch Jews, went into hiding to avoid being sent to the death camps, ultimately they were discovered, deported to one of those barbaric camps, and met their death. After the war, however, Anne Frank's father, the only member of the family to survive, discovered his daughter's diary. This intimate chronicle has become one of the most important and eloquent accounts of wartime experiences. The house where the Frank family hid is now a museum, offering glimpses of life during the German occupation. This part of our trip deeply affected both Luke and me, and for the rest of the day we were subdued, thinking back about the sorrows we had endured ourselves between 1942 and 1945, in a place so far away yet still so fresh in our memories.

Upon our return to The Hague, we thanked my parents for the opportunity to see these interesting and eloquent sites in Europe. We got a fascinating perspective on the Old World that we would never forget.

We brought home little souvenirs for Opa and Oma: chocolates and silver knickknacks from Brussels and Delft blue earthenware we picked up along our journey. We bought little wooden shoes for Peetie and Lisa and a wooden windmill for ourselves. We thanked my parents for taking care of the children, and they declared that they had the time of their lives. But we could see that they also looked somewhat tired. Peetie and Lisa, like most small children, were a handful most of the time. They had their friends and all their toys at home to keep them busy, but with their grandparents they had only a couple of new books and a favorite toy or two. Opa and Oma had bought them more toys, which they took everywhere they went.

My parents cried when we left for home. They understood that when they saw us next would be the last time for a very long while. I was their only child, and Peetie and Lisa their only grandchildren. They brought us to the train station and waved us goodbye with tears in their eyes.

FAREWELL THOUGHTS

At home in Halsteren, more letters from the emigration Bureau waited for us, with a plethora of procedures and instructions. Somebody had already looked at our house, which they wanted to rent. Everything now pointed to a speedy departure. It was the middle of April, so there was just a short three months before we would leave The Netherlands.

Peetie, now five and a half years old, and Lisa, almost four, were treated like little celebrities by their friends. "You are really going to America?" I heard them ask in awe, several times a day. It was of course the America that they knew from all the TV series they were allowed to watch. Halsteren was close to the Belgium border, and most TV series we were able to get came from Belgium TV stations. Peetie would then parade importantly in front of his friends, dressed in his Western attire, cowboy hat and all. And for once Lisa was willing to wear her Indian headdress. I explained several times to Peetie and the others that America was not really like what they saw so often on TV. There were no wild Indians, no boisterous cowhands shooting anything in sight while sitting on drunkenly on their hard-to-handle horses. But the power of television and movies was too powerful, and the children continued their imaginary play.

With a million and one things to do before our departure, I had to put some sort of schedule together. I made lists for priority items to be packed and tagged our furniture with the names of friends and acquaintances who had bought pieces from us. In that respect, we were quite fortunate, because everything we had was sold within a reasonably short time span. People had paid in cash well before the day of our departure.

In the middle of all the hustle and bustle, my grandmother often came to mind. Although she never really was long out of my thoughts, even after all these years, she was even more present in certain stressful times in my life. All her grandchildren felt the brand of her nature, which was strong and which lived on through us. I reflected on how she would have handled a situation like this. Her smiling face came to mind and gave me confidence, and with it her inimitable brand of efficiency and her ability to concentrate totally on the matter at hand. My grandmother Tina would just plow ahead, making elaborate arrangements and lists of priorities. She would have worked diligently and meticulously down her lists, covering the smallest details.

During these weeks of transition, scenes of the plantation flashed across my mind. I especially recalled those times when all of Tina's grandchildren surrounded her, staying with her for the duration of a vacation. She made sure that we all learned something about responsibilities. It was our job to care for the animals that she and my grandfather Alfred had given to us. She also taught us the simple things, such as not to leave our clothes on the floor, to be picked up by our nannies, as we all were inclined to do. She even taught us to cook a little, so that we would not be totally helpless without servants.

Oma Tina showed us how to care for plants and anything that grows. She had a piece of land that she had divided into as many sections as she had grandchildren. Each of our names was painted on a flat rock to identify the piece of land that belonged to us. Everyone planted whatever he or she wished in the little piece of land. Eric, whose piece was right next to mine, planted corn, and I planted mine with cassava, which I loved. Oma taught us how to prepare the land before we could plant anything, and I can still picture how we worked and worked, and how we all balked when the steer manure was brought in, and how we had to mix the stinky stuff into the earth with our rakes.

At the end of the day, we complained about imaginary pains and real aches and showed her our blistered hands. She would take care of them lovingly, smiling in sympathy, but the next morning we were all back doing our chores, until the project was finished. The end results of our plantings were amazingly neat and turned out to be delicious after the produce was cooked.

Oma Tina made us do the cooking ourselves. "From the good earth onto your plate," she would call the project. The kitchen drill she gave us was at first disastrous. We charred pots and pans and created unpalatable meals, some so vile that we had to discard them immediately—even the dogs turned up their noses. We grumbled about burned fingers and so on. She would kiss our wounds lovingly and then gently prod us back into the kitchen. Behind our backs, our nannies groaned, *"Adu kasian betul,"* meaning. "Oh, I feel so sorry for them." My grandmother would give them a piercing stare and they would return to their chores, still shaking their heads.

During the first weeks of our vacation at the plantation, we settled into a steady routine. The girls made good progress in their housework chores, and the boys soon excelled in weeding and yard work. My grandfather and grandmother would take us out on picnics at the nearby beaches fringed with palm trees. We would swim and have a blast. They also took us to the movies as a reward for our strenuous endeavors, with an ice cream party afterwards.

That very special vacation, when I was 8 years old, will stand out forever in my mind. Afterward, as adults, we understood that, slowly but deliberately, my grandparents, especially my grandmother, had striven to instill in every grandchild the importance of team spirit, being a good sport, and abiding by the rules. Duty and responsibility were words frequently used by both of them. And Oma was determined to arm each and every one of us with sound principles and the proper attitudes when we became adults.

My grandparents taught us the meaning of honor, integrity, honesty, and truthfulness, among so many other things. But my grandmother's often strong and tough teachings were always spoken with underlying kindness, giving us love and understanding. And this has stayed with most of us throughout our lives. It was those years spent at the huge plantation house, in 1940-1941, just a year before the war came to destroy our family home, that were most meaningful to me and would live in my heart and mind always.

So much for reverie about the past. With a snap I was brought back to the present when Peetie and Lisa came into the house carrying all sorts of toys they had found in the little shed in the back yard. "Can we bring these with us to America," they asked, looking up at me. I explained that we could bring only one good-sized box of toys and they could choose what they wanted to take with them. But they had to be few, since their scooters were going and they took up a lot of room. They ran outside again and I concentrated on packing up the kitchen. Next I planned to go into the dining area to continue packing some of the glass work I cherished the most, mainly wedding gifts. We could not take too much, but enough to sustain us until we were completely settled.

We would have three suitcases of clothes and a big trunk with our belongings. Some people took more with them than others, and a few even had their furniture shipped with them. We preferred to travel light, since we were not sure what to expect. Although we were in continuous contact with the Reverend Snyder, we did not want to burden ourselves with too many of our belongings, preferring to have the money we made from selling them in our pockets. It gave us a feeling of some security, since we had heard stories about emigrants who were left stranded with no sponsor to receive them. Presumably this happened only if an emigrant had found a sponsor on his or her own. I am not too sure what the real reason was for such a terrible situation, but these unfortunate events did happen in several cases.

In mid-June we quickly celebrated Lisa's fourth birthday. Proudly she announced that she was now all grown up like Peetie was and ready to make the ocean voyage with her family and many others on a great big ship. Some weeks later, our friends and acquaintances organized a farewell party for us. It was an extremely pleasant surprise for Luke and me, especially the generous money donations, which moved us to tears. We would really miss them all and promised to keep in contact as much as we could and as soon as we were able.

Our house was quite empty once the various pieces of furniture were carried away. The children tumbled through the empty rooms excitedly, apparently unconcerned about the future, strongly believing, as well cared for children do, that all will be well as long as they are with their parents. This time the parents were not so sure as they wanted Peetie and Lisa to believe they were.

Yes, we did have doubts and fears, and our feelings went back and forth about the entire plan. Luke and I had not the slightest idea what the future held for us. It was a risk we were willing to take in spite the comfortable existence we had created for ourselves and the children in our ten years in

Holland. The idea that you know what you have, but you don't know what you are going into, played through our minds repeatedly.

It was now quite late to change our minds, with all our furniture sold and Luke discharged from the Air Force. We could still refuse the emigration opportunity if we wanted to. Responsibility, especially for the children, weighed heavily on us. What if Luke could not find a job quickly enough? What if we were sent to one of the many ghettos in the big cities? That happened to some of the people we knew, and there was no guarantee that it would not happen to us. Who could really say what would happen to us? Every time we received a letter from the Reverend Snyder, our fears dissipated for a while, since he wrote nice, upbeat letters. And with the relatives and friends surrounding us prior to our departure, we controlled our agitation and doubts.

LEAVING HOME ONCE AGAIN

We left Halsteren at the beginning of July. Again there were tearful farewells, hugs, and promises of staying in touch, although everyone knew that this was a promise of little permanence. A huge ocean separated us, and I knew in my heart I would never return to the land whose people had so grudgingly taken the Dutch-Indonesian people into their midst, although their motives were understandable at the time.

We had ten days to spend with my parents, relatives, and friends in The Hague. Several people from my mother's side of the family had come to the Netherlands from Indonesia. Two of her sisters came with their husbands and their children, none I was really close with. My father's youngest brother, Ben, and his family often came to visit when we were at my parents. Longingly, I would ask if he had heard anything more about Eric and his family, still in Indonesia. I still corresponded with him on a regular basis, but lately, with all our moving and emigration priorities, I had lost track of their whereabouts and their plans.

It turned out that Eric had applied to come to The Netherlands with his family. They fell into the category of *Spijtoptanten*, meaning literally people who regretted staying behind in Indonesia. *Spijtoptanten* got a second chance to come to The Netherlands to live. Eric was scheduled to arrive with his family on the July 1, but government red tape delayed his arrival until a month later. Since we were leaving in mid-July and could not postpone the date, we would miss him by just two weeks' time. He and I would never meet again, and we never got to know each other's spouses and children. I was so disappointed, I cried.

After my grandmother had passed away in 1954, Eric's parents left Indonesia immediately. But Eric still refused to come to The Netherlands, even though he was already feeling the pressure and precariousness of being less than a first class citizen of Indonesia. He felt it at work most noticeably, and his children in their schools. Twice Eric was passed over for promotions, and full-blooded Indonesians, younger and less capable, had gotten both positions. But his love for the country he had been born in was so great that he took the humiliation in stride. Finally, after being passed up a third time in his career and line of work, he made the necessary steps to ask for permission to enter The Netherlands with his young family, and it was granted to him rather quickly.

After a hectic ten days of saying our farewells to friends and relatives, we arrived at the most difficult moment of all, saying goodbye to my parents. Luke's parents, the van Larens, had left Holland 6 months earlier. His father had been assigned to a job in Papua New Guinea, as the head of forestry in Manakwari, for a two-year term. With them they took Luke's youngest brother Peter and his only sister Letty.

FINAL GOODBYES

The night before we sailed, we huddled together in the living room, with my parents hovering near their grandchildren. Peetie and Lisa, feeling our suppressed emotions intensely, clung to their Opa and Oma even more than usual. They both wanted to sleep with their grandparents one more time. Luckily both children slept soundly, perhaps exhausted from the overly busy days. Everyone awoke early in the morning, the day of our departure. Both my parents were extremely quiet and mechanically helped us to get ready for our great adventure. We decided that they should stay home, and other relatives and friends would escort us to the ship in Rotterdam. It would be too painful for my parents to see us slowly leaving the harbor. We wanted our farewells to be private and quick.

The doorbell rang. It was one of our friends, ready to drive us to Rotterdam, where our ship lay waiting. My father pulled me against him, tears streaming down his cheeks. My mother hugged and held on to Luke as if she wanted to detain him from going. The children started to cry when they saw us in tears and clung to their grandparents. Our friend John grabbed both of them and carried them to the car. I turned to my mother, hugged and kissed her mutely, with tears blinding my eyes. No one knew when we would see each other again, or if there would ever be an opportunity to do so. I ran to the car and jumped in, but not before I heard my father ask Luke to take care of his daughter and his grandchildren, his voice thick with emotion. Luke nodded, not trusting his voice. He hugged my father and turned and leaped into the car. I looked back one more time and saw my parents standing in front of their house, my father's arm protectively around my mother's shoulders. They looked so forlorn.

Another farewell scene flitted through my memory. Another last goodbye, ten years ago, in another place so far, far away. I saw my grandmother again standing in front of her driveway, waiting for us to pass by, in the military truck with so many others, on our way to Tanjung Priok, the harbor of Batavia, the Jakarta of now. She missed seeing us by a split second. I heard myself screaming, "Goodbye Oma, Goodbye Oma"' to no avail, for she could not hear me over the racket of the traffic. She too had looked so small and forlorn, although she stood as straight as she always had.

We arrived at the Rotterdam Harbor around one o'clock and found all our friends and relatives waiting for us in the huge spaces of the harbor halls. They had gathered tables and chairs, as many as they could find, for everybody to sit together. Luke and I were touched to see that so many people had come to see us off. Luke's brother Carl, who was in the military and the only one of Luke's immediate family who had not left for New Guinea, stood close-to us. My Aunt Laura and her husband Frank, my cousin's Erna's parents, Erna herself and her new husband Ted were all present, plus our many friends. Peetie leaned against Aunt Laura, who had her arm firmly around him, and Lisa sat on my Uncle Frank's lap, while Luke and I filled out a short form at the emigration counter further down the great hall.

Someone had ordered sandwiches and drinks for everyone, which we ate nervously. Suddenly a piercing whistle sounded, followed by an announcement for all the passengers to say goodbye to friends and relatives, after which the embarkation started almost immediately. The final goodbyes were hasty, and perhaps this was for the best. No time for more tears and intense emotions. We walked up the gangway of the ship that was taking us to a new life, turning to wave to all the people we left behind—again.

We were led to the cabin we were to share with others, and as on our earlier voyage to Borneo, and from Indonesia to the Netherlands, the men were separated from the women with their small children. The cabins were adequate—we had seen worse. We shared our cabin with a young mother, Ivonne Hennings, and her three-year-old son, Bertie. There were three lower bunks and two high up. Ivonne and I gave the children the lower bunks; we would climb the ladders to the beds above them. Peetie chose the single across from Lisa and me. He made himself comfortable and pretended to sleep—but not for long. The moment I told him that we still had to go back on deck to wave goodbye to all our relatives and friends on shore, he was out of bed and moved toward the long hallway with Lisa and me closely behind him.

We hurried to the upper deck on the shore side to seek out familiar faces. Luke was already there and made room for the children to stand in front of him, while clinging to the railing. I squeezed next to him with a firm grip on Lisa, while Luke took care of Peetie. The ship's railings had spaces between the bars wide enough for a child to slip through. The ship's horn sounded deafeningly, and the space between shore and ship slowly widened.

As we threw serpentines, coiled rolls of paper, to the ones on shore, holding on to them as long as we could before breaking contact, I silently compared our departure from our beloved country, the Dutch East Indies, with this one. How different were the emotions I felt ten years ago, all heartbreak and shattering losses. When I left the country of my birth, I left behind a huge part of me. At this moment, although I felt a deep sadness at leaving my parents and other relatives and friends, I was not devastated as I was then.

As the ship drew away from the shore and the faces of the waving people became vague and unrecognizable, we walked over to the many deck chairs that lined the ship's wall and sat down, preoccupied with our thoughts. Even the children were quiet. It had been a long and emotional day for everyone. One chapter of our lives had been closed again and another was starting. I was assaulted by a mixture of emotions—great relief at leaving Holland, but also worry for the future. I was excited and scared at the same time. Another blast from the ship's horn startled us and an announcement was made for all passengers to regroup on the boat deck for a safety drill. "Are we going to sink?" Lisa wanted to know. Luke explained that this was just to teach everybody how to use their swim vests in case of emergency, an explanation she accepted hesitantly. Peetie just looked around with big round eyes. He just found everything extremely interesting.

The nine days on the ship were grueling. The children's room was twenty-five feet square, equipped with two baskets full of toys, a rocking horse, and a blackboard on the wall—an extreme minimum to occupy and entertain 300 children. Fighting over a few books or a piece of chalk was unavoidable, with so many children in a small space, and it occurred throughout the day. The children had no fun, and Peetie and Lisa begged me not to take them there. Instead Luke and I held onto our twosome watchfully, since the thought of them slipping through the spaces of the railings and disappearing into the churning waters brought chills of terror down our spines.

A NEW HORIZON

On Day 5, a black dot appeared on the horizon behind us. We were being followed by a ship called the S.S. U.S.A., a brand-new ship that was huge in comparison to our old and weary M.S. Grote Bear. We had noticed the ship when we left the harbor in Rotterdam. It had just come from the United States, and it left again two days later to return there loaded with new passengers. It was known to cross the Atlantic in four days, while it took our ship nine full days. By midday she sailed in stately fashion by us, blowing her whistles as a greeting in answer to our ship's whistle. She passed so closely that we could see the passengers' faces clearly. It was an impressive moment and a happy one at that, knowing that there was another ship not too far away on this vast, empty sea.

Early in the morning of July 22, 1960, our ship reached Hoboken, New Jersey, and was about to enter the harbor of New York. We sailed passed the Statue of Liberty, an impressive symbol of welcome and freedom. Seeing the lady and her torch, which we had seen so often in magazines and the movies, in actuality, all kinds of emotions and questions once again played through our minds. Will this be the land in which we grow old in and end our days? Will our children grow up in safety and comfort? Did we do right to emigrate? Realizing that these questions were unanswerable, I concentrated on the moment and my children. Peetie exclaimed, "Look, it's the lady we've see in the movie house, just before a movie starts." "Yes," Lisa agreed, "she's so tall." Luke told her that perhaps someday we could climb all the way up into her crown and look at the world from way up high. "Can we do it today," Peetie wanted to know.

No, not today, we had a lot of other things to get done. First, we had to go to the Grand Central Station, to catch a train to Boston, where we were to meet one of our sponsors. Looking at Peetie more closely, I noticed a feverish glitter in his eyes and a flush on his face. His face felt hot and dry. I remembered hearing him sniff and cough a couple of times during the morning, but in all the excitement it had not really registered. Peetie had a cold and was running a slight fever. I took him to the cabin, gave him some children's aspirin, and sat with him until the emigration authorities came on board to lead people ashore. Luke took care of Lisa while I was occupied with Peetie. The little fellow really did not feel well and fell asleep almost immediately after I had put him to bed. It would be hours before we were called forward, since the process was alphabetical, and our name, which had always been alphabetized on the L, was now pushed back to the V. This was wrong, since the "van" of van Laren simply means son or daughter of Laren. But then, who wants to argue on the first day in a strange country, with a sick child in our midst.

Luke came twice into the cabin to see how Peetie was doing, which gave me the opportunity to get sandwiches and something to drink for all of us. Two hours later, we woke Peetie gently and were happy to notice that his temperature was normal. The little boy felt much better after his long nap and was almost himself again. We left the cabin with our bags packed and gathered on the deck, where the other immigrants stood waiting to be called. Most of the group we traveled with were already on shore when our name was finally called and we walked off the gangway onto American soil. We disembarked at Hoboken, New Jersey, so close to Ellis Island, where thousands and thousands of immigrants have come before us, through so many years.

PART III

UNITED STATES OF AMERICA

Chapter 7

New England

The hangar-like buildings we walked through in Hoboken were cavernous and echoed with all sorts of sounds—voices, male and female, as well as children's high-pitched ones, their cries, and everyone's footsteps. The loading and unloading of the baggage and the sounds outside on the busy docks also reverberated through the buildings. Each of us had a tag pinned to our clothes with our name and group number. As in Europe, long tables had been set up lining the walls, behind which two officials per table were sitting to receive the immigrants. Everything seemed quite orderly and smooth. By one of the door openings stood another official, who pointed us the way to the many buses ready to transport us to Grand Central Station in Manhattan, the point of departure for everyone's journey to his own destination. Arriving at the station, we were ushered as a group to long, empty, solid-looking benches. Each of us made ourselves as comfortable as we could, since the train for Boston would not arrive until 9 o'clock pm.

At 6:45 p.m., officials came around with baskets of sandwiches and soft drinks. We could also buy small baskets of French fries and a hamburger or a hot dog—our first taste of America's number one fast foods. Unfortunately for myself, I took to such questionable delicacies right away, especially the pizza, which ranks to this day high on my list of

American favorites. The children also liked it very much, but Luke needed time to adjust to American tastes.

Peetie, with his fever returning, wanted only a few bites of hot dog. Although he liked it well enough, he did not have an appetite. He preferred huge amounts of ice cold Coke, which helped to cool him down. From the lady emigration official who took care of our little group Peetie got another children's aspirin. She also laid down a couple of folded blankets, which miraculously appeared from nowhere, to make a soft bed for him on the hard wooden benches, and Peetie fell asleep almost immediately.

We would arrive in Boston at five in the morning and I prayed fervently that someone would be there to meet us, since once the train arrived at Grand Central, we would be on our own. The helpful immigration official assured me several times that a member of the church guild would be there to assist us. He would be responsible for driving us to our new home, the small but picturesque town of Hamilton, some 20 miles north of Boston.

Hamilton was a very wealthy town. How wealthy it actually was, we learned soon enough. The plan was for us to stay temporarily in the house of the second minister of the Episcopal Church in Hamilton. He and his family had been transferred to another state, and for a few months the house would be standing empty. The church guild arranged for us to live there for three months, which would give us time to look for jobs and permanent housing.

The train was quite full when it arrived. Luke sat with Lisa some five rows down the aisle from where Peetie and I found a seat, right next to a friendly elderly black man. When Peetie saw the old Negro, it was our family's first culture clash in our new country. The only black men Peetie knew was *Zwarte Pieten*, the costumed helpers who always appeared with Saint Nicolas. He started to howl. "*Ik wil niet naast die zwarte Piet zitten,*" he cried. "I don't want to sit next to Black Peter. He will take me to Spain," he screamed. Luckily the man was sweet and understanding and offered to move to the front of the car, where his friends sat—or so he murmured, hastily vacating his seat by the window and letting Peetie take his place. It was utterly embarrassing for me, but I did not yet have the English vocabulary to explain to the old gentleman why Peetie reacted the way he did.

Peetie stopped crying as soon as the man left and was happy with the unexpected opportunity to sit by the window. I at once explained to him that in this country he will see many more Negro people than just the old gentleman. Some are intensely dark and some are lighter, but they had nothing to do with the helpers of Saint Nicolas. I told him that many of them are people with children of their own whom they love very much. They would feel hurt if Peetie acted the way he just did. Peetie listen to me intently, staring at me with his huge dark eyes, which flashed as he innocently commented, "Some of them stay in the sun too long. Maybe they do it every day, Mama," he concluded, happy now that he had found a reasonable explanation for the blackness of the old man's skin.

The train rolled smoothly into the Boston station just before 5 o'clock in the morning. Nervously Luke and I scanned the platform for a person carrying a sign with our name on it. Thank the Lord, we did not have to wait long. Almost immediately a neatly dressed gentleman in a well-tailored light gray suit, waving a good-sized sign, drew our attention. We recognized our name in bold letters on the sign he carried way up into the air. I had no idea how nervous I had been until I saw him, when tears of great relief sprang to my eyes.

Gerry Van Houten stood on the station platform waving his sign with a huge smile on his face. A Dutchman born and raised in the Netherlands, he had moved to the United States in his early twenties to open a branch of his father's vast flower bulb business in Hamilton, Massachusetts. He'd married an American young woman not long after he established the bulb business in Hamilton. The branch was now fifteen years old and flourishing. He spoke English fluently but with a strong Dutch accent, which Luke and I, in our anxiety, failed to notice at first. He welcomed us with a wide grin and open arms and ushered us to his waiting car, a sable brown Cadillac, immediately giving the porters instructions as to where to send our heavy trunk and how to put our suitcases into the trunk of his car. He then opened the doors for us and said in fluent Dutch, *"Welkom in Amerika, mijn naam is Gerry van Houten"* ("Welcome to America, my name is Gerry van Houten.")

Luke and I gaped at him in total surprise and confusion. He laughed cheerfully and Peetie and Lisa exclaimed in unison, *"Deze meneer spreekt Hollands"* ("This gentleman speaks Dutch"), whereupon Gerry ruffled their hair and said, *"Ja dat doe ik al voor heel lang"* ("Yes I do that already for a long time"). He explained to us then that the church guild had chosen him especially for the job of meeting us because of his knowledge of the Dutch language. He too belonged to the Episcopal Church in Hamilton. He said that now he spoke Dutch with an English accent and English with a Dutch one—which was exactly true and with which we could identify ourselves years later. It does not matter how long one has been in a country: the accent of the country in which one was raised will always be detectable, in some people more than others. It is otherwise only if one arrives in a country at a very young age, way before the grammatical drilling has taken place in school. Tired and overwhelmed, we all settled into the car for the half hour drive to Hamilton. Peetie was very quiet and looked all around him for some time. Suddenly he asked out loud, *"Maar waar zijn toch al die Indianen en de cowboys, Mam?"* ("Where are all those Indians and cowboys, Mom?").

I reminded him what I had told him before we left Holland, that many things had changed and that the movies he had seen on TV were stories about people who had lived a long time ago. Gerry explained that now, except for a very few, there were no cowboys or Indians anymore, at least not the way they looked in the movies, whereupon Peetie, although disappointed, immediately turned his attention to the things he observed as the car drove through the busy Boston streets. It was a clear and glorious day and Lisa, who sat close to me, fell asleep as soon as the car came into motion. Peetie, who fought his tiredness with great determination, succumbed to it after a while. The people inside the car grew silent and Gerry, understanding how physically and mentally exhausted we must have been, pointed out landmarks in a soft voice so as not to disturb the children.

Gerry increased the speed as we left Boston behind us, reaching the highway or turnpike, as they are called back East. It was even hard for Luke and me to keep awake. We were both exhausted and to our embarrassment dozed off, waking with a start when the car stopped in front of a large and comfortable-looking Victorian house, painted white with soft blue trim. It stood in a quiet neighborhood surrounded by lots of trees. At the end of the driveway was a large yard surrounding the house and the two-car detached garage.

A NEW HOME

With the sleeping Lisa in Luke's arms and a half-asleep Peetie clinging to mine, Gerry ushered us into the quiet house, made ready for us by guild members days ahead. He also unloaded the trunk and brought everything inside the enclosed front porch. Gerry then showed us to the bedrooms upstairs. There were three large ones and a smaller one in the back, which was used more as a storage room. Gerry guided Luke to a little girl's bedroom, which had belonged to one of the young daughters of the departed minister. It was freshly redecorated for our use with white furniture and a pink-and-white gingham bedspread and curtains. On the window seat rested a big basket full of all sorts of toys, the kind a little girl of Lisa's age would love to play with, including several dolls. The bed was made up and ready. I opened it and removed Lisa's shoes, while Luke laid her down and tucked just the sheet in around her. Oblivious to all the commotion, Lisa slept the sleep of exhaustion.

Peetie, who had found his bedroom immediately, sat on his bed, surrounded by all sorts of toys he had found in the basket in his bedroom, also placed in the window seat. The toys of both children were not new, but all were in impeccable condition. Peetie's room was also newly decorated in blues and reds, and he was totally absorbed in a Lassie book he had found in his basket, together with a football and a baseball glove with baseball and bat. All these things were extremely strange to a 5-year-old boy from Holland, who had never seen such toys up close, but only fleetingly on television. He had no idea of what to do with them, since Europe's favorite sports are soccer, volleyball, and tennis. Gerry whispered to him that he would send some boys over to teach him how to play. Peetie nodded eagerly and showed us the other toys, including cars and a train set.

After he had seen us settled, Gerry took his leave. With a glance at our tired faces, he advised us to take a long nap, since the morning was still young. We walked him to the door, thanking him profusely for all his help. When we came back upstairs, Peetie was already sound asleep in the middle of all his newfound toys. He had somehow recovered from whatever had been ailing him the night before. It was perhaps the unfamiliar that had caused him to fall ill. We went to our bedroom, removed our shoes, lay down on the bed, and almost instantly slept. It was only a little past eight in the morning.

Three and a half hours later, Peetie woke us up. He too had just awoken from his nap. "Mama, Papa, wake up! There were people in the house, their voices woke me up," he exclaimed excitedly. "They're gone now, but they brought something in and I heard them put stuff on the table in the dining room." The four of us, now all awake, went downstairs together, crossing the hallway into the dining room. In the middle of the round dining table stood a huge vase of summer flowers, with a card stuck in it from the guild who had sponsored us with the sweetest note of welcome. The flowers were all kinds of bright colors—they were beautiful. A large tuna fish casserole, a big bowl of tossed green salad, and a huge apple pie surrounded the flowers, along with a bowl of all sorts of fruits. We could not believe our eyes. What a wonderful and sweet welcome, and how different from the one we got when we arrived in Holland. Ten years earlier, we were just a number among so many others, then more of an obligation to the Dutch government than anything else.

Hungrily we sat down around the table to eat, only to realize that we needed silverware, plates, and placemats, which we'd seen in our brief tour of the kitchen. The kitchen was newly redecorated and remodeled with lots of stainless steel and a black-and-white Armstrong linoleum floor. It was beautifully done and very spacious—awaiting the arrival of the new second minister and his family, no doubt. But we were to use it first, which gave me the nerve-wracking responsibility to be most careful with someone else's new kitchen.

We found the silverware in one of the drawers and placemats in another. The food was unfamiliar, but everything looked and smelled wonderful and we were ravenously hungry. Luke heaped food on Peetie's plate, since he always had a healthy appetite, and I poured lemonade that I found in the refrigerator into glasses for the children. We then sat down and helped ourselves to the bounty, saving the apple pie for dessert after the evening meal. The casserole was so big that there was enough left over for the evening, and salad left over as well. After lunch the children went back upstairs to play with their toys, while I washed the dishes and Luke dried them. We later discovered that the chrome-colored door beneath the kitchen counter was the household luxury of a dishwasher. Not being used to such a convenience, Luke and I decided to leave it alone for a while until we had read the operating instructions, which we were sure we would find in one of the many kitchen drawers.

We continued our investigation of the house, opening several cabinets above the many kitchen drawers. They were fully stocked with all sorts of cans, cereals, coffees, teas, and chocolate drinks. On every door were short notes telling us to feel free to use whatever we wanted, since the groceries had been put there for us. To our even greater delight, the refrigerator was also filled with fresh milk, eggs, butter, and loaves of bread. In the freezer compartment, we found a chicken, pork, and beef. All the packages were oversized, in our eyes. And in the two drawers in the refrigerator, we found all sorts of vegetables. It was like a Christmas feast in July; everything we could imagine was there. The guild had even thought of ice cream and cookies—especially for the children, the little note read.

Luke and I were overwhelmed by all the food, especially by the thoughtfulness of those who provided it. Off the kitchen and next to the downstairs bathroom, we found more surprises: a vacuum cleaner, electric iron, and ironing board in a small utility closet and a array of cleaning materials. Furthermore, we encountered a clothes washing machine and a dryer on our discovery tour. We had no knowledge yet of how to use these convenience gadgets, but I was planning to learn about them as soon as possible. What an enormous help they would be! Whereas in Indonesia we had servants, there was no one to help the housewife with her numerous daily tasks in Holland.

We continued our discovery tour and found a small library, tucked away in a corner near the living room at the end of the hallway. Many of the books were about theology, but others were novels and history books that I promised myself to read the moment I was in a position to do so. I was sure a dictionary would be needed, but that was one of the ways one learned to speak a language.

Luke and I now continued our walk-through up the stairs, where we found Peetie and Lisa engrossed in their new toys, games, and books. Next to our bedroom was a large bathroom. I could not get over the fact that we now had the use of two whole bathrooms in our house, whereas in Holland for years we lived in homes with none, except for the tiny cubicle in Blaricum, our first house, and in Halsteren, our last. I shuddered briefly, remembering the grimy bleakness of those long years. Even in the concentration camp in Indonesia, we at least had plenty of water behind makeshift *gedek* walls where we had fabricated a *pantjoran* or shower.

Across the hallway we found a deep built-in linen closet with clean but used towels and all the linens needed for the household. There were even extra blankets, one of which I still have in my closet. They all were in excellent condition and spotlessly clean. In the fourth bedroom next to the bathroom, the small one used as a storage room, there was an old black rolltop desk, an old-fashioned highboy with drawers in it, a broken chair, and other castoffs. From the room's two windows we had an excellent view of the backyard, where we could see the two-car detached garage. On the left was an iron garbage container built into the ground with a heavy lid attached to it. We learned later from our neighbors that it was for the deposit of food waste.

We were just about through with our tour when the doorbell rang. Luke ran downstairs to answer the door and greeted someone who had just entered the house. Looking over the balustrade, I glimpsed two men, a short and balding one of some 50 years and another one, tall and slender, also in his early fifties. When the tall man spoke, his voice sounded deep and warm. The short man had a permanent smile on his roundish face. Slowly I came down the stairs, already practicing how to greet them in correct English. The tall man with the deep voice turned out to be the Reverend Snyder himself, and the roundish man with the warm smile was an elder from the church, one of the main people we were to deal with later. His name was Harvey Hawkins, and later we learned that he had a wife and three daughters ages 16, 18, and 20, all still living at home. They became among our dearest friends, and we always felt cherished and protected when we were with them.

A NEW JOB

Harvey told Luke casually that he would stop by two days later to escort him around to certain companies where he had lined up job interviews. He arranged to stop by at eight in the morning on that day. All this he announced matter-of-factly and with the smile on his face that we came to know so well. We chatted with the two men a short while, until, satisfied with our well-being, they left. When Luke and I were alone, Luke said to me, "Did you hear that, he's taking me on a job interviewing tour! And did you see all the company names on that list in his hand?" I just nodded speechlessly.

Harvey Hawkins did considerable business with the Lockheed Corporation on the West Coast, we learned much later, and traveled frequently to and from San Francisco, where he would stay for weeks at a time. He was high up on the corporate ladder, and he also knew well many other electronics companies, with which he had dealings on a daily basis. He also knew many companies in our immediate area. That was why he had such a long list with all the names of companies he wanted to introduce Luke to.

Two days later as promised, Harvey knocked on our door a little before 8 o'clock a.m. and took Luke on the job-hunting expedition. It was a short one, since the second company they visited offered Luke a job. He was to start the next week on a Monday—that would give him a little time to catch his breath. Of course, Luke realized that, without Harvey's help, he would not have been hired so easily. The man who did the hiring was a old business associate of Harvey, and the two men had exchanged a few words before Luke had been called in. But that the company needed a technician was indeed a certainty, and Luke's diligent and observant nature was quite apparent. The two men noticed his quick eye for detail, as well as his eagerness to learn and get started.

Luke was home from the interviewing trip much sooner than I expected and entered the house with a huge smile on his face. "I've got a job," he exclaimed happily. Our future looked bright and secure, at least for the moment. I ran out to thank Harvey, but he waved to me from his car and drove away, hurrying back to whatever he had to do that day.

McKinley was the name of the company that hired Luke, and it was not too far from where we lived. Luke was to ride every day with a fellow employee, until we could afford a car of our own.

A NEW CAR

That Saturday, a phone call from the church guild informed us that two ladies wished to take us for an orientation tour of our surroundings around 2 o'clock in the afternoon. We readily agreed. The children were excited at the prospect of riding in a big, beautiful car and were waiting on the front porch long before the ladies were due to arrive. Eventually, a beautiful white Lincoln Town Car drove up our driveway. One lady, named Mary Chandler, got out of the car and entered the front porch where Peetie and Lisa were waiting. We heard Peetie say in perfect English, "I'll get Mom and Dad for you." How he had picked up that phrase so quickly we'll never know. Lisa too had started to say short sentences in English. The next door neighbor's children had been playing with them since the day we'd arrived, which may help to explain their progress in learning the language so quickly.

We got into the car and introduced ourselves, and as Mary drove off she introduced us to Ann Hastings, who sat quietly in the passenger seat.

She was a lovely lady of about 65 years. Whereas Mary was somewhat loud in her friendliness, Ann was soft-spoken and calm. It was clear which of the two ladies was the leading figure. As we drove along, both of them in turn pointed out several shopping areas, health clinics, the church, and all the necessities of life in a small town.

They drove to where Gerry Van Houten and his family lived and where he had his Dutch bulb business set up. Mary then drove slowly passed two car dealerships, turned around, and made a complete stop before one of them, waving her jeweled hand to one of the salesmen who were standing in front of the showroom. She seemed to know him and, calling him by name, she asked, "Hey Jack, how much is that secondhand Buick over there?" pointing to a dark green car.

We sat and observed the exchange without comprehending what was taking place. Luke had indeed told both ladies the good news about his new job, although I'm sure they already knew about it. He also told them about the arrangements for the temporary ride he had found with one of the men who worked at McKinley. Mary mumbled something like, "Oh no, that would take too long, and it would be inconvenient for both parties." She said this fast, and the meaning of it did not register with us at the time.

Mary asked Jack more softly about the price of the two-year-old car, and Jack, taking her cue, answered in an equally low voice. Mary then took out her checkbook as she quietly continued to haggle about the price. Ann, who had followed the negotiation with great interest, now turned to us and said, "Do you like the car?" Suddenly the full meaning of what was going on hit us, and Luke and I exclaimed at the same time, "Are you buying a car for us?" Our amazement was clearly noticeable in our voices. "Yes," they both said, also astonished, "You need a car to get around. Especially you, Luke, you need to get to your work."

Speaking carefully but firmly, we thanked the two ladies for this wonderful gesture but explained that we had some money and, for such an important necessity in life as one's first car, we wanted to buy it ourselves. When she saw how serious we both were, Mary turned to Jack and said something like, "We'll talk about this later, Jack." Ann, who had quietly observed the entire conversation, smiled at us and said, "I admire the two of you for this very much," adding softly, "Enough is enough, right?" And with that she winked at us.

Two weeks later we received a phone call from Jack, the salesman from the car dealership, announcing that he had just gotten in a nice 1957 black-and-white Pontiac station wagon, and it might be a car that we would be interested in. He urged us to come in as soon as possible. Luke told him that the car was way too new, only three years old, and that we could not afford a car that new. Jack insisted that we come over anyway, saying that he would make us a good deal. Knowing that we had no other transportation, he offered to pick up the four of us after Luke got home from work to look at the car. We promised each other not to get too excited. The car would be too expensive and we would have to resist the sales pitch.

As we waited in front of the dealership, Jack brought the car around to us. It was parked somewhat separately from the others. He asked us if we liked it. Of course we did, but we explained to him in halting words our financial situation. Luke had worked only a few days and we had only a small amount, which would certainly not be enough for a 3-year-old Pontiac station wagon. Jack just smiled and prodded us to step into the car for a test drive, just to see how it behaved on the turnpike. Peetie and Lisa jumped up and down. "Yes, yes, let's do it," they shouted in unison. Jack then excused himself for a moment and went inside the showroom and office building. We could see him walk to a phone on the table, dial a number, and speak briefly. We then saw him nod a few times and smile and then return to us. He gave Luke the key and opened the car doors for us. We all stepped in with Luke in the driver's seat, while Jack urged us to take a spin, still smiling widely. Luke and I looked at each other and thought, well, let's give it a try, why not, knowing very well that we could not afford to buy the car anyway. The children clapped in their hands in excitement and cheered as Luke drove off the parking lot.

We drove around for a little while, then turned into the dealership to return the car. Jack was outside waiting for us. Before we knew it, he had ushered us into the building and over to his desk. He had papers for us to sign, whereupon he said, "The car is yours." He accepted our $350, giving Luke back the keys he had put on the desk. We did not have printed bank checks yet, so we gave him the cash, which I had in my purse. Then he led us back outside, thanked us for our patronage, and again opened the car doors for us. Overwhelmed, we stepped in for the second time, but now as new car owners. Jack exclaimed "Drive safely and enjoy!" Luke drove the car away in a daze, and none of us could believe that we now were the proud owners of a 1957 black-and-white Pontiac station wagon. The children cheered, and Luke and I, infected by their happiness, cheered with them.

We drove home in a festive mood, stopping on our way to celebrate with some soft ice cream at the Dairy Queen. When we finally got home and the children were asleep, we communicated to each other the one thing that was clearly on our minds. We would have never gotten the car if someone else, perhaps by the name of Mary Chandler, had not added quite a bit more money to our $350 to make the deal work. We remembered Mary's conversation with Jack the day she and Ann drove us to see the dark green Buick, as well as Jack's quick telephone call the moment we admitted that we liked the Pontiac station wagon. We also remembered the swift acceptance of our offer. In the meantime, our transportation problem had been miraculously lifted from our shoulders. We had a wonderful, reliable car that drove like a dream. What generous people we had fallen in with!

A NEW CULTURE

Slowly we were adjusting to our new life in the USA and the customs and culture of a people, who had accepted us so generously. We had been in America a little over two weeks, and August was about to begin, when we encountered a small problem in the upstairs bathroom. While everything else seemed to have been refurbished, this bathroom, although it looked to be in good condition, was actually not. The showerhead was leaking and sprayed water every which way except on the right spot. The threads on the head were apparently stripped and it needed to be replaced. Not wanting to bother our sponsors with such a small problem, we decided to handle it ourselves. After discussing it with Luke, I agreed to go to the hardware store the next morning.

The hardware store stood conveniently near the town square, in a little shopping area surrounding the square. There were benches near the walking paths and a children's play area partly surrounded by trees. On one of our orientation tours we had stopped to let the children play on the seesaws, swings, and little carousel. That's when we'd noticed the hardware store.

Peetie, Lisa, and I headed toward the square on foot. It was a bright morning and the children wanted to play as soon as they saw the swings. I explained that we would first go to the hardware store and they could play afterward. Lisa had already come down the slide, and Peetie wanted to have a turn on the monkey bars. Finally we continued our walk and reached the hardware store. I was full of confidence about what I needed to buy and how I was going to ask for it.

We stepped inside the store, and immediately a young man of about 25 came toward us. With a friendly smile, he asked if he could be of any help. "Yes," I answered brightly, "I would like to have a douche." Although I said this somewhat haltingly, I felt proud that I had managed to find the words to ask for what I wanted correctly. So I was completely surprised to see the young clerk's face become bright red with confusion and embarrassment. He turned his head and, while looking over his shoulder to someone in the back room, bellowed "Tony! Tony!" Hearing these apparent shouts for help, a heavyset man in his early sixties walked rapidly toward the front of the store where we stood, concern on his face. At his approach, the young man dove into the back room.

Tony asked me what the problem was, and I repeated what I wanted. He too became visibly embarrassed, but, presumably noticing my heavy accent, he walked me quietly to the door and pointed across the square to a drugstore, complete with a wooden statue of an Indian in front with his tongue out. He politely said, "I think the people in the drugstore can help you better with what you want than we can." With that, he ushered the three of us out the door and closed it firmly behind us.

I was a little puzzled, by now remembering Luke telling me clearly and explicitly to go to the hardware store. "Well, maybe they do things differently in this country," I thought, bewildered. I walked with my two children to the drugstore across the square, entered the building and for the third time I repeated what I wanted, this time to the druggist. He smiled and cleared his throat a couple of times and led me to a shelf stocked with all kinds of feminine hygiene products and pointed to a few boxes.

Immediately I understood the great discomfort I had caused the two men in the hardware store, especially the friendly young clerk. I became deeply flushed myself, and then the comical side of it struck my funny bone and I started to laugh. I explained to the druggist what I really wanted, making him understand that I wanted to buy a showerhead, but that I had incorrectly used the French and Dutch word *douche* for shower instead. The druggist earnestly advised me to go across the square once again, pointing out the hardware store. Visualizing the look of the two men at the hardware store when the three of us reentered their store made me chuckle all the way back.

The young clerk looked up from his work and scurried away as soon as he recognized us, almost tripping over a chair in his haste to get away. Tony, the older man came out, and asked, "Did you find what you were looking for at the drugstore?" "No," I answered, "I need a showerhead" and spotted a rack against the store wall full of what I needed. Haltingly I explained that in Dutch the word for it was *douche,* which I had used incorrectly, whereupon we both burst into laughter. But the young clerk never even stuck his head out to see what all the commotion was about. I had scared him out of his wits forever—or for the rest of the day, anyway. I apologized to Tony and left the store with the object that had caused such embarrassing confusion tucked safely in a box in my hands, hoping never to return. When Luke asked me that evening if I could easily find a showerhead at the hardware store, I answered, "Don't even ask!"

LANGUAGE LEARNING

I should say a word here about the language. People in the United States are sometimes baffled by Europeans' fluency in speaking English. In most European countries, English is mandatory in secondary school. Dutch students can take French and German in addition to Dutch and English. Because the Netherlands are surrounded by France, Germany, and Belgium, with interconnected borders, these languages are a necessity to learn, even if only for simple conversation and communication with one's closest neighbors.

English is taught all over the world. And American movies, television, and song lyrics have helped familiarize all of Europe and its colonies with American expressions and terminology. Teenagers, especially, are connoisseurs of popular culture—but not always to good effect. Along with the good aspects of language, in their adolescent desire to be "cool," they pick up the ability to use English swear words and curses, which they use with as much facility as those of their own languages.

I studied English during my school years both in the colonies and in Holland, so when I arrived in the United States, I had a rudimentary ability to speak and understand the language. In addition, after we moved to California and my children were in school, I took a job with an electronics company, which paid the tuition for a two-year course at Diablo Junior College in Concord California. Other courses that I took to expand my skills, including medical terminology and religions of the world, also improved my English and widened my vocabulary.

BLOCK PARTY

August went by quickly, with so much for us to learn and absorb. For Luke's birthday at the end of the month, we planned a quiet and relaxing day for the four of us at a lake we had heard of from our neighbors. This plan, however, did not materialize. A day before Luke's birthday, the church group announced that it had organized a neighborhood party for Luke's first birthday in the USA. Our street would be blocked, and there would be a good all-American barbecue cookout, which was already being prepared for us. More than one hundred people were participating, and it would be on the enormous front lawn of a house across from where we lived. The next day, early in the morning, benches and picnic tables arrived and were placed under and near the huge shade trees. Our feelings of appreciative surprise were matched by genuine bafflement, as the implications behind the actions taking place became clear to us. Luke and I were assaulted by a mixture of emotions.

We were flattered by the efforts people were making on our behalf but also overwhelmed, grateful but worried about how to act and how to have conversations with so many people we did not know in our halting English.

The conversational obligations would rest mainly on my shoulders, since Luke was not much of a talker in any language, not even his own. The party started at 5 o'clock p.m. There was plenty of sunshine until 8 o'clock or later in the late summer. We were told not to bring anything but ourselves and just enjoy. During the afternoon we could see young men and women dressed in white shirts and black skirts and pants setting up huge barbecue grills, and big containers filled with food and ice chests full of drinks were put out on long, sturdy tables. They were from the catering service the church had engaged for the party.

At precisely 5 o'clock, someone we had never met before knocked at our door. He introduced himself as Jim Morrell, a church elder, and jovially escorted the four of us to the party across the street. Everybody had already gathered, probably in anticipation of meeting us. As soon as we arrived, everybody clapped their hands in welcome. The children circled Peetie and Lisa and led them away toward the drinks and snacks. Luke and I found drinks in our hands before we could even blink, and everyone welcomed us with genuine pleasure. We made our way slowly to the appetizer table, halting every few feet to greet someone who introduced himself or herself to us. Of course, after the first few introductions, we completely lost track of everyone's names. I glanced worriedly to where my children were sitting and found to my relief that they were enjoying themselves tremendously.

My concern went more to Peetie than to Lisa, because his temperament was more like his father and my father, always keeping themselves in the background, observing more than participating in games and conversation. Peetie was shy and easily embarrassed and therefore quickly hurt. Later in life he learned to camouflage this characteristic by joking or by applying biting sarcasm to his speech. Lisa was different, more matter of fact, although like most adults she too learned to cope with life's cruel ways. But at the moment the two were in the midst of a group of children who welcomed them. And Peetie, who liked to eat, had his mouth stuffed full with things he liked very much: in one hand, a celery stick stuffed with cream cheese, in the other, a can of soda. In a month and a half in America, Peetie and Lisa had picked up enough words and short sentences to play with the neighborhood children, but now that they were the center of attention, their faces showed some consternation as more lemonade and snacks were pressed into their hands by so many children who wanted to make them feel at home. But children are adaptable, and now and then throwing glances toward Luke and me, they both succumbed to the children's attentions and the ice was broken.

An hour went by and we held up without any embarrassing moments. We tried hard to understand the conversation and at the same time remember who was who. The catering staff went to and fro, and two cooks handled the grills beautifully, their forks turning the steaks to brown and juicy perfection and the marinated chicken breasts lined up right next to the steaks. For the children, there were hot dogs and hamburgers and grilled buns. The women servers took ears of boiled corn out of the big cooking container and laid them on a rack to dry so they wouldn't drip onto the plates. Huge bowls of tossed salad were uncovered and potato salad was put on the tables.

We, who had never seen a full-fledged barbecue, were astonished to see so much food—especially the beef. We were used to good food, but our dishes in Indonesia called for small pieces of meat, and in Holland a family of four would eat for several days from one of the servings that I received on my plate. Luke and I looked at our plates with concern. I worried about whether it would be impolite to take most of my portion home after the party. That was seldom done in Europe, as far as I knew. Luke and I did our best to eat it all, which was not a hardship, since everything was so new and so delicious. But at some point I could not eat another bite, especially of the meat. Hesitantly I asked for another plate and a piece of foil. I quickly wrapped my leftover food and Luke's, and before Luke could say anything I ran across the street into our house to put it into the refrigerator. I returned to my seat before anybody could have missed me—or so I thought. The Reverend Snyder came over to where I sat and whispered, "That was a lot of food they put on your plate, huh? I could barely finish mine, and I'm a big guy." He said it with a smile that put me at ease.

Now came the desserts: brownies and huge chocolate chip cookies for the kids and a delicious Indian pudding served with vanilla ice cream for the adults, a New England specialty. To this day, this dessert is one of my very favorites. I loved it from the start. Huge slices of watermelon, along with coffee and iced tea, topped off this great dinner. At the end, an enormous birthday cake materialized with 28 candles on it, and everybody sang Happy Birthday to Luke.

It was all a wonderful gesture of welcome, and it was also a gesture of acceptance into their midst. Luke and I have never forgotten those people and through the years have kept in regular contact with many of them. Even before the applause died down, I could see Peetie wolfing down a huge piece of chocolate brownie. Lisa, who carefully looked over the table with all the desserts, could not decide which one she wanted. Her eyes kept going to the birthday cake, and Julia Fargo, who was in charge of cutting the cake, saw this and cut a big piece for her, which she of course could not finish. Luke had to help her out. We, who lived through a war and lived for ten years in postwar Europe, will not waste a crumb of food. Our children were taught that daily all through their growing years.

People lingered a little longer over the coffee and tea, but finally, a few at a time, they started to leave. After thanking everyone profusely, we said our goodnights and crossed the street to go home. A little later Luke and I could see the catering service putting all the pots and cooking utensils into their vans parked on the side of the road, then tidy up the lawn. After a while we put the children to bed, who were tripping over their own feet from tiredness. Luke and I were tired too, but enormously grateful for the wonderful day and for all the wonderful people who made it possible—our sponsors, the Episcopal guild.

September soon made its entry, and Peetie prepared to enter the first grade. During the summer, I had a meeting with the principal of the nearby school, and Peetie was given tests to see if he was ready for the first grade. It was amazing to see how this principal, Mr. Williams, got through to Peetie, who spoke just a little English. After a couple of hours, Mr. Williams declared Peetie more than ready for first grade. The little boy and the experienced educator communicated quite well with each other. Mr. Williams was articulate and precise about what he wanted Peetie to do, and the little boy understood the tests perfectly. He started the first grade in the first week of September, when he was only five years old, since his birthday was at the end of October.

Lisa started kindergarten a week later. Peetie had had a hard time adjusting to kindergarten in Holland, perhaps because of his young age, so I was afraid the same would be the case with Lisa, but she could not wait to enter school. She did not want to stay behind her brother. After dropping her off, I waited anxiously in the school's long hallway for my daughter to come running out of the classroom, crying for me. Lisa did come out after a while, accompanied by a girl of her same age. The two went over to drink from one of the fountains in the hallway. Noticing me sitting on one of the benches along the wall, she came to a dead stop and asked, "Why are you still here, Mom? I thought you had gone home already." Well, what a letdown, I thought wryly. I picked up my purse and trotted down the long school hall with mixed emotions. I was of course glad that Lisa had adjusted so easily yet was somewhat disappointed that she did not need me as I had expected. The school bus brought them both back to me at different times that day. Lisa came home at 11:30 and Peetie followed an hour later. Both had many enthusiastic stories to tell.

Slowly we adults acclimated and settled into our new country. Our children did this much faster, being completely at ease with the tremendous changes. The flexibility of children is indeed remarkable. And so September came and went. The many trees lining the streets of our neighborhood started to turn beautiful colors, from light yellow to bright orange and maroon red. It was a gorgeous sight.

On one side of our house, our neighbors were a plumber, Ray, his wife, Annie, and their six children. Ray and Annie were extremely hospitable and kind. Ray would drive us around town for hours, showing us the sights. His wife made all kinds of dishes for us to try and patiently taught me how to prepare them. Ray's family had owned their property long before more well-to-do people started to buy up the land in the neighborhood and build their houses. Ray and his family stayed, keeping their small house as neat as they were able, with their growing brood. Ray even added on a couple of bedrooms to accommodate his family. Often I would send over a chicken or some of the eggs or cheese that we got on a regular basis from our sponsors. Not being used to so much food, we shared it with the neighbors.

Regularly for months we found near our front door a basket filled with food—fresh eggs, fresh vegetables, chicken, beef, or a ham, butter, sugar, coffee, tea—you name it. Someone, whom we never saw, would put a basket near the door on the front porch early in the morning, even before we were up. This happened like a ritual once a week, but never on the same day. We had asked our sponsors about it, of course, but they would just smile and said, "Oh, people take turns." I also told them that it was way too much, whereupon they answered, "We don't want you to get hungry." So I gave up arguing about it and simply shared the food with my neighbors.

One morning in early October, a Mercedes stopped in front of our house and three people from the church guild got out. They had come to visit, which happened often, to see how we were getting along and to exchange thoughts and ideas with me. I knew them from several church meetings and had talked to them often. The husbands of two of the ladies visiting us were partners in a well-to-do real estate firm in Boston, and the other one owned a beautiful, very large art gallery stocked with gorgeous pieces. They took me for a visit to the gallery once, and I was flabbergasted by the prices. These people lived in enormous houses on the north side of Hamilton, with acres of land surrounding their homes. Millie McDuffey was originally from California, and so was Carol Miles. They were the two ladies whose husbands were in real estate. Evelyn Barton was born and raised in the Boston area. Her husband's father had traveled all over the world to gather beautiful antiques and gorgeous paintings and vases from the China and the Far East. When visiting with these women, I sometimes felt somewhat inadequate to have them in my home, knowing their background and the luxury that surrounded them. But I would remind myself of my own upbringing, which would immediately make me square my shoulders and become more at ease with them. I might not have the money any more, but I surely had innate style and class of my own, and with these thoughts my self-confidence would always return.

We talked about Peetie and Lisa, how well they both were doing in school, and also about Luke and his work and his recent raise. They complimented me on how well I had decorated the house with the few things I had. I served them tea and cookies that my sweet neighbors had brought me just the day before. The ladies carried more of the conversation, since my vocabulary was still quite limited at this time.

Suddenly, the conversation shifted. Artfully cloaked in interest for our neighbors' well-being, the ladies asked me carefully how well we got along with Ray and Annie and if our children played with their children very much. They also asked if Luke and I liked them a lot. In turn I told them how helpful Ray and Annie had been from the first day we moved in, and how well our families got along. I noticed the look of concern each gave the other. All three ladies agreed, with smiles on their faces, on how fortunate this was for us. Then Evelyn Barton said carefully, "Yes, they are very nice people, and we are thankful for all the help they have given you, but just be nice and pleasant to them. You don't have to be friends. They actually do not belong in this neighborhood," she added, apparently oblivious that Ray's parents had lived here long before it had become such a plush area. "After all, Ray is just a plumber, you know," she concluded. "We brought you here to come up in the world," Carol explained.

I could only look at them as if I had swallowed my tongue. My vocabulary was not developed enough to spring to our neighbor's defense. Oh, the snobs, I thought. What terrible snobs! I could not believe my ears and was reeling from the meaning of their words, which were slow to penetrate my brain. Our minister should see them now, these church-going and supposedly God-fearing people, I thought. Ray and Annie were the sweetest and kindest people and shared with us almost everything they had. It was very clear to me that no one was going to choose our friends for us.

That evening, after telling Luke about the morning's visit with the three ladies, we discussed moving away from Hamilton to Ipswich, a neighboring town, to be more on our own. We could afford to be more independent now, since just two days earlier I had been hired as a clerk in the front office of a hospital in Ipswich. I had forgotten to mention this to our sponsors and now immediately started to plan how to communicate the news to them without hurting their feelings. I knew they would object to the idea of our moving away, thinking us not ready financially to be on our own. But Ipswich was only ten minutes away from Hamilton and Wenham, where all our sponsors lived, so it shouldn't be a problem, Luke and I reasoned.

So far, it was our sponsors who paid the rent on the big house in Hamilton, for which we were extremely grateful, but it was time for us to move on and be on our own. Actually it might have been a little sooner than we had anticipated, but we were ready. Our sponsors, at least some of them, had started to rule our lives a little more than we were comfortable with. If they felt they could dictate with whom we could associate and with whom we could not, this might be just the beginning, we thought with concern. We did realize that everything they did was done with the best of intentions and for the our well-being. By the same token, we also realized we were a pet project, so to speak, of a bunch of very rich people, and they were beginning to expect us to live by their rules. So we felt we had to show them our independence and be on our own.

The next day Luke and I and the children drove to Ipswich, a town a bit bigger than Hamilton, still with a small town atmosphere. It took us only minutes to get there. The streets and houses were not as impressive as the ones in Hamilton and Wenham, but it seemed warmer and a whole lot friendlier. We noticed a white church on top of a hill just before the beginning of the town square, where there was a supermarket and a bank, and next to it an old-fashioned soda fountain with the high stools in front of a red counter—just the type I'd often seen in American movies in Indonesia and Holland. We also drove by the hospital where I was going to start work in another week. We went through streets and housing areas and found a crisp-looking white painted duplex building, with a For Rent sign in front. A large man stood on a ladder painting the trim dark green. Luke stopped the car and got out to talk to the man, who immediately climbed down the ladder. After a while he walked up to our car with Luke beside him, after putting his brush on the plastic sheet he had laid down on the grassy lawn.

I opened the window and he stuck out a large hand to me, after wiping his hands on a towel hanging from his belt. His name was Tom Brielle, a

French Canadian who had married a American girl some 30 years earlier and settled in Ipswich near his bride's parents. He was the owner of the duplex and suggested for us to see the place. He also told us about his two sons and said that his eldest lived in the big house next door with his wife and six children. He worked for the police department so we should feel safe with him living next to us. I laughed and said that we haven't even looked at his place yet. "Well come on in, what are we waiting for," he exclaimed. The side of the duplex that was for rent had three floors, with a big kitchen and a living room and a half bath on the first floor, two big bedrooms and a large bathroom on the second, and a loft bedroom on the third. It was big enough for the four of us, and it had a nice big basement with a washer and dryer and an old piano in it. Luke played a melody on it with just one hand as he passed by. The sound was not very good, because the piano needed tuning badly. The house looked very clean and fresh, and the price was within our budget. If we wanted to rent it we could give him some money to hold it, and then we could move in a week later. It sounded good, and so we agreed.

We were especially pleased after Tom showed the children the little pond in back of the house, which would freeze over every winter and children and adults from the neighborhood would skate on it. He also pointed out an old estate across the street, a huge Victorian house set on a hill with six acres surrounding it, standing white and lonely and empty. It belonged to an old New England family; the owners had died and the house was under the care of a man who lived in a small house set back on the property. There was a well behind the house and, to avoid accidents of children falling into it, the caretaker had spread the rumor that the grounds and the house were haunted. At least I'm pretty sure that that was the reason. Signs were put everywhere, "Do Not Enter, Private Property" but of course children pay no attention to such warnings. They were, however, in awe of the rumor.

We could move in on the first of November, Tom Brielle said, after he heard us mention our Reverend's name, whom he knew very well and whom we had used for reference. It was all so easy back in those days in small towns where everyone knew one another. Happily we said goodbye and congratulated ourselves on finding a house in a nice neighborhood that we could afford.

As I predicted, our sponsors reacted with surprise and some hurt. But some, especially our Reverend, could understand our need to be on our own. Ray and Annie were heartbroken and promised to visit us when they could, our new home being only ten minutes away.

NEW CELEBRATIONS

Before we moved and just before Halloween, we celebrated Peetie's sixth birthday, his first in the USA. Our sponsors sent over a beautifully decorated chocolate cake with "Happy Birthday Peetie" written on it and six candles. We invited ten boys and girls to his party and everyone came. The usual party hats and noisemakers had also been brought over by one of our sponsors, along with ice cream, all sorts of snacks that children favor, plus several types of fruity drinks. Even the games were organized by the church guild ladies, although many were familiar to us.

The party was a great success, and Peetie had never in his life seen so many presents all at one time. He stood there dumbfounded, then decided to play tag with his friends instead of opening the presents. We let him do this for a while and let him open the presents a little later. Peetie was, as you might imagine, ecstatic.

We never celebrated Halloween in Holland, although I think that there is a day resembling the event on the same date, called Saint Maarten's Day, but I'm not sure. It was a negative sort of celebration, and teenagers especially do all kinds of nasty things, like hanging dead cats or rats on somebody's front door or leaving bags full of garbage at the doorstep. However, do not take my word for it; I'm not entirely sure. Halloween was brand new for Peetie and Lisa to experience.

For their first Halloween celebration, they were given costumes by our sponsors. Peetie wore a lion's suit and Lisa was a pussy cat. Both were equipped with Halloween lanterns and pillowcases for the "loot" they collected. The outfits were sturdy and thick, for which we were thankful, since the temperatures in late October dipped down quite a bit. All the children in the neighborhood stayed in a group, escorted by three adults. Trick or treating was great fun for Peetie and Lisa. When they returned, they emptied their bags on the floor to show us what they had gathered. There were lots of candies but also fruits, like apples, pears, and oranges, cookies in wrappers, and lots of nickles, dimes, and quarters.

Almost before we realized it, it was time for people to ready themselves for Thanksgiving. This quintessentially American celebration was totally unknown to us immigrants from Europe and elsewhere, where celebrations were generally low key. In Holland, people tended to be tight-fisted with their money, and celebrating of course means spending extra cash. A reputation for penny-pinching is not limited to the Scottish! I found that people in the Netherlands turn their dime over a thousand times before spending it. This was to me a most irritating habit, and I try to avoid people with such attitudes. They make me nervous and uptight and spoil the fun.

A family was chosen by the church guild to introduce us to the customs of Thanksgiving and to entertain the four of us in their home on that special day. Betty and Frank McCoy and their two teenage sons, Randy and Brian, 17 and 15, were lovely people. Their house was large and sprawling, with tennis and basketball courts and a swimming pool on their five acres, much like the other members of the church guild. Luke, the children, and I were their only guests that Thanksgiving, since they wanted to give us their undivided attention.

The meal they served was the traditional turkey with all the trimmings, and, so as not to confuse us, they kept it simple. These people were sweet and considerate, soft-spoken and calm. They urged us without any pressure to try cranberry sauce and other dishes that were foreign to us and so gently introduced us to their culture. Like the other members of the guild, they were extremely well off, but quite down to earth in their ways, which reminded me very much of my grandparents, and allowed me to relax.

Their soft and cultured speaking voices were quite different from the general shrill and somewhat nasal New England manner of speech. They taught us, in a unpatronizing way, how to make certain dishes, and most of all they introduced us to the meaning of Thanksgiving and its origin. The evening flew by, and we felt almost sorry to leave the peaceable atmosphere. These people became one of our favorite families in the six and a half years of our life in Massachussetts. We stayed in contact with them for years, even after we moved to California. As they escorted us to our car and we said our goodbyes, Betty whispered to me an invitation to come for Christmas dinner, which we later shyly but gratefully accepted.

Again I find myself automatically making the comparison between these people and the people in the Netherlands. What an enormous difference in our welcome. In Holland I had always felt out of place in an already overpopulated country. Although we were citizens with a great deal of Dutch blood pumping through our veins, we were still "those colonials from the Dutch East Indies." It was these colonies, by the way, which had much to do with making the Netherlands one of the richest countries in the world. And I, coming from a proud family whose standards of integrity and rectitude were stringently taught, suffered enormously from the cold shoulder we got in Holland, especially from the lower middle class with whom we came in contact.

In all the years I have been in America, I have never returned to Holland. Perhaps I may relent and visit the Netherlands briefly, just to show my grandchildren a part of their heritage, which I can neither renunciate nor deprive them of.

INDEPENDENCE

We moved into our duplex apartment on December 1, and I started to work at the hospital not long thereafter. Peetie and Lisa were registered in their new schools in Ipswich, and Elana Brielle, our landlord's daughter-in-law, babysat for them while I was at work, which was three days a week from 8 to 5 o'clock. Elana charged me the minimum and many times even refused to accept payment. She used to say time and time again, "When you already take care of six kids, two more are not going to matter much." Of course I did not agree. The paycheck I brought home was not a large, but it helped quite a bit with buying groceries.

We were very happy to be on our own. It was not ungratefulness that we felt toward our sponsors—not at all. However, we had begun to feel uncomfortable about being fed, clothed, and given a big house rent free, already for three months. We were extremely grateful for such a fortunate start, but it was time to be on our own.

The members of the church guild were reluctant to let us go, but slowly they acceded to our wishes. They rented a moving truck and filled it with four single beds and a queen-sized one, a dinette set with four chairs, a long sofa, and an upholstered easy chair. They even had a refrigerator for us loaded into the truck with an old washer and dryer set. Everything was preowned, of course, and nothing matched, but it was all in very good condition and satisfied our basic needs. We were excited and pleased with the gift of furniture and appliances, especially since we had been wracking our brains, trying to figure out how to afford some furniture ourselves.

Our sponsors kept saying, "Don't buy anything, we'll see what we can come up with." The beds especially would come in handy, since we were expecting my parents to arrive. Frank and Betty McCoy had promised to sponsor them, and they'd already started the procedure of filling out forms. I was estatic at the prospect. There was a chance that my parents would be with us the next year in July, exactly a year after we had arrived in the USA.

I of course kept in regular contact with both my parents and had already discussed the possibility of emigration with them if they wished to come. I had set the wheels in motion, and my mother's constant prodding kept them turning. My father was more reserved and, although he wanted to be with us as much as Mom did, he thought that one huge uprooting in a lifetime was as much as he could handle. He thought it was a risk to emigrate to a foreign country at their age, and he did not wished to burden us.

There were pluses and minuses for an older couple to emigrate. As it turned out, when they arrived, they had a higher income than we did in the beginning. They had their Dutch pension, which they could rely on, as well as their A.O.W., a kind of social security, later on. Their coming to America was no risk to the sponsor, but a great help to us in our first years of building up for the future. On the down side, they spoke very little English, which was a handicap, and they had to leave behind relatives and friends, which was very hard at their age. My mother was in her sixties, and my father was sixty years old. But Mom could not live without Luke and me and her grandchildren. After all, I was their only child.

We urged them to take English lessons as soon as they could and make serious efforts to learn the language. It would be to their own benefit to be able to speak well, if they chose to make this country their home. As we learned years later, many of our Dutch-Indonesian people clung together, some insisting on conversing in their own language as much as possible. Maybe immigrants from other countries do the same thing. It is therefore not surprising that their English speech and vocabulary are inadequate, even after living in the United States for decades.

Some of my people may have considered it an insult or disloyalty to their heritage to stop speaking their native language. Some may even have perceived a streak of hautiness in those who developed a facility for expressing themselves in English. Such thinking is wrong, in my opinion, an attitude to which I've never given the slightest credence and have always ingnored. Needlessly to say, such an attitude does not improve a person's English and usually results in a very limited way of speaking, clumsily uttered and primitively expressed, even after a lifetime of living in one's chosen country.

My parents studied hard in the beginning, but their efforts and good intentions evaporated once they had arrived in America and had us to rely on. As a result, they were never able to get beyond the most basic phrases in their English and were therefore limited in their ability to express themselves.

As mentioned before, our apartment had three floors. The top one had an attic bedroom, quite comfortable and nicely decorated, with the roof sloping down on both sides. It had cottage-type windows with colorful window coverings. The second floor had two bedrooms and a bath, and the bottom floor a living room, a large eat-in kitchen, and another bath. There was a door and steps leading downstairs to the basement. Our half of the basement still had the old piano in it, still out of tune, but later my father and sometimes Luke got some melodies out of it. The washer and dryer stood in one corner, as did an old sofa with its springs protruding from the seat. The apartment was just right for us, especially with the pending arrival of my parents the following year. The furniture was sufficient for now. Our sponsors had also given us sheets, pillowcases, blankets, and towels. As I said, some of those blankets I still have, after all these years.

They also gave us pots and pans, silverware, plates and glasses, and the like, some of which we kept for many years.

HOLIDAY TIME

Ten days before Christmas, a truck stopped in front of our house and the driver got out to haul a Christmas tree to our front door. It was so big that it needed some heavy trimming all around and on the top just to get through the doorway. Stephanie Bradley, one of our sponsors, had followed in her shiny black Mercedes and stood by to see that he did everything right. The driver left after installing the tree near the window, just where I wanted it to be. She asked me then to follow her to her car, which was stuffed with all sorts of beautifully wrapped packages, decorated in the most elegant way. The passenger seat was loaded high with presents, as was the back seat and the car floor.

The two of us went back and forth from the car to the house, laughing and slipping on some icy spots on the footpath. When everything was put inside the house, I asked her to sit down for a cup of coffee. "Oh no," the lady said, "We are not through just yet. There is more in my trunk." And so we went back again to her car.

I was astonished and did not know what to say. I had never in my life seen so many gifts. Christmas was not celebrated like this in either of the countries I grew up in. As I have described in earlier chapters, the gifts we gave each other were modest. Even with Saint Nicolas on December 5, a celebration actually for the children, the gifts were usually small and few. This shower of presents was so bountiful that the thought crossed my mind that somehow we would have to explain the difference to the children, for this bounty could not continue when the time arrived for us to live without our sponsors nearby us. But for the moment I pushed the thought aside and indulged myself in full admiration of the beautiful tree, the decorations, which came in separate packages, and the gorgeously wrapped presents, which were piled in stacks all over the living room floor. They were all given from the goodness of one family's heart, rich or not. I thanked her profusely for everything she and her family had done. "This is from all of us," she announced happily, after which she hugged me affectionately and hurried off to attend one of the many social functions she regularly gave. She waved as she left, leaving behind the soft and pretty scent of the perfume she wore.

Later we learned that her husband, Mark Bradley, was one of the most prominent lawyers in Boston at the time and the only son of an extremely wealthy old New England family. Stephanie, his wife, was born and raised in Texas and the oldest of two daughters of an oil baron and his chic Italian wife. The following spring, while visiting the Bradley family in their great mansion, we got a glimpse of how immensely wealthy these people actually were. You could smell the old money, so to speak, and it was literally hanging on the walls.

By the time Peetie and Lisa came home from school, I had the tree half decorated and there were a few wrapped presents in the living room. The rest I had put in the basement and locked the door carefully. I planned to add them later to the ones in the living room, everything arranged under the tree after it was decorated. The children became wild with excitement. All this was overwhelming, both for me and for them, and I had the hardest time calming them down. Eventually they sat on the carpet and gaped at the tree and the packages, watching me finish decorating the tree.

On Christmas Eve, we went to the McCoys for dinner and spent a wonderful evening with our favorite sponsor family. We had modest presents for everyone, which they received with the greatest joy. Peetie was given a whole train set, complete with a station house. Lisa got a small bed with a doll in it and an entire set of doll clothes. After dinner the children played quietly in one of the nearby rooms, where the McCoy boys kept them occupied by setting up Peetie's train set. Even Lisa found it interesting and followed the boys' every move while carrying her new baby doll around.

In beautifully wrapped boxes Luke and I received cashmere sweaters, and for Luke a matching silk shirt and tie. Mine was black with a matching tank top, as well as a strand of pearls and earrings that were a perfect complement. We were overjoyed but also a little dazed by all the gifts and attention we received. Silently I was thinking of all the other presents we still had to open the next morning, which the Bradley family had brought to us. I seriously considered keeping a few hidden until next Christmas, because there were so many. The thought also crossed my mind to share some of them with Ray and Annie's children. Stephanie could not possibly remember everything that she had given us. Yes, perhaps just a few, I thought happily.

In the meantime, dinner was served and Rosie, the McCoys' cook, brought in the turkey and a deliciously aromatic ham. There were green beans, small baby carrots, a dish with sweet yams, rings of gelatin salads, and of course the unforgettable cranberry. Wine was served with the meal and, for the children, glasses of fruit juice and water. Afterward the dessert was a choice of several pies, served with coffee or cognac, for those who wished it. The festive evening was beautifully put together and delightfully spent. The McCoys had the gift of creating a relaxing holiday atmosphere. From the start, we loved them dearly—they were like family away from home.

As we were about to leave, Frank announced that the immigration officials had given their approval for the McCoys to sponsor my parents. They had received the official notice three days before and had deliberately waited to tell us, wanting it to be another Christmas present. Tears of joy sprang into my eyes, and I thanked them both happily. I missed my parents and worried about them constantly. What wonderful people the McCoys were, always so considerate and loving. That Christmas Eve spent in their company was a very special one for us. I fashion our holiday celebrations in

America somewhat after that first Christmas celebration with them, even after all these years—only not as lavishly done, of course.

ELEGANCE OUTSIDE HAMILTON

Winter passed into spring. In early May, we received an invitation by telephone to have lunch with Mark and Stephanie Baily at their home. We knew vaguely the area where they lived, although we'd never been there. Stephanie told us not to worry about the children. "Just bring them with you," she urged. "My five-year-old grandson Bobby is spending some time with us while his parents are in England on business. And Bobby has his own nursemaid with him and has brought plenty of toys to keep an entire group of children occupied for hours on end," she added cheerfully. Looking at her, it was hard to believe her a grandmother and Mark a grandfather. Both looked vibrantly young and very fit and trim, and I told them so. "We have two grandchildren," Stephanie explained with pleasure. "Bobby is our son Jack's boy, and little Megan, who is only two, is Mia's, our daughter's, little angel. Mia and her family live in New York, and next month we will have little Megan for a while. We'll show her to you when she is here," she promised with a smile. "By the way," she added, "lunch is at one o'clock, but please come around noon, all right?" I thanked her for the invitation and said we were looking forward to it very much. "Good" she answered, "We'll have a great time," and hung up the phone.

On the appointed Saturday, Luke and I and the children drove to the Baileys, whose estate was located a little outside Hamilton. Luke followed the directions easily and before long we arrived at the entrance gate of a long and winding driveway. "Sunny Meadows" we read on a scrolled cast iron sign, and then "The Baileys" in small letters underneath. Two giant spruces stood like sentinels next to the two stone columns on which the sign was fastened, reminding me strongly of the entrance to my family's plantation, except that the scenery and the setting had been tropical. Instead of spruces, there had been palm and coconut trees.

The gate opened automatically before us, and we drove on to see a truly magnificent white colonial house at the end of the driveway in the distance, with four big pillars and a high front porch. The grounds spread out around the mansion for more than a mile. I saw men trimming the bushes and others riding lawnmowers. In the distance behind the house, trees formed a solid wall of green against the blue horizon.

Luke drove to the imposing front steps and, as from nowhere, a man appeared to open the car doors for us with a warm greeting and a big smile. After we got out, Luke parked the car a little way down the drive. We rang the door chime, and a maid in a dark blue uniform and a white apron opened the huge double glass and lead doors. "Right this way, please," she said pleasantly, waiting while we took off our light spring jackets and coats. Standing in the huge foyer, we saw two curving stairways with dark, shiny mahogany balustrades leading to a big upstairs landing and eventually to the other rooms of the immense house.

Stephanie, hearing our voices, came down one of the staircases. She greeted us warmly, hugging everyone, genuinely happy to see us again. In one glance I noticed the two big oil paintings hanging on the foyer wall. I recognized them as the work of the English artist, J.M.W. Turner. There was a meadow scene and another landscape with the vibrant colors and rich textures that could only be a Turner. The floor was of Italian marble, and there were enormous, elegant vases in the corners. In the room we next entered, one of many sitting rooms in the mansion, were more vases, some of Oriental design and expensive looking. They were set on dark wooden marble-topped tables, and here and there was a statue nestled among vibrant green plants.

Stephanie ushered us to a group of sofas, arranged near a huge hearth in which a small fire burned to fight off the chill of spring, asking us to sit down. I noticed how elegant she looked in her black pinstriped suit, how chic with her dark hair in a French twist, adorned with a brilliantly made comb. The suit she wore managed to look both businesslike and utterly feminine. Her face was not beautiful in the usual sense of pretty, but more classical and arresting. It was a golden olive triangle, dominated by large dark brown eyes with prominent cheekbones. Her face had a sculptured look.

As we sat on sofas cozily arranged around low tables, a small boy of Peetie's age rushed into the room, a young woman immediately behind him. "It's quite all right, Peggie," Stephanie exclaimed, noticing the flushed and worried look on the nursemaid's face. She continued, "He can say hello to everyone, and then perhaps you can take the children for a glass of lemonade, and then Bobby can show them the ponies." After giving his grandmother a big hug, Bobby smiled and waved to us while leading Peetie and Lisa out of the room.

Stephanie made sure we were comfortably seated and busied herself with the wine she had offered us. The maid brought in a platter of appetizers. In the meantime I looked around and saw that the room had a singular grandeur, with high ceilings decorated with elaborate plasterwork and tall leaden windows flanking the large carved fireplace of beautiful bleached oak. Yet for all its imposing detail, Stephanie had introduced a soft charm and comfort plus a subtle elegance, which must have taken lots of time, superb taste, and a vast amount of money to create. The priceless paintings, sculptures, and vases were in perfect harmony with the Georgian antiques, which she had collected with loving care. The Savonnerie carpet brought a delicate beauty to the room, and in the Chippendale cabinet I could see delicate figurines that added to the graciousness of the room. This afternoon especially, the spring-like mood of the setting, created by the soft and light color scheme and the brightly patterned chintz of the sofas, was enhanced by glass bowls filled with tulips, hyacinths, and daffodils spilling their yellows, reds, and pinks and lightening the darkly gleaming wooden surfaces of the tables. Their fragrance wafted on the air. I spied another Turner painting, which hung above an impressive mantelpiece. Another landscape, it was a superb example of the artist's poetic interpretation of rural and pastoral scenes.

My survey was interrupted by Mark's entrance, who came in greeting us warmly. He had met the children at the pony stalls, he told us, and had put each child on a pony and Bobby, whose riding skills were already quite developed, on a sweetly tempered mare. In a flash I remembered myself on my own pony so many years ago, with my cousin Eric at my side galloping across my grandfather's lands. I forced my attention back to Mark, who described the children making the rounds in a big circle around the stalls, each with a stable boy walking next to each pony.

At 6'2", well built and trim of figure with long legs, Mark Arthur Bailey cut quite a figure. He was always fashionable, never anything but faultlessly dressed, right down to his handmade shoes. Like his grandfather before him, he had a penchant for elegant clothes and for wearing them with dash. He was fair with light brown hair, a handsome face, full strong lips, and gray-blue eyes. Born and bred a gentleman, he had a natural self-confidence and handled himself with aplomb in any situation. He had a quiet charm and a ready smile.

This same man in the courtroom could turn to steel, it was said, and those friendly gray-blue eyes could be piercingly direct, cutting right through the soul of the unfortunate one sitting on the witness stand. He was nicknamed The Bulldog by his peers and officers of the law. Once he had chosen to defend someone, he bit into the case with great determination to prove his client innocent. However, his determination applied only when he believed it himself. His fees were very high, but he seldom lost a case. He was well known for his cunning ways and therefore much feared by his opponents. I looked at him closely and could see only a warm and friendly man giving his guests his utmost attention.

Lunch was another new experience. It was served at precisely one o'clock p.m., as Stephanie had annouced it would, in one of the smaller dining rooms in the huge house. Reflecting Stephanie's heritage, the meal was entirely Italian cuisine. Maria, Stephanie's Italian cook, had prepared the delicious meal, smartly and beautifully put together. For the children she baked a bubbly lasagna, dripping with cheese, knowing that the other dishes might be too sophisticated for their simple tastes. After seating us, Stephanie and Mark sat down, and Peggy took the meals for the children upstairs into the nursery. We could hear their squeals of laughter and pleasure. "Maria is a real jewel," Stephanie confided. "She cookes and prepares dishes with infinite care and decorates the plates beautifully as well." Stephanie told us how Mark made it possible to bring Maria and her sister Gina, as well as both their husbands, into this country legally about ten years earlier. Their husbands worked as gardeners; neither couple had children. Gina and her husband Giorgio went to work for Stephanie's parents in Texas, and Maria and Antonio came to work for the Baileys in Hamilton.

The lunch started with a delicious Portobello salad with roasted red and yellow peppers. It was followed by a roast chicken stuffed with polenta and another delicate-looking dish of eggplant and parsley, cheese, and marjoram. The dessert was a compote of pears steeped in red wine, flavored with cloves, topped with a creamy sauce, and sprinkled with walnuts. For the children there was apple bread pudding, which they apparently loved, since their demands for seconds were clearly heard downstairs where we sat. Maria had outdone herself.

The afternoon went by quickly and, after coffee and a long walk through the large Bailey estate and the beautiful manicured grounds, we said our thanks and goodbyes, but not before we promised to come back sometime for another meal. In spite of their busy lifestyle, Stephanie and Mark had us over many times in our years in New England. We stayed in contact with them and the McCoys for many years after moving to California, until Stephanie's death from cancer in 1980, when she was 73.

FELLOW EMIGRÉS

In the meantime, we got in contact with some of the Dutch-Indonesians in the Boston area. Around that time, a Dutch-Indonesian club came into existence. We all joined, hungry as we were for contact with our own people, with whom we had so much common history and culture. But in this, it seems, we made a serious mistake. In almost any group, one encounters people from all stations and all walks of life. Nevertheless, one's upbringing and social behavior, which influence one's thoughts and actions, are fixed and potent characteristics. The fact of being all thrown together in a strange and faraway country does not erase this reality. A common history does not create long-lasting friendships, just because two people came from the same country. Acquaintances, yes—but friendship is something very dear and precious and reserved for a very special few.

We had a handful of wonderful Dutch-Indonesian friends, and the rest of the group became people that we "just know." From this small group of Dutch-Indonesians emerged a couple who proclaimed themselves its leaders. They surrounded themselves with followers and seemed to continuously run a popularity contest. They wanted to be on top of things and found it highly important to be the herald of the latest news. It did not seem to matter whether it was bad or happy tidings, as long as they were the ones who knew about it first. The pettiness and superficiality of these people made me incredibly tired and I ignored them as much as I could.

There was also a young woman of about my age, blessed with a pretty face but not much else. She had a husband and a child, a beautiful little boy. She seemed to be constantly aware of her face and much less aware of her husband and child. She used her prettiness to manipulate people, mostly the dimwitted who were not aware of her self-centeredness and only saw the pretty face. She could not pass a mirror without admiring herself. She too was continuously running a popularity contest, the point of which was easily perceived. Her choice of female friends seemed to confirm her selfish, shallow, and insecure character: only the plain, unimaginative, and easily impressed became her friends. She was a restless soul, and a very unhappy one. Years later I heard that her marriage had fallen apart and that she had died alone. She had taken her own life with a bottle of sleeping pills when she was only 42.

By the end of June 1961, our church guild was sponsoring another young family. Rob Berings was Dutch-Indonesian and his wife Emily was English. They had a adorable little two-year-old girl, a tiny doll with dark brown hair and blue-grey eyes. Emily got pregnant again shortly after they settled in the United States, yet she was upset at the thought that her baby would be born on American soil, an attitude that both hurt and irritated the church members, with good reason. One wonders why they were here if such feelings prevailed. Later we heard that it was primarily Rob's desire to emigrate and not Emily's. She had given in reluctantly since he wanted it so badly. This couple returned to England a short six months after they arrived in the United States. Rob returned to his job at Shell Oil, where he had met Emily some years before they were married.

In the meantime, in July, my parents arrived in America, to my great joy. We were thrilled and thanked the McCoys from the bottom of our hearts, since they were the ones who made it all possible. The two families, the McCoys and the Baileys, became our closest friends, our stabilizers, and our safe haven. We felt comfortable and protected with them in those first years in our new environment. Yes, these two families who lived in great prosperity were proud, dignified, and very powerful, but they also were warm, sweet, and caring to us.

The McCoys and the Baileys reminded me of my grandparents. Self-assured, capable, and intelligent in their dealings with others. Always cool and collected and in control in any circumstance, but also kind and loving, with infinite social grace. Many a time, I've heard unkind remarks uttered against wealthy people, usually by those who were not as privileged financially. People are sometimes hateful in their resentment. However, my experiences have taught me otherwise. I've often wondered, when I hear such envious utterances, what leads people to these bitter conclusions. Perhaps they experienced prejudice, snobbery, or aloofness and so formed their unkind opinions. Or maybe it was just plain envy. I don't know, and in any case generalization is meaningless.

A HOME OF OUR OWN

In the summer of 1962, we were able to purchase our first house. It was modest: three bedrooms, a large open living room with a beautiful view through a large bay window, a dining area, a kitchen, and one bath. It was not fully insulated when we bought it, since it had been used as a summerhouse by the former owners. Luke, the children, and I were elated with the little house. Many friends helped winterize it, including our former neighbor Ray and a friend, and Luke labored at it every spare moment he had. It took two full months, and when it was done it sparkled with a new coat of white paint plus light blue trim. It was finished just in time for winter, which was fortunate. We were snug in our little home, overlooking the marshlands of Ipswich.

During these years in New England, when the children were small, they developed a love for the outdoors and nature as a whole. Especially

Peetie, who learned to swim quite well, not in a swimming pool but in one of the many small, picturesque lakes dotting the area, one in particular with a huge boulder jutting out into the water as a diving board. He often wandered with his friends through the woods. The lakes, the rivers, the beauty of the coastline all had his attention, although it was in the forests that he felt most comfortable. Later, as a teenager in California, while wandering through the mountains, fishing in lakes and streams, he would suddenly stop and make a quick, roughly done sketch in a notepad with a piece of charcoal he always carried with him, to catch a fleeting image of the wildlife he encountered.

In Ipswich, when Peetie was nine or ten years old, he and his companions would go to the marshes and dig for clams. Luke and I and sometimes my parents, who rented a small cottage at the beginning of our street, rejoiced to see them returning home with buckets full of clams, which I scrubbed and then steamed. We all loved to sit around the table, eating clams dipped in a buttery, garlicky sauce.

It always was a challenge for me to wash Peetie's clothes and tidy up his room. Foul odors would rise from the hamper into which he had tossed his jeans, usually forgetting to empty his pockets first. I never stuck my hand in his pockets without checking carefully, warily, from the outside first. Once I forgot and a slimy creature curled around my finger inside a pocket. Another time, while tidying Peetie's room, a couple of horseshoe crabs crawled over my feet—luckily they were slippered.

When Peetie was ten, he had an accident that would affect the rest of his life. He loved baseball and football and played both. In baseball he became an admirable little pitcher, whom the coaches often praised for his swift and accurate throw. One day, at one of his practices, he stood carelessly behind the coach who was demonstrating how to handle the bat correctly. As he swung out, Peetie was in the way and got the bat with full force against the side of his head, losing consciousness for a few seconds.

The coach, deeply concerned, brought Peetie home immediately and called the doctor right away from our house.

At this time, there were still physicians who made house calls. The doctor came promptly and examined Peetie carefully. The bump on the side of Peetie's head was as large as a woman's fist. The doctor advised me to keep Peetie calm and in bed for the time being. "But don't let him fall asleep," he warned, cautioning me to watch for convulsions that might occur. "And keep an ice pack on the bump as long as possible," he said as he was leaving. We followed his advice. In the morning Peetie seemed fine, although he had slept fitfully. The ugly bump on the side of his head was gone, becoming an ugly black and blue discoloration instead. I kept him home from school for a day just to make sure. This was very much against Peetie's wishes, who for some reason felt proud of the incident and wanted to show off his markings, I think. The bruise soon healed, and we all forgot about the accident.

A NEW LIFE

The busy years passed swiftly, and, at the beginning of Febuary 1965, I knew that I was pregnant with our third child. Surprise, surprise—after almost ten years, our family would again have a baby in its midst. Lisa was ecstatic and wished for a baby sister. Peetie did not say much but just accepted the news in his usual quiet way.

There was a problem to be solved, however. Our house had only three bedrooms. With a baby on the way, Peetie and Lisa would have to share one for the time being. Both were quite put out about this decision, not wanting to give up their privacy. They reluctantly gave in when Luke promised to build a fourth bedroom as soon as the baby was born. This was really the only solution, since the bedrooms were too small to add the baby's crib to the space. Lisa's room was the biggest of the three, and I wanted Peetie and her to get a good night's rest without the disturbance of a baby's crying.

The baby was born in early October, a girl we called Marcy, just two weeks short of Peetie's twelfth birthday. Lisa, who had turned ten in June, got her wish for a baby sister and was thrilled. It was Peetie who sat with me all through the night when the pains started. Luke was fast asleep when it began, and when I woke him, he opened one eye and asked how far apart the pains were coming. When I told him that it was just the begining stage, he turned over and snored away. Peetie made me a cup of tea and and a piece of toast with marmalade and one for himself. He sat with me all through the night and into the early morning hours. At 8 o'clock, Luke drove me to the same hospital that I worked in and, precisely at 11 o'clock a.m., the baby was born without any complications. She was 9 lbs, 2 oz., and 21 inches long.

When we brought her home from the hospital three days later, Peetie, Lisa, and my parents were waiting at the house, along with all the children in the neighborhood. Lisa wanted to hold her immediately, so after she sat down, I gave her the baby. Soon Peetie wanted to hold her, too, and I was amazed to see how tenderly and adroitly he handled the tiny baby. He was twelve years old, most of his movements were usually rough and somewhat clumsy, as all boys of that age are. He took Marcy in view of all his friends, who stood surrounding him and the new baby. Peetie was totally absorbed in his little sister and could not get enough of looking at her as he held her.

When Marcy was not quite a month old, late one night I was awakened by a noise in the living room. I jumped out of bed, ran out, and found Peetie with Marcy over his shoulder, patting her back in an effort to make her burp. He had given her a bottle, which he'd warmed up first, and she had taken it greedily. "She was crying, Mom, so I picked her up and warmed her a bottle and gave it to her," he said proudly. At that point

Marcy gave the loudest burp ever. And after I changed her diaper, she slept all through the night into the early morning.

Peetie certainly had a nurturing streak as a boy. Although his sister Lisa, only 20 months younger, would not, of course, abide his care, I remember when they were both much younger, Peetie about six and Lisa four, Peetie tried to prevent his sister from sucking her thumb. He had overheard adult conversations about how children who sucked their thumbs would grow up with protruding front teeth, and he was not letting this happen to his sister. Tirelessly he rose from his bed to pull Lisa's thumb out of her mouth, time and time again. And Lisa would just turn on her other side in her sleep and suck her other thumb. Peetie complained that he could not keep up with her, but he never gave up and always kept a watchful eye on her.

MORE CALIFORNIA DREAMING

The bedroom Luke wanted to build on never materialized, because our thoughts began to turn toward the West. I had been reunited with an old girlfriend from Indonesia who had settled in California with her family. We corresponded frequently and also had numerous telephone conversations. California had been one of our top choices on our immigration forms, but we were given New England instead. Luke and I saw our chance now, ready for the taking. My friend, Ellen Haas, her husband Carl, and their two children lived in Northern California and loved it. She also said that there were many work opportunities in the electronics field for Luke. California stood at the very top in electronics.

We thought about it long and hard before making the decision. It would be almost like a second emigration, and we would be leaving our sponsors behind. How to inform them of our decision without hurting their feelings was a big question. For them, Massachusetts was the only state worth living in, and all the others were extremely inferior, in their assessment. We decided to speak to the McCoys and the Baileys first about our intentions. It was the right decision. They were saddened by the thought of our departure, but they knew that after, the first five years, we were free to do what we chose. We were not their responsibility any more in a legal sense; however, Luke and I knew that they would always be there for us and our children, no matter how much time had elapsed and no matter where we decided to settle. Both families were delighted when Marcy was born. They outdid each other with gifts and loving attention, so much so that it irritated my parents, who became jealous. Every time they came to visit their new granddaughter, someone else was already there, holding her.

And now, with the prospect of our upcoming citizenship, the Baileys organized a celebration dinner for our family, the entire church guild, and the Reverend Snyder and his wife. The McCoys elected themselves to drive us to Boston and be with us for this special moment. They also appointed themselves to arrange the time and day with the Immigration and Naturalization Services office. In the meantime, Luke and I had studied American history and the Constitution, attending evening classes for adults at the high school for many weeks. Eventually we felt secure enough to take the test.

On a Monday morning in July 1966, the McCoys picked us up at the appointed hour. Our appointment with Immigration was at 9 o'clock. It was a gorgeous day, and we enjoyed the half hour drive to Boston, feeling confident with the McCoys at our side. There were only ten other people pursuing their applications for citizenship that morning, and one by one they were called in. Before too long our turns came to be summoned to one of the small rooms by an official. The procedure was fast and utterly impersonal, almost like being on a citizenship conveyer belt. Luke and I were interviewed separately. Each of us was asked three or four questions, and that was that.

Somehow we expected more of a test. We felt relieved but also a little let down. We expected it to be harder, to have many more questions, at least to make the long hours of study we put in worthwhile. Before we knew it, all twelve of us were gathered together to recite the Pledge of Allegiance, and we were sworn in as citizens of the United States of America. The McCoys, beaming and wildly proud, hugged us again and again. They took us to an elegant restaurant overlooking the Charles River for a luncheon celebration, complete with the best champagne the restaurant had to offer. Despite the bureaucratic dispatch with which our cases had been handled, Luke and I were glad we had dressed up for the occasion.

During the drive home, our friends enthusiastically discussed the party that the Baileys were planning to celebrate both our becoming American citizens and our leaving for California. Peetie and Lisa and my parents were, of course, included. A total of 38 adults had been invited, plus their children and grandchildren, for whom a separate menu and entertainment were going to be provided.

In the meantime, Luke and I were extremely busy finding a buyer for our house, which we fortunately came up with in a few days. A man who worked with Luke and his wife were immediately interested. They had come from England six months earlier with two small boys, and were looking for a house. They had no furniture, so we sold what was in the house to them, making a nice profit. There was no real estate agent involved in the sale, and the Baileys gave us the services of one of their lawyers to arrrange the legal aspects. We never got a bill from the lawyer, even after making numerous phone calls. We understood that, once again, we were the recipients of the Baileys' generosity.

Our friends in Northern California invited us to stay with them for a while, at least until we found a house we liked and could buy. We accepted their offer gratefully, and so did my parents. We promised to try to find a small home, enough for the seven of us, as soon as we could. After all the years under the watchful eyes—and protective wings—of our sponsors, this was another uprooting. We were starting from scratch again, although for a second time we were doing it willingly. Now we could speak the language much better and were acquainted with the customs of the people. We also had more money in our bank accounts, which was a reasuring thought.

All we had to do now was to pack our suitcases. Marcy and I would fly to California, and so would my parents. To make sure of that, our sponsors gave us first class tickets. "For the baby," they exclaimed in unison when Luke and I protested. "You'll have so much more room to move around when Marcy gets fussy," they said with concern, "and you can change her easier when you have to." They all were so sweet and so deeply concerned, and we accepted with tears in our eyes. Luke, Peetie, and Lisa were to make the trip across the country by car, with the suitcases and linens packed into the station wagon. The car underwent a careful inspection at a dealership the McCoys suggested, and four brand new tires were installed. Again, the bill never reached our hands. How could we leave these sweet people? They were all genuinely concerned for us and still felt responsible for our well-being. But deep in our hearts we knew we had to leave. They would always treat us as their charges if we stayed.

AN ELEGANT FAREWELL

The Saturday of the farewell party arrived. In addition to attending the festivities at the Baileys' home, we were going to spend the night there. My parents at first wanted to decline, but the Baileys announced that the rooms were all ready for them, and they were talked into staying as well.

The Baileys had asked our family to come at four in the afternoon, so we could settle into our rooms and relax with them before the others arrived at seven. When we arrived, Elvie the housekeeper opened the door and a young man took our overnight bags and dress clothes for the evening ahead, preceding us up the broad staircase. Even before we reached the landing, a flurry of arms and legs came rushing toward Peetie and Lisa in the form of Bobby, now eleven years old. After quick hugs for everyone, he, Lisa, and Peetie ran down the stairs we had just ascended and out the front door, disappearing as they always did when we came to visit. Elvie opened a door on the left of the wide hallway and showed my parents their room. Ours was right across, and Lisa's next to us with a connecting door. Peetie would sleep in Bobby's room, sharing with Bobby for the night, which they had done many times during the years of our friendship with the Baileys.

I opened the door and, as always, the size of the spacious room and yet its coziness astonished us, although we had been in the same room many times before. Our feet sank into the luxurious cream-colored thickness of the carpet, which made me want to take off my shoes and nylons and wiggle my toes in the feel of it. The room was done in cream-colored overtones, and the wall against which the headboard was situated was of the softest green. The bed itself was a king-sized four poster. All done in cream with accents of the same green, as was repeated throughout the mansion in all sorts of fashionable decorations. Above the headboard hung yet another Turner, Stephanie's favorite artist, the English master of light and color, this original as priceless as everything else throughout the enormous house. Before Elvie left, she announced that Stephanie would be waiting for us in the informal smaller sitting room.

I took another look around the bedroom before closing the door, admiring once again the cozy sitting area, with its cream-colored marble hearth, cold now and stuffed with potted plants, but blazingly hot in winter. A large television screen loomed in front of the sofa. Off the sitting area was the dressing room, where the young servant had deposited our overnight bags and hung up our clothes. Each bedroom had, of course, its own bath as well. The mansion had ten guests rooms and one great master bedroom on the other side of the house, completely private from the others. All the rooms had about the same setup, but different splashes of color from the pillows and paintings and other artifacts gave each room a different light and ambiance of its own.

After checking on my parents, we descended the stairs. They wanted to rest a while before the evening stir set in. Stephanie already knew this, and Elvie planned to bring up refreshments that they could enjoy in privacy, they told us. Downstairs we heard Stephanie's voice directing the servants how she wanted things done. We entered the grand dining room where she stood, looking as elegant and stylish as ever in a soft yellow pantsuit, gold earrings dangling from her lobes. Her brown hair was again pulled away from her face in a French twist, the rage in the early 1960s and 1970s. "I'm so glad your parents decided to come, too," she said warmly, hugging my shoulders affectionately. "It wouldn't be complete without them," she continued with a smile.

She turned and hugged Luke for a welcome also. Entering the immense dining room, we saw it in its glory, richly decorated and ready for the evening. The long table was set and three floral centerpieces were evenly spaced along it. I recognized a painting by Raphael on one of the walls next to the enormous marble fireplace. On two slender marble stands I saw a pair of ginger pots from the Ming Dynasty, also original. The pots were gorgeous in soft peach, gold, and greens flanking the tall windows, which had creamy gold-edged drapery framing them, looking out over the beautifully kept grounds. A large and elegant chandelier hung above the center of the dining table. The facets created sparkling light in the evening when it was turned on. Under the table was a luxurious Aubusson carpet, thick and soft and lush in cream, green, and peach. The whole was just so elegant and soothing to the eye, it was a pleasure to be part of it.

We were about to leave the dining room when Mark came in, dashing even in old jeans and rumpled white shirt. He had been busy with the gardeners all day, who were replacing part of an old wall surrounding the estate that had fallen down. He was also needed in the huge five-car garage, which housed three Bentleys and the two Mercedes that he and Stephanie drove, and whose roof needed to be replaced. The daily pressures of his job and the burden of a large estate did not seem to bother him. He was completely in control, once again greeting us warmly and sincerely glad to see us.

As usual, he had met the children in the pony stalls, where they were "helping" Carlo the stable boy to brush the ponies and the horses and to comb their manes and tails. After Mark freshened up, the four of us entered the small sitting room, where refreshments were waiting for us. There was white wine in a silver bucket filled with ice, and for the children lemonade in pitchers filled with ice cubes. Coffee, tea, and cream were set out on a long, slender serving tray on wheels. Elvie no doubt had seen to it all.

It was nearing 5 o'clock and delicious whiffs of cooking food reached us. Stephanie, always the considerate hostess, had shown me the menu some days before, making sure we would enjoy it, although time and time again we assured her that there wasn't much we did not like. The menu was all Italian again, giving Maria the cook and her helpers a chance to demonstrate their skills. There was to be a garlicky soup, with lots of garlic and onions thickened with a potatoe puree, stock, and thyme. "Have no fear of the garlic," Stephanie commented, "the cooking process attenuates the strength but leaves the flavor." I did not believe this but it did not matter, because we love garlic. People who omit such an important ingredient in recipes that call for it, in my view, don't know how to cook. There was also antipasto of red, green, and yellow bell peppers mixed with a balsamic vinegar and oil, fried zucchini flowers, turkey breast with black and green olives, small red potatoes, basil lemon chicken (the chicken roasted first before all the ingredients were added and then put back in the oven), and for dessert folded peach tarts, hazelnut cake, and cherries steeped in red wine. For the children—and there were many, ranging from age four to thirteen—there was pizza loaded with sausage and veggies, macaroni, green beans, and ham. Dessert for the kids was Maria's famous chocolate cake and all sorts of ice creams.

After a chat and refreshments with Mark and Stephanie, we retired to our rooms for a little rest before people arrived at seven. Luke and I decided to walk the grounds for a while, rounding up Peetie and Lisa on our way back to the house. As we walked, the peace and solitude were palpable. The rush of water in a nearby creek could be heard making its own music. Above that sound, we heard peals of laughter and soft voices of the children from the direction of the stables.

There was a large patch of vegetables behind the stables and I was promptly transported back to another time and place, back to the plantation where Oma taught her grandchildren to plant our own vegetables. That place was also located near the horse stables, far removed from the house.

Surprising as it may seem, since we were far from our rooms at the house, I heard my infant daughter cry. We had put her in the care of the nursemaid, Debbie, who was delighted to see her again and insisted on taking care of her while we stayed with the Baileys. I sped toward the house, raced up the stairs, and opened the nursery door. Yes, I had heard right, Marcy was crying big tears. Debbie was trying to feed her dinner and, from all the tiny jars of baby food, had chosen the one Marcy hated the most, soft rice and spinach. She spit out the first bite, which explained the green spots on Debbie's white uniform and face, and pushed away Debbie's hand holding the hated little jar, screaming. Many a time the same thing had happened to me when I fed her spinach, but I knew how to distract her for a little while until she really had her fill from the green mushy stuff. She blew it all in my face and would clamp her little mouth shut and that was the end of it.

I picked Marcy up from the high chair and she stopped crying immediately. Debbie, after cleaning herself up and changing her clothes, came back laughing. "My, oh my," she said, shaking her head, "What a temper that little one has, and she looks so cute and soft." I took Marcy into my room, fed her some carrots, which Debbie had warmed, and gave her a bottle. Marcy fell asleep immediately and was totally herself when she woke up, happily going with Debbie into the nursery.

I, too, took a nap and, when I woke, saw Luke on the sofa, snoring softly. Peetie and Lisa were sprawled on the thick carpet, sound asleep with the television set on, the volume turned low so as not to awaken the baby or me. I let father and children sleep a little longer as I showered and dressed. Luke and the children then took their turns getting ready for the party.

The guests started arriving around seven. After all these years, we knew everyone well and had been in their homes at least a few times. Bobby, Peetie, and Lisa ran ahead to greet the children who were arriving with their parents. I heard squeals of pleasure when they stood with Stephanie and Mark at the door to welcome their friends. Luke looked handsome in his dark suit. Taking a last inspection before descending the stairs, my parents right behind, I nodded with satisfaction at my own reflection in the mirror. My dress was a deep blue silk and quite tailored. My hair was done in a French twist and adorned with a cluster of tiny silvery silk flowers that Stephanie had given to me, together with drop earrings also in silver clusters in a flower design.

After lots of hugs and warm greetings, we gathered in the large drawing room for wine and champagne and lemonade for the children. The adults were then summoned for dinner by Stephanie, elegant in her black and white Gucci dress, her arms around Luke's and my shoulders. As we walked into the dining room, Maria and her helpers, two pretty young Italian women, were loading the enormous sideboard with dishes. Stephanie sat at one end of the table and Mark at the other. She put Luke and me on either side of her as honored guests, with my parents right beside me. I could pick out Lisa's and Peetie's voices among the others in the smaller dining room. They seemed to be enjoying themselves, and I could hear their laughter several times during dinner. Champagne and wine were poured, along with water, and were replenished at frequent intervals. Reverend Snyder, who sat across from my mother with his wife, stood up and made a brief but touching speech. After him, Mark and then Frank McCoy said theirs, and their tributes moved Luke and me to tears. The Reverend then said a short blessing, and Stephanie gave Maria and her helpers a tiny nod to start serving the food.

As we ate, I let my eyes roam over the details of the room, probably for the last time: the ceiling's elaborate carvings, the creamy color repeated in the draperies dressing the tall windows. The ceiling and draperies were edged in gold. Everywhere I noticed potted palms and tall, slender marble stands topped with big vases filled with fresh flowers. My childhood memories rushed at me again, and I saw the plantation house and the hotel dining room filled with astonishing similarities. Different in appearance yet quite the same. There, too, guests had sat at long tables graced with plants and fresh flowers, laden with delicious foods, prepared and served by caring, well-trained cooks and servants. I came back to the present swiftly when Stephanie, touching me lightly on the arm, announced dessert. She knew by looking at me, after all these years of our friendship, that something had triggered a memory.

After dessert she gave the sign for everyone to gather in the smaller sitting room, knowing my preference for that particular area of the house. It was indeed my favorite of the two sitting rooms. It was a little smaller than the other and more intimately arranged. I stood for a moment, pausing to soak up for the last time the gentle beauty of it all. It was the loveliest spot in the entire house, I thought, with its peach and cream color scheme and exquisite paintings. Although Mark and Stephanie had sold some of their renowned collection of Impressionists, they still had two Monets and two Sisleys on the walls, giving the elegantly decorated room its great beauty. I gazed at the enormous Sisley landscape a little longer. I had never coveted anything so much as this painting, which of course would never be possible. The painting is priceless and belonged in the kind of huge and elegant surroundings that this house provided.

The evening flew by. People soon were gathering in the grand foyer near the front door. Elvie handed the ladies their purses and light evening wraps and some of the gentlemen their hats. Hugs and tears flowed, and promises were made to stay in touch. Well, we all know how that goes. The children were gathered, and little Marcy, deep asleep, was carried out for a last kiss and caress. The baby slept through it all. Before long we were alone with the Baileys and the McCoys, who were also staying the night. The servants were complimented for their excellent work. My parents and the children went upstairs after expressing their thanks several times. It was near midnight, and it had been a wonderful evening, filled with liveliness, happy moments, and some sadness because of our departure and leaving so many kind people.

A week later, we would be leaving New England and an important part of our life behind once again. In particular, we would be leaving the two special families who made it possible for us to live through the difficult first years of adjustment and learning. They and the guild helped us to acclimate to American life and American culture. Never pushy or overbearing in their teachings, no one could have better sponsors than we had. This particular part of my book is thus a loving tribute to all of those here in the USA who kept us well cared for and gave us their understanding and gentle guidance.

Chapter 8

California

As we made our way from New England to California, we often realized with astonishment that few were as lucky as we were in our assignment of sponsors. There were reports of Dutch-Indonesian immigrants who suffered from severe negligence at the hands of their sponsors. Stories were told of people waiting in vain at points of embarkation for their sponsors to claim them and who never appeared. Luke and I knew a family whose sponsor literally dumped them in one of the worst neighborhoods of Oakland, California, and then took off, never to reappear. At the time of their arrival, this family had three small children and a total of $300 in their pockets. They ate peanut butter sandwiches or bread dipped in a little sugar for weeks and months. The husband was forced to look for the lowest kind of work available. These people, relying solely on an individual sponsor for guidance and assistance, had no church group behind them, as we did.

Other Dutch-Indonesian immigrants came in contact with rough and uneducated people, people who barely could sustain an existence for themselves, much less help recent immigrants. They met this class of people at work on a daily basis and had to deal with them constantly in low-paying, inferior jobs, like janitorial work in public buildings, cleaning public transit buses, working hard, sweaty hours in box and paper factories, and the like. Some came to work in gross environments with cockroaches crawling over their feet.

People who found themselves in these circumstances were bound to feel unhappy. Some even felt betrayed by a people and a country that they had thought they could trust. Especially after World War II, for many people in Europe and elsewhere in the world, America represented protection, a certain amount of security, and a great deal of trust. Those of my people who struggled with poverty became embittered, and the bitterness grew slowly into acute resentment. For them, Holland became a haven to return to, and many of them went back to the country they had left so gladly, with so much hope in their hearts for a better future for their children and themselves. Others in this situation stayed in the United States, nursing their resentment, for they did not want to uproot their children for a second time. Many more factors were intertwined with the decision to go, of course, and also with the decision to stay. A lot of Dutch-Indonesian immigrants in this country are still very involved with Holland and visit it yearly. Others are confused and don't know where they want to live, changing their decision, going back and forth many times.

Luke and I were lucky. We always knew where we wanted to be. Perhaps not in the same region, but for certain in the same country that we had chosen so long ago. There was never any doubt about it. We were here to stay.

Once we arrived in California, we went about the task of making a new start. We were fortunate in being able to stay for a few weeks at the home of our friends Ellen and Carl Haas in Pleasanten. This gave us the opportunity to look for housing and employment for Luke. He found a good position in two weeks' time, and shortly thereafter we found a house we liked at a price we could afford. Both the house and Luke's work were in Walnut Creek, a community about 40 to 45 minutes from San Francisco to the north. Not long after we moved into our first house, my parents found a house in Contra Costa County. Their small but cozy home was not too far from ours. It had a big piece of land that my father could work and plant to his heart's content. It kept him busy and healthy for a long time.

The children, however, missed the freedom that small towns on the East Coast provided. Especially Peetie, who now that he was an adolescent wanted to be called Peter or Pete. He missed the open marshland and the many ponds and small lakes of New England, which he used to explore with his friends. Lisa, too, missed the freedom of small town living and her many playmates. New England was so green in the summer, kept fresh by frequent storms that drenched the land, then cleared up and disappeared, leaving the air, the flora, and the soil replenished.

The golden brown scenery of California in summer took some getting used to. To newcomers, the surrounding hills looked scorched. It took us a while to appreciate the contrast of the golden brown with the massive, dark green oaks that dotted the Californian landscape. It was strikingly beautiful once we got used to the color scheme, so different from the all-green masses in the East. The pleasant temperatures made up for whatever was missing, however. There was plenty of sunshine and very little humidity. Even the higher temperatures were much more tolerable, we found, than the humid summers of the East Coast.

And San Francisco—Luke and I fell instantly in love with it. The City by the Bay is absolutely gorgeous, especially when approached from the San Francisco Bay Bridge. It is such a pretty sight, with all its buildings and houses built into the hills. They seem to shimmer in the sunlight, the green of the trees and red tile rooftops glimmer in between, and the deep blue of the bay surrounds the whole. It all contrasts strikingly with the orange of the Golden Gate Bridge as a backdrop.

We fell hard for California, especially after we saw the soaring Sierra Nevada Mountains, with azure Lake Tahoe in their midst, and sculptured Yosemite Park, with its deep valley surrounded by sharp-edged mountains.

But not before we saw the Central Coast, from the Big Basin to Big Sur, did we realize how totally we had fallen for the beauty of the state and its diversity. Year after year, we have returned to these areas of the Central Coast for summer fun. First with our children when they were young, and then just the two of us when the children grew older, and later again with our children, their spouses, and our grandchildren as well.

From Santa Cruz all the way north to Monterey, Pacific Grove, Pebble Beach, Carmel, and Big Sur, the beaches are impressive and dramatic in their beauty. The surrounding areas and coastline shrouded entirely in fog gives it a mysterious feel of its own. Monterey, known as the Sardine Capital of the World, is also known as the Butterfly Town. Butterflies seem to gather there at certain times of the year.

Just tour the gorgeous neighborhoods of Monterey and its close neighbor, Carmel, and notice the celebrated residents. There are stretches you can walk with splendid stands of redwoods, or you can watch the mighty gray whales as they migrate south in the winter for warmer waters and then watch them coming back in the spring. The rich sandy soil of the Monterey Bay area also produces all kinds of fruits and vegetables, which have brought fame to the region as well. Artichokes, cauliflower, and Brussels sprouts are harvested here and transported to supermarkets all over the United States. There are strawberry fields that seem to go on forever, and many produce stands line the highways selling locally grown products. Driving the Californian coastal highways overlooking the cliffs of Big Sur, the rugged beauty of its isolated beaches and sweeping vistas is unforgettable.

Point Lobos State Reserve Park, in the Carmel area, is one of our family's favorite spots. It has more than a 1,000 acres of discovery. We used to hike along the oceanfront trails and along the craggy cliffs and sometimes along the sheltered coves, where sea life hides and flourishes. Sea otters hide in the maze of kelp and often can be spotted leisurely floating on their backs with their babies on their chests. The otter pups sleep peacefully, rocked by the gentle motion of the water in the cove. We often watched pelicans drop straight from the sky into the water to catch a fish they had spotted from way up high. I never tire of seeing them perform, almost always catching their prey.

Sometimes we encountered rabbits hopping into the thickets and, later in the afternoon, we could hear sea wolves or sea lions barking, the animals for which Point Lobos is named. At one time in history, the area was home to American Indians, the vigorous Rumsien tribes lived here for over 2,000 years. The shell mounds and bedrock mortars are all that remains of their existence.

The steep forest of the Santa Lucia Mountain Range is impressive, its steep ridges rising in some places more than 5,000 feet into the sky, with V-shaped valleys in their midst, all carpeted with chaparral. Fortunately, the remoteness of Big Sur has discouraged many developers and saved this densely wooded paradise from overpopulation. In some places, Highway 1 soars as much as 1,000 feet above sea level, if I'm not mistaken, and comes as close as 50 feet of the water's edge.

Carmel by the Sea, my most favorite town, is known for its picturesque village and white beaches. It is also known as the Clint Eastwood City; he was once mayor, and many visitors still go on a Clint watch, hoping to see him at one of his two restaurant-bars, the Hog's Breath Inn or the Mission Ranch. The soft-spoken, gracious actor is as friendly in person as his Hollywood screen image is tough and unbendable. Luke and I met him once. His neighbors are Doris Day, whom we have seen driving through the narrow streets of Carmel in her Mercedes, and James Garner.

I read somewhere that over 40 movies have been shot in this area. The ones that I know of are *A Summer Place* with Sandra Dee and Troy Donahue in 1959, *The Sandpiper* with Elizabeth Taylor and Richard Burton in 1964, and I think *Blind Date* with Bruce Willis and Kim Basinger in 1987. The area is fantastic for picture taking, although I'm always disappointed with the ones we take. They don't do justice to what we see: there is no depth in them, and the perspective is too limited. So now we just go there and gaze at the beauty. Pete, Lisa, and Marcy love these areas as much as Luke and I, and when he was older Pete made many a sketch of this region.

LIFE IN CONCORD

Our family settled into life in California slowly but surely, and the days and years went by quickly, occupied as we were with new work, new schools, and a new home. We furnished it as well as we were able, which we had to do very carefully and slowly, since our sponsors were not around to help us out anymore. We missed them dearly, as well as the protective feeling they surrounded us with. We spoke on the phone often.

The children made friends quickly, mainly neighborhood children with whom they went to school. Luke was busy getting acquainted in his new job and before long was making swift progress.

All was well, except for Peter. He developed the habit of "sleepwalking." It was occasional and sporadic at first, but slowly the habit increased to at least two episodes a night. It wasn't until he was about fourteen years old that we took him to a doctor; that's how slowly it progressed. The doctor said that hormones sometimes cause strange things to happen in teenage bodies and made us promise to bring him back if the sleepwalking increased.

We started to notice in Peter a forgetfulness, which gradually increased, although it was quite subtle, almost too small to be detected. Peter was sixteen by now, a strapping boy of about 5' 8" tall, sturdy and quite healthy in appearance. When he got his driver's licence, we bought him a used car. He was very proud when we gave him the key and drove away for a spin with a friend. Not knowing what lay ahead, Luke and I waved at him happily and proudly. In a sudden premonition, I saw Peter in a series of small accidents. I shook off the thought and stepped back into the house, somewhat subdued. After the euphoria of seeing one's oldest drive away for the first time, a strange depressive mood came over me, something I could not explain. Pete came back about a half hour later, very pleased, with a half-eaten ice cream cone in his hand. He had dropped off his friend Randy at his house before returning home.

Shortly after Peter got his car, something happened to him that shook me to the core. I was working in the front yard and saw it all. He came home one day from school, and just as he reached the front door, he spun around. One look at his face told me that he was about to have a seizure. After he spun a couple of times, he fell to the ground, but got up in a split second in one fluid motion. He looked at me then, and I knew that he was not aware of what just had happened. He reached for the doorknob and stepped into the house. I told him what had happened and reached for the phone to report this to the doctor.

After I described the incident, without leaving anything out, the doctor gave us the address of a neurologist nearby and telephoned ahead of our coming. Luke took Peter to the neurologist that very same day. Tests were done, and we waited for the results and diagnosis with great apprehension and anxiety. Two days later, we received the diagnosis: Peter suffered temporal lobe seizures.

The doctor asked if he had experienced any head injuries in the past, and Luke mentioned the baseball accident. It had happened six years earlier and been long forgotten, since the physician at the time had declared Peter to be fine, so no one made a connection. The neurologist told us that often there was a delayed reaction. Many things can suddenly develop, especially during puberty with its hormonal changes. I mentioned the sleepwalking that started when Peter was twelve and how it gradually increased in frequency. The neurologist commented that sleepwalking is not a normal activity and people take it way too lightly. In Peter's case, he experienced tiny little seizures that grew worse through the years and finally developed into full-blown seizures. The doctor agreed that the slug against the side of his head did have everything to do with it. Later still, Peter was sent to the Department of Neurology at the Stanford University Medical Center for intensive tests. The tests revealed an old scar exactly at the spot where the baseball bat had hit him on the side of his head. The doctors prescribed a new medication that would allow Peter to function normally and lead a healthy life—or so they said.

Peter was quite shy, although he would never admit this to anyone, and was easily embarrassed, more so than other children of his age. The seizures must have happened at school as well, I imagine. But at that time they were not severe, and Peter could cover them up. He was an excellent student, sharp and very witty. Also, because of his atlethic abilities, a group had clustered around him, both males and females.

Yet more and more, we detected increasing forgetfulness in him. He began to miss football meetings, classes, and the like because of it. At first we thought him careless about his studies. Since it was the 1960s when Peter and Lisa were growing up, the possibility of drug use crossed our minds on many occasions. I started to observe him surreptitiously, or so I thought. But Peter's own quick-wittedness had already noticed my constant observation of his every move. He confronted me bluntly one afternoon. "Mom, do you think I'm on drugs? You're watching me all the time!" I was taken by surprise for just a split second and then answered him straightforwardly. "Yes, it has crossed my mind. You would worry too if you were a parent these days." Grimly he admitted that he would and then softly said, "No, Mom, I'm not doing drugs. It's just that I forget to do things."

Peter found it annoying to have to take his pills exactly as prescribed, and many a time he would skip a dose, and a seizure would occur during the night in his sleep. And he was annoyed to have to grab for his pills in front of his peers, which seemed denigrating and sissy-like to him. He did not like anybody to know about his disorder and became quite uptight about it. He became involved in numerous minor car accidents, because of the carelessness with which he took his medication. All through those years I became more and more nervous about his driving, at times even threatning him to take away his car keys and driver's license unless he was more faithful about taking his medication. All to no avail. I worried every time Peter stepped into his car, wondering if I would see him back alive.

Peter appeared splendidly well and robustly healthy. He was tall and handsome, and daily life in our household was disturbed by constant phone calls from girls who wanted to talk to him. But he became more and more reticent about his disorder, and along with that the carelessness about taking his medicine the right way increased. His personality was changing gradually, too. He covered up his innate shyness with a quick, sarcastic wittiness of a sort. Because of his illness, he felt a need to create a tough image. He strove to always prove himself capable and knowledgeable, which he was in most cases, and in full control, which he was not—that is what aggravated him the most.

To us, his parents, he became most reproachful, especially when he forgot something after I had reminded him about it. He would become frustrated with himself and then would blame it somehow on me. He knew that only I was totally aware of the seriousness of his disorder. No one else in the family knew or understood the strength of his inner battle as I did. Not his sisters, not his father, and later not either of his wives. But I saw my child, my only son, change from a loving and deeply caring boy into a frustrated man, and I could only sit back and let it happen. I felt so helpless through those years. Luke saw only the rough side, the reproachful and bitter personality that his son had developed. He did not know the pain and struggle inside his heart. He saw only a robust good-looking young man and was not aware how strongly his son's illness had affected his character.

Bereft of self-esteem, Peter now hid behind a tough image. Although he cared for his family deeply, he was by now unable to show his affection. It was only at family gatherings, birthdays, or Christmas that he would relent, and then he would overload us with cards and expensive presents. His deep affection and love could not be put into words.

When Peter was 28, he married a young woman named Demmi, whom Luke and I cared for very much. She was petite, dark blond, and pretty and as quick of wit as Peter himself. Her college major was English, and she studied at the University of California, Santa Barbara. The marriage lasted two years. Luke, Lisa, Marcy, and I were deeply disturbed by their divorce.

Not long after, Peter remarried, this time to a statuesque blonde named Dianne. Their marriage lasted nine years and from it was born our eldest grandchild, Nicolette, called Nikki. We went wild with her, our first grandchild. Lisa and Marcy were aunts for the first time. She was so pretty, with big deep brown eyes and rosy skin and deep auburn hair. By the time little Nicolette was eight, this union too disintegrated. Knowing from experience how difficult life with Peter was, we never blamed his wives for the breakups. My only regret is that neither woman was able to understand Peter's deep-seated emotional trauma. He still tried to ignore his condition and avoided speaking about it—there was no acceptance. In the first happy years of his marriage to Dianne, he did his best to take the medication regularly and for years the seizures subsided. His love for Dianne and the responsibility for his child subdued his rebellion against his illness.

No one else can ever fully understand a couple's intimate relationship. I have a first cousin living in Australia who was in an automobile accident years ago. He, too, most unfortunately, hit the side of his head against the car door and was afterward extremely difficult to live with. His wife of 20 years, when the accident occurred, had an enormous task to put up with him. But she was of the old world and better equipped and far better trained in that respect than the younger generation. Today, for many young people, the promise "for better or for worse" has become an automatic phrase, mumbled on their wedding day, the meaning of which does not even slightly penetrate their souls.

PACIFIC PLAYGROUNDS

But I am getting ahead of myself. Let's go back to the time before the children left our house. When Marcy was thirteen and the other two children were away at school, Luke, Marcy, and I went to Hawaii for the first time. We loved it so much as a vacation spot, or spots rather, that we decided to buy into a condominium time-share. The arrangement was that we had several condos at which we could stay for two weeks a year, spread over the four major islands. Watching the surfers one brilliant afternoon, admiring their agility on their polished surfboards, I was transported back to the time when I was in my teens, swimming and romping in the tropical waters of a bay and surfing. Our surfboards were not manufactured but were freshly cut from a banana tree trunk. The banana trunk peels in huge layers; when cut to the size of your body, they make fantastic body surfboards, since the inner core of the trunk layers are light and filled with air like a beehive comb. What fun we had, and it did not cost a penny.

Often in Hawaii and also at other places in California, we watched the kite fliers. Up went the elaborate kites in all their expensive store-bought glory, with tails yards long drifting in the wind, then swooping and rearing way up high into the sky. Again in my mind's eye, I saw myself as an 8-year-old, following my older boy cousins around when they were playing kite-war. And a serious thing it was. The cousins layered the kite string with ground glass. They ground up pieces of broken bottles and added a foul-smelling glue, mixed it well, and drew the kite string through, then let it dry. After that they were ready for war.

I tagged along with the cousins and their friends, trying to do everything the older boys did. I did it myself, too—well, with a little help from Ben, my oldest male cousin, who had a soft spot in his heart for pesky little girls like me. He would help me with the grinding of the glass, afraid I would cut myself on the sharp pieces. If properly done, the area of the string closest to the kite itself, which had been drawn through the glue and glass mixture, was as sharp as a razor.

Now the waiting and watching started. We scanned the area over the house rooftops and treetops—yes, there was a kite way up high. Quickly, two kites in our group went up into the air and drifted in the enemy's direction. Ben made a quick movement with his fingers holding the string. Closer and closer came his puny little kite with a short tail attached. Ben made another swift motion and "Yes!" we yelled, "Gotcha!" Quickly he pulled in his kite so as not to give away our location. Of course we too lost a good kite many a time—it was all part of the game and good fun.

We returned to Hawaii year after year, for at least fifteen years. Although they are tropical, the Hawaiian Islands are nothing like Indonesia, and tiny in comparison. The foods and dishes are extremely different, although many of the fruits we knew in childhood grow there, transplanted to Hawaiian soil from different places in Southeast Asia many years ago. Authentic Hawaiian dishes are quite different. The language is totally different and unrelated to anything with which I was familiar. At first, the sound of it was strange, reminding me of someone speaking and hiccuping at the same time. Each vowel is pronounced separately, with an extra push of air through the lungs. Buddy Holly must have been quite a bit in Hawaii when he was writing and singing his songs.

On another vacation trip, back on the mainland, we spent a week in beautiful San Diego. Marcy was again with us, and the zoo was a number one attraction, the old and legendary "haunted" Hotel Del Coronado another, and for me of course the exclusive La Jolla area, with its beautiful homes and well-kept gardens, with bougainvillia creepers spilling over the walls and against the houses. We spent one afternoon on one of the many wonderful beaches in San Diego. When a group of young men in Marine uniforms sauntered by us, my thoughts fleetingly returned to the end of World War II, when I was still in my Dutch East Indies. It came to my mind that our army, the K.N.I.L. (*Koninklijk-Nederlands-Indies-Leger*), was one that was totally dissolved and ceased to exist with the independence of Indonesia. The quiet gravestones in military graveyards are silent symbols of the brave men who fought in that proud and valiant army and gave their lives in the Dutch East Indies, so many years ago. A quiet and respectful salute goes to those who fought for us in the past.

FAMILY GROWTH AND CHANGE

Meanwhile, the years sped by, as our lives in the United States became more and more intertwined with the American way of living. Our children grew up, went to college, took jobs, and chose their partners. Peter became a proud father of his beloved daughter, was happy and settled in his family life with his second wife Dianne, and enjoyed the security of a well-paying job for many years.

Lisa married but after three years divorced and remarried someone else. She and her tall, blond husband James gave us two wonderful twin grandsons, now ten years old. They are healthy and full of life and mischief and quite a twosome. Although they are twins, they don't even look like brothers. As different as they look from each other, they are also different character-wise, but both as cute as they come. Palmer, who was born first, is fair of skin with hazel eyes and freckles on the bridge of his nose. Parker has dark brown big eyes and olive skin tones and always a rosy glow on his cheeks. Active in all sorts of sports, they keep their parents hopping from early morning to late into the evening. Lisa is a chauffeur, organizer of games, classroom Mom, nurse, mother, and wife as well. Also she is deeply involved in community and neighborhood activities. James, who often works more then ten hours a day, manages to scrape up the energy to join the boys and Lisa at baseball, soccer, and football events. He and Lisa are wonderful parents to their two boys.

Marcy met her husband in Switzerland, while on vacation with her girlfriend Sandy some fourteen years ago. Her husband Gordon is from Montana, where they live with their two adorable little girls. Adia will be five soon: she has light brown long hair with golden highlights, blue-grey eyes with thick dark lashes, and a rosebud mouth that seems permanently rosy pink colored. Her sister Sofia, our darling living baby doll and youngest grandchild at the moment, has dark hair and a very fair complexion. She has big round dark brown eyes as of now, which can slightly change since she is only seven months old. She has the cutest button nose and a button mouth you want to squeeze and kiss at the same time. Marcy and Gordon adore them both.

Marcy too is extremely busy with her children. Adia loves to ski and is very good at it. She started when she was not even three years old, on the tiniest skies I have ever seen. She loves music and takes dance and piano lessons as well. As young as she is, she has already won a trophy in athletics and loves to perform. She is never nervous or stiffens in front of an audience, at least that we can tell. Marcy, like her sister Lisa, runs from one point to another with baby Sofia in tow, to get her daughter to all the different classes and of course preschool as well.

Both our daughters are wonderful mothers and their husbands are great fathers. We could not have wished for better for our daughters or for Luke and me. Our sons-in-laws are pretty darn nice to have in the family. Thank heaven for that!

EPILOGUE

It was now much later, and the air had turned cool. It seems odd, but the fragrance of flowers play a powerful role in my memory. The strong fragrances of jasmine and gardenia transported me thousands of miles, into a world that once had been, so very long ago. A lifetime of scenes drifted across my mind's eye, so clear and real I could almost touch them. Fragrance operates like music on my sensibilities. It stirs up long forgotten emotions that rush through me like a strong tide. Perhaps the primitive memory of fragrances floats in the canaliculi of the brain, forming a powerful connection between the past and the present.

"Nora? Are you home?" Luke's voice rang out as he stood at the glass patio door. The sound of his voice startled me out of my long, long reverie. I blinked my eyes, focusing on the final blaze of my beloved hibiscus and gardenias as the lowering sun struck them, raising my forearms up on the edge of the pool and back into the present. I looked about, once again grateful for the quiet beauty, then sank back into the water and slowly swam toward the concrete steps. Luke walked over to the edge and looked down at me.

"You're home early," I said as I climbed up the steps, presenting him with a wet cheek for his kiss. He looked at me with concern and asked "Are you all right? You look as though you've seen a ghost." I shivered, picked up my towel from a chair, and replied, "I have. Many ghosts—many ghosts of the past. Maybe I'll tell you about them," I said lightly as I passed in front of him toward the house. At the door, I turned briefly and said, "I'm going to take a quick shower, then dress and fix dinner. Ok?" "I'd like that, you know," he said quietly. And, as the light left the sky and turned the fiery plants to shadows, he put his arm around my shoulders and we turned together into the house.